LAUER SERIES IN RHETORIC AND COMPOSITION

Series Editors: Catherine Hobbs, Patricia Sullivan, Thomas Rickert, and Jennifer Bay

LAUER SERIES IN RHETORIC AND COMPOSITION
Series Editors: Catherine Hobbs, Patricia Sullivan, Thomas Rickert,
    and Jennifer Bay

The Lauer Series in Rhetoric and Composition honors the contributions Janice Lauer Hutton has made to the emergence of Rhetoric
and Composition as a disciplinary study. It publishes scholarship that
carries on Professor Lauer's varied work in the history of written rhetoric, disciplinarity in composition studies, contemporary pedagogical
theory, and written literacy theory and research.

Other Books in the Series

*Writers Without Borders: Writing and Teaching Writing in Troubled
    Times*, Lynn Z. Bloom (2008)

1977: A Cultural Moment in Composition, by Brent Henze, Jack
    Selzer, and Wendy Sharer (2008)

The Promise and Perils of Writing Program Administration, edited by
    Theresa Enos and Shane Borrowman (2008)

*Untenured Faculty as Writing Program Administrators: Institutional
    Practices and Politics*, edited by Debra Frank Dew and Alice
    Horning (2007)

Networked Process: Dissolving Boundaries of Process and Post-Process, by
    Helen Foster (2007)

Composing a Community: A History of Writing Across the Curriculum,
    edited by Susan H. McLeod and Margot Iris Soven (2006)

*Historical Studies of Writing Program Administration: Individuals,
    Communities, and the Formation of a Discipline*, edited by Barbara
    L'Eplattenier and Lisa Mastrangelo (2004). Winner of the WPA
    Best Book Award for 2004-2005.

Rhetorics, Poetics, and Cultures: Refiguring College English Studies
    (Expanded Edition) by James A. Berlin (2003)

Stories of Mentoring

Theory and Praxis

Edited by
Michelle F. Eble
Lynée Lewis Gaillet

Parlor Press
West Lafayette, Indiana
www.parlorpress.com

Parlor Press LLC, West Lafayette, Indiana 47906

© 2008 by Parlor Press
All rights reserved.
Printed in the United States of America

S A N: 2 5 4 - 8 8 7 9

Library of Congress Cataloging-in-Publication Data

Stories of mentoring : theory and praxis / edited by Michelle F. Eble, Lynee
Lewis Gaillet.
    p. cm. -- (Lauer series in rhetoric and composition)
 Includes bibliographical references and index.
 ISBN 978-1-60235-072-4 (pbk. : alk. paper) -- ISBN 978-1-60235-073-1
(hardcover : alk. paper) -- ISBN 978-1-60235-074-8 (adobe ebook)
 1. Mentoring in education--United States. 2. English language--Rhetoric-
-Study and teaching--United States. 3. English language--Composition and
exercises--Study and teaching--United States. I. Eble, Michelle F., 1974- II.
Gaillet, Lynée Lewis.
 LB1731.4.S76 2008
 378.1'25--dc22

                                2008033416

Cover design by David Blakesley.
Printed on acid-free paper.

Parlor Press, LLC is an independent publisher of scholarly and trade titles
in print and multimedia formats. This book is available in paper, cloth
and Adobe eBook formats from Parlor Press on the World Wide Web
at http://www.parlorpress.com or through online and brick-and-mortar
bookstores. For submission information or to find out about Parlor Press
publications, write to Parlor Press, 816 Robinson St., West Lafayette,
Indiana, 47906, or e-mail editor@parlorpress.com.

Contents

Part II: Mentoring Relationships

Part III: Mentoring in Undergraduate and Graduate Education

Part IV: Mentoring in Writing Programs

For Win

Photograph of Michelle F. Eble, Winifred Bryan Horner, and Lynée
Lewis Gaillet by Wendy Sharer. Used by permission.

Acknowledgments

A project of this magnitude depends upon the generosity, dedication, and knowledge of a great many people. We wish to thank David Blakesley at Parlor Press, as well as Patricia Sullivan and Catherine Hobbs for supporting this collection. For editorial help and assistance, we are grateful to Delisa Mulkey at Georgia State University for her early assistance organizing both contributors and contributions and to Megan Roberts at East Carolina University for providing invaluable help with the index and final submission details. Finally, we wish to thank the seventy-six authors who religiously adhered to deadlines (even when we couldn't), willingly revised and trimmed their pieces, and inevitably challenged our assumptions about mentoring theory and practice.

Michelle F. Eble: I would like to thank my colleagues and mentors in the Department of English at East Carolina University for their consistent support, willingness to collaborate, and inspiring conversations. I could not ask for a more collegial, smart group. In the course of editing this collection, Lynée was a fabulous collaborator and friend especially when a hurricane and my wedding took my attention away from this collection; I will always be grateful for her patience and wisdom. I also want to thank Shane and our web of family and friends for their support in anything and everything I do.

Lynée Lewis Gaillet: I wish to thank the Georgia State University College of Arts and Sciences and Department of English for their constant support over the years. I am also indebted to the scores of students who have mentored me over the last two decades. I have learned far more than I've taught, and I am constantly awed by my students' knowledge, energy, perseverance, and drive. From my students, I have learned humility and the true meaning of what Eodice and Day label (first person)[2] collaboration. Finally, for their generosity and understanding when I've ironically ignored them to mentor others, I am forever grateful to my family—Philippe, Helen, John Rhodes, Charlotte, and Stormy.

Stories of Mentoring

1 Introduction

Lynée Lewis Gaillet

This collection seeks to define the current status of *mentoring* in the field of composition and rhetoric by providing both snapshots and candid descriptions of what that term means to those working in the discipline. Contributors offer a wide array of evidence and illustrations in an effort to define the scope of this ubiquitous and ambiguous term. In the pages of this collection, then, the reader will find program descriptions and critiques, testimonials and personal anecdotes, copies of correspondence and e-mail messages, term projects and assignments, accounts of forged friendships and peer relationships (some good; some bad), both new paradigms and familiar constructs for successful mentoring, tales of pregnancy and mothering, chronicles of both administrative nightmares and dream solutions, and stories giving insight into the character of those rare individuals who embody the term *mentor*.

Our experiences, both as mentors and mentees, led us to the present investigation. Within two months of issuing our call for papers, we received ninety queries and abstract submissions. Interestingly, over ninety percent of the proposals were multi-authored; obviously, the topic touched an academic nerve. To include as many representations of mentoring within the field as possible, we elected to accept shorter reflective pieces as well as longer chapter-length studies. The result? A chorale of seventy-eight voices whose experiences depict current theories and practices of mentoring. In this study, we do not draw definitive conclusions or posit a theory of mentoring based on the contributors' work. Rather, we compiled these stories, anecdotes, reflections, analyses, descriptions, and discussions of mentoring to serve as a representative sample of mentoring as it is theorized and practiced in the fields of rhetorical, writing, and literary studies during a moment in

time. When viewed collectively, these essays help define and complicate conceptions of mentoring within English Studies.

The term *mentoring* proliferates the field's recent scholarship, and
is most often associated with teaching assistant training programs, the
preparation of graduate students to meet the demands of professional
development, gender and tenure issues, and the enculturation of new
faculty members and administrators. The concept of mentoring, dat-
ing back to Homer's *Odyssey*, currently signifies a range of practices
and responsibilities within rhet/comp studies, but definitions of the
term are hard to come by. Although the term figures prominently both
in the pages of our field's scholarship and as a primary component of
graduate education, *mentoring* did not make Heilker and Vandenberg's
list of important *Keywords in Composition* back in 1996.

While rhetoric and writing faculty boast a long and rich heritage
of mentoring, scholarship specifically addressing the act is a rather recent occurrence. Nearly a decade ago, Theresa Enos challenged the
master-apprentice, male model of mentoring, suggesting alternative
strategies for incorporating mentoring and role modeling within graduate education ("Mentoring"). Enos also alludes to the importance of
mentoring throughout her book-length study *Gender Roles and Faculty
Lives in Rhetoric and Composition* (1996). In "Graduate Students as
Active Members of the Profession: Some Questions for Mentoring"
(1997), Janice Lauer applauds faculty who encourage graduate students to develop themselves as professionals within the field, but she
claims those mentoring efforts aren't always adequate. Although we
have the responsibility to train our students for the rigorous demands
of life in academia, Lauer, a generous mentor, says we must also adopt
an "ethics of care" approach to mentoring, which promotes modeling
the effective ways in which professionals relate to each other within
the field (234). Recognized as master mentors, both Enos and Lauer
further explore the ramifications of mentoring within the pages of this
volume.

Perhaps the best source for examining the significance mentoring
holds within Composition Studies lies in the work of Writing Program Administrators (WPAs). Given their university-mandated responsibility to train teaching assistants, experienced WPAs have published an important body of work related to mentoring and mentoring
programs. With the growing recognition that WPAs are engaged in
intellectual inquiry, mentoring has become more programmatic and

systematic. This paradigm shift in part replaces the individualized professor/protégé construct of the past and has led many WPAs to disseminate information about the programs they helped form. Recent edited collections targeted to WPAs address the challenges of training TAs, particularly those new writing teachers with little or no training in writing instruction. *Preparing College Teachers of Writing* (Pytlik and Liggett 2002) outlines histories, theories, programs, and practices of writing teacher preparation, and several chapters focus on the act of mentoring teaching assistants as well as preparing them to teach writing (see chapters by Rickly and Harrington, Ebest, Martin and Paine, Das Bender). Likewise, *Strategies for Teaching First-Year Composition* (Roen, Pantoja, Yena, Miller, and Waggoner 2002) discusses the training and mentoring of new writing instructors. Other important book-length volumes addressing writing program administration include *Kitchen Cooks, Plate Twirlers and Troubadours: Writing Program Administrators Tell Their Stories* (George 1999); *The Writing Program Administrator as Researcher: Inquiry in Action and Reflection* (Rose and Weiser 1999); *The Writing Program Administrator's Handbook: A Guide to Reflective Institutional Change and Practice* (Brown and Enos 2002); *The Writing Program Administrator as Theorist: Making Knowledge Work* (Rose and Weiser 2002); *The Writing Program Administrator's Handbook: A Guide to Reflective Institutional Change and Practice* (Brown and Enos 2002); *Don't Call it That: The Composition Practicum* (Dobrin 2005); and *Writing Program Administration* (Susan McLeod 2007). Three excellent new collections—*Culture Shock and the Practice of Profession: Training the Next Wave in Rhetoric and Composition* (Anderson and Romano 2006), *Untenured Faculty as Writing Program Administrators: Institutional Practices and Politics* (Dew and Horning 2007), and the forthcoming *Feminisms and Administration in Rhetoric and Composition* (Ratcliffe and Rickly 2008)—critically and extensively explore ways in which the profession is reinventing its identity, in large part through (post)doctoral training.

In addition to providing excellent teacher-training advice, WPA-led scholarship also addresses both faculty and peer mentoring of junior WPAs. Collaborative models of writing program administration advance a decentered administrative structure, while providing increased opportunities for mentoring and for the professional development of graduate students as they attempt to make the transition from graduate school to professorships. Often controversial constructs, junior administrative positions are economically beneficial to the university (read cheap labor). Associate and assistant WPA positions—commonly held by graduate students, lecturers, or instructors—are designed to prepare apprentices for full-time administrative positions. However, as James Sosnoski and Beth Burmester contend, the master/apprentice traditional model of education has long outlived its usefulness for the training of graduate students. Burmester explains,

> Mentoring as a practice was always connected to education and the welfare of the less experienced person, but apprenticeship was never constructed to apply to education, nor to look out for the apprentice's rights or growth; instead, apprenticeship helped maintain the distance between masters and apprentices, in the conditions of their labor and wages. (328)

In a thematic issue of *Rhetoric Review* (2002) devoted to administrative work and the professionalization of graduate students, contributors agreed that their graduate school experience in administration gave them useful, practical experience that prepared them "for the intellectual work of being a WPA"; however, they didn't feel adequately prepared for the "institutional politics of this very difficult job" (Mountford 42). In describing "collaborative efforts between teachers with different amounts of institutional power" (66), Margaret K. Willard-Traub argues that

> formal opportunities [to engage in administration and assessment] would not only help to improve the quality of teaching and of learning; opportunities for graduate students to theorize the politicized nature of their positions within the institution would help serve the aims of scholarship as well, providing emerging scholars with occasions for the kind of epistemic reflexivity that Pierre Bourdieu argues for in support of the pursuit of disciplinary knowledge. (68)

Perhaps the most significant benefit that results from the kind of mentoring that occurs naturally within collaborative administration is the increased opportunity for significant reflection—an important facet of mentoring illustrated by the experiences of Susan Popham, Michael Neal, Ellen Schendel and Brian Huot (working together both as GTAs and program administrators). Having found a way to successfully combine theory, practice, and program policy, Popham, et al. claim that writing programs benefit from collaborative reflection that leads to revision in policy and curriculum and that informs the intellectual work of writing program administration (28). These voices suggest new paths that mentoring might take. In addition to preparing students for the triumvirate of activities most commonly associated with faculty work (research, teaching, and service), mentoring within WPA programs can potentially provide mentees with the tools to negotiate institutional politics while helping them conceive of administration as intellectual inquiry.

Collectively, works in the tradition of the ones cited above provide a foundation for this volume; however, these studies address mentoring tangentially (i.e., in the course of describing a faculty member's job responsibilities, offering ideas for building programs and training students, or discussing tenure and advancement). Existing scholarship doesn't attempt to collect and capture specific theories, practices, stories, and reflections of mentoring—the goal of our collection. In a field that likes to define keywords, concepts, and best practices, no extensive treatment of *mentoring* currently exists. The overwhelming response to our call for papers—which included queries from undergraduate and graduate students, business professionals and technical writers, lecturers and instructors, professors and emeritus faculty—attests to the widespread interest in mentoring practices. Building on the last ten years of research and scholarship addressing mentoring, the essays in this collection provide a wide range of examples for assessing the implications and applications of mentoring, while documenting existing research and practice on the subject. We think both undergraduate and graduate students, faculty, department and college administrators, and those interested in assessment/documentation of faculty work will find *Stories of Mentoring: Theory and Praxis* of interest.

We divide this work into four sections realizing that these divisions are a bit arbitrary and permeable. Interspersed within the traditional chapters, readers will find shorter reflective pieces highlighting unique perspectives on mentoring. The four sections include (1) definitions of mentoring by and multi-voiced tributes to model mentors, (2) tales of mentoring relationships, (3) descriptions of mentoring pedagogy from both undergraduate and graduate education, and (4) analyses of mentoring that occurs within program administration. Winifred

Bryan Horner, my dissertation director and mentor for nearly twenty years, provides an extended definition of the term *mentoring* in the opening essay and offers a first-hand account of the development of mentoring within the field of rhetoric and composition. Professor Horner is recognized nationally (and internationally) as a master mentor, and scores of women and men claim her as a career-long friend and "guiding light." Recipient of the 2003 CCCC Exemplar Award (presented to a professor who represents the highest ideals of teaching, scholarship, and service within the profession), Professor Horner is never content to rest on her laurels, but serves as a model for emulation and an avid mentor well into her retirement. Distinguished Professor Emerita of English at Texas Christian University in Fort Worth, where for a decade she held the first Radford Chair of Rhetoric and Composition, Professor Horner remains interested in her colleagues' projects, eager to collaborate with former students on new projects, and concerned about both the professional careers and personal lives of so very many of us in the profession.

In "Educating Jane," Jenn Fishman and Andrea Lunsford (1994 CCCC Exemplar Award recipient and mentor extraordinaire) both define and complicate traditional connotations of *mentor*. They forego this nebulous term and instead opt for *colleague*—a term that implies shared inquiry, collaborative research and writing, and true professionalization between and among partners. The next three essays in this section are multi-voiced tributes to influential mentors and the programs they established. In "Their Stories on Mentoring: Multiple Perspectives on Mentoring," Janice Lauer (1998 CCCC Exemplar Award winner) and seven of her former graduate students, who entered the program at Purdue in 1994, describe and discuss the primary components of a successful mentoring program. In this dialogue, the participants discuss composition instruction, academic advising, collaborative dissertation groups, professional development sessions, community building experiences, and job search preparation. In the next chapter, "Mentorship, Collegiality, and Friendship: Making Our Mark as Professionals," Steven Bernhardt and nine of his mentees offer a range of individual perspectives on what it means to be mentored within a PhD program. The collaborators discuss the metamorphosis of their relationships from that of professor-to-student into colleagues and friends. In the final essay of Part I, Anna Leahy, Stephanie Vanderslice, Kelli L. Custer, Jennifer Wells, Carol Ellis, Meredith Kate Brown, Dorinda

Fox, and Amy Hodges Hamilton document ways in which Wendy Bishop and her work mentored colleagues and students. The authors discuss Bishop's call to collaboration and the legacy she leaves for the next generation of academics through those whom she mentored in person, via correspondence, and through her scholarship.

The second section includes chapters describing and analyzing diverse mentoring relationships. In these pages, the contributors discuss mentoring in the contexts of friendships, mothering, collaborating, conducting research, and observation. In "Mentoring Friendships and the 'Reweaving of Authority'," Diana Ashe and Elizabeth Ervin argue that multifarious, mutual, and generative relationships—friendships—can offer a potent model for mentoring, especially relationships frequently advocated in the literature on critical pedagogy. Catherine Gabor, Stacia Dunn Neeley, and Carrie Shively Leverenz explore the important role that mentors can play in the careers of young women attempting to combine motherhood with academic labor. In "Mentor, May I Mother?" the three collaborators, mentored by Andrea Lunsford, weave recent research on motherhood and academia within their own stories of becoming mothers. In the next chapter, "The Minutia of Mentorships: Reflections about Professional Development," Katherine S. Miles and Rebecca E. Burnett explore qualitative longitudinal data from worklogs, collected over more than two years, and provide narrative reflections from their own mentorship to chronicle its initiation and growth—and to demonstrate ways in which it has evolved over time and in specific contexts. Next, Wendy Sharer, Jessica Enoch, and Cheryl Glenn highlight the importance of professional and personal respect enacted and taught within a collaborative mentoring relationship in "Performing Professionalism: On Mentoring and Being Mentored." The final snapshots in this section capture unique mentoring relationships. Susan Thomas and George Pullman reflect on their international mentoring relationship and advocate mentoring by modeling, while Doug Downs and Dayna Goldstein describe a long-term, ongoing mentoring relationship that privileges everyday practice and mutual benefits over career advancement

Part III, "Mentoring in Undergraduate and Graduate Education," includes seven chapters that examine opportunities for mentoring in both undergraduate and graduate education. The first two essays describe writing groups: Lisa Cahill, Susan Miller-Cochran, Veronica Pantoja, and Rochelle L. Rodrigo illustrate how graduate student

writing groups serve the function of community building, and Angela Eaton along with seven of her undergraduate students describe a
mentoring experience that began as a course in research methodologies and culminated in several publications and professional presentations for the group. The next three essays explore the role of mentoring
within graduate studies. Adopting a web metaphor, Jennifer Clary-
Lemon and Duane Roen define mentoring as a scholarly practice and
graduate school as the locus of that practice. And in "Mentor or Magician: Reciprocities, Existing Ideologies, and Reflections of a Discipline," Barbara Cole and Arabella Lyon remind readers of the tensions and obstacles involved in mentoring literature-trained graduate
students to teach writing, pointing out ways certain ideologies function within disciplinary practices such as the composition practicum.
In the next essay, Amy C. Kimme Hea and Susan N. Smith outline
the transition from graduate student to faculty member that many
TAs experience. The co-writers report on issues of power and authority that surfaced when they piloted a co-taught, graduate course. The
final two reflective pieces in Part III specifically address mentoring
pedagogy. C. Renée Love outlines a teaching plan that asks students to
explore the benefits of mentoring relationships, and Nancy Myers argues convincingly how a text can function as mentor, providing access
to disciplinary habits and institutional responsibilities that are often
viewed as the role of a human mentor.

Part IV of the collection explores mentoring practices associated
with writing program administration. Alfred E. Guy Jr. and Rita
Malenczyk recount their experiences working within New York University's (NYU) Expository Writing Program. In describing the history, structure, and strengths of the program, the authors speculate on
the implications the NYU program may have for mentoring within
current writing programs. In "Mentoring Toward Interdependency:
'Keeping It Real'," WPAs Krista Ratcliffe and Donna Schuster argue
that writing programs must address five key factors in order to provide a pragmatic vision for mentoring: local institutional situations,
writing staff needs, curriculum design, staff personalities, and training opportunities. Joan Mullin and Paula Braun explore the notions
of reciprocity and risk-taking in successful mentoring relationships,
followed by Cinda Coggins Mosher and Mary Trachsel's analysis of
how mentoring programs, based on attention and response, negotiate the distinction among panopticism, oversight, and surveillance by

paying attention to individuals and their needs as instructors. In the final program description, Holly Ryan, David Reamer and Theresa Enos chronicle the three-year revision of their faculty and peer-mentoring program in the Rhetoric, Composition, and the Teaching of English at the University of Arizona. The co-authors critically discuss the research, evaluation, and continual development of this highly acclaimed mentoring program. Tanya Cochran and Beth Godbee close this section by proposing in "Making It Count: Mentoring as Cultural Currency" ways to document mentoring as a scholarly activity of value in CVs and tenure and promotion materials.

In the coda, Michelle F. Eble critically reflects upon this volume, discussing the implications *Stories of Mentoring: Theory and Praxis* might hold for future scholarship. Like Telemachus's Mentor in the Odyssey, present-day mentors are commonly viewed as teachers, coaches, counselors and protectors, parental figures, role models, advisors and motivators trusted with the care and education of younger and less-experienced mentees. But as the contributors to this collection demonstrate, professional mentoring relationships are much more complicated and often hold high-stake repercussions for individuals, local programs, and the discipline at large.

Collectively, the essays in *Stories of Mentoring: Theory and Praxis* illustrate diverse ways in which *mentoring* is defined in everyday practice. However, the multiplicity of views that compose this collection is by no means exhaustive; we attempt only to provide discipline-specific, candid snapshots of mentoring within the field of rhetoric and writing. Areas offering particularly rich opportunities for research include: mentoring and distance learning, undergraduate mentoring, viewing mentoring as intellectual inquiry, and issues of race/gender and mentoring. We hope other researchers, mentors, and mentees will share their tales of mentoring in these areas, adding their voices and experiences to the stories shared in this collection.

Works Cited

Anderson, Virginia, and Susan Romano. *Culture Shock and the Practice of Profession: Training the Next Wave in Rhetoric and Composition*. Cresskill, NJ: Hampton, 2006.

Brown, Stuart C., Theresa Enos, and Catherine Chaput, eds. *The Writing Program Administrator's Handbook: A Guide to Reflective Institutional Change and Practice*. Mahwah, NJ: Erlbaum, 2002.

Gebhardt, Richard C., and Barbara Genelle Smith Gebhardt, eds. *Academic Advancement in Composition Studies: Scholarship, Publication, Promotion*. Mahweh: Erlbaum, 1996.

Das Bender, Gita. "Orientation and Mentoring: Collaborative Practices in Teacher Preparation." *Preparing College Teachers of Writing: Histories, Theories, Practices, and Programs*. Ed. Betty Pytlik and Sarah Liggett. New York: Oxford UP, 2002. 233-41.

Dew, Deborah Frank, and Alice Horning, eds. *Untenured Faculty as Writing Program Administrators: Institutional Practices and Politics*. West Lafayette, IN: Parlor Press, 2007.

Dobrin, Sid. *Don't Call it That: The Composition Practicum*. Urbana: NCTE, 2005.

Ebest, Sally Barr. "Mentoring: Past, Present, and Future." *Preparing College Teachers of Writing: Histories, Theories, Practices, and Programs*. Ed. Betty Pytlik and Sarah Liggett. New York: Oxford UP, 2002. 211-21.

Enos, Theresa. *Gender Roles and Faculty Lives in Rhetoric and Composition*. Carbondale: Southern Illinois UP, 1996.

—. "Mentoring—and (Wo)mentoring—in Composition Studies." *Academic Advancement in Composition Studies Scholarship, Publication, Promotion, Tenure*. Ed. Richard C. Gebhardt and Barbara Genelle Smith Gebhardt. Mahwah, NJ: Erlbaum, 1997. 137-46.

George, Diana, ed. *Kitchen Cooks, Plate Twirlers and Troubadours: Writing Program Administrators Tell Their Stories*. Boynton/Cook, Heinemann, 1999.

Heilker, Paul, and Peter Vandenberg. *Keywords in Composition Studies*. Boynton/Cook, 1996.

Lauer, Janice M. "Graduate Students as Active Members of the Profession: Some Questions for Mentoring." Ed. Gary A. Olson and Todd W. Taylor. *Publishing in Rhetoric and Composition*; Albany, NY: SUNY P, 1997. 229-36

Martin, Wanda, and Charles Paine. "Mentors, Models, and Agents of Change: Veteran TAs Preparing Teachers of Writing." *Preparing College Teachers of Writing: Histories, Theories, Practices, and Programs*. Ed. Betty Pytlik and Sarah Liggett. New York: Oxford UP, 2002. 222-32.

McLeod, Susan. *Writing Program Administration*. West Lafayette, IN: Parlor Press, 2007.

Mountford, Roxanne. "From Labor to Middle Management: Graduate Students in Writing Program Administration (In Memory of Eric Walborn)." *Rhetoric Review* 21.1 (2002) 41-54.

Popham, Susan, Michael Neal, Ellen Schendel, and Brian Huot. "Breaking Hierarchies: Using Reflective Practice to Re-Construct the Role of the Writing Program Administrator." *The Writing Program Administrator as Theorist*. Ed. Shirley K. Rose and Irwin Weiser. Westport, CT: Heinemann Boynton/Cook, 2002. 19-28.

Pytlik, Betty, and Sarah Liggett, eds. *Preparing College Teachers of Writing: Histories, Theories, Practices, and Programs.* New York: Oxford UP, 2002.

Ratcliffe, Krista, and Rebecca J. Rickly, eds. *Feminisms and Administration in Rhetoric and Composition.* Cresskill, NJ: Hampton Press, forthcoming.

Rickly, Rebecca J., and Susanmarie Harrington. "Feminist Approaches to Mentoring Teaching Assistants: Conflict, Power, and Collaboration." *Preparing College Teachers of Writing: Histories, Theories, Practices, and Programs.* Ed. Betty Pytlik and Sarah Liggett. New York: Oxford UP, 2002. 108-20.

Roen, Duane, Veronica Pantoja, Lauren Yena, Susan K. Miller, and Eric Waggoner, eds. *Strategies for Teaching First-Year Composition.* Urbana, IL: NCTE, 2002.

Rose, Shirley K, and Irwin Weiser, eds. *The Writing Program Administrator as Researcher: Inquiry in Action and Reflection* Portsmouth: Heinemann-Boynton/Cook, 1999.

—. *The Writing Program Administrator as Theorist: Making Knowledge Work.* Portsmouth: Boynton/Cook Heinemann, 2002.

Sosnoski, James, and Beth Burmester. "New Scripts for Rhetorical Education: Alternative Learning Environments and the Master/Apprentice Model." *Culture Shock and the Practice of Profession: Training the Next Wave in Rhetoric and Composition.* Ed. Virginia Anderson and Susan Romano. Cresskill, NJ: Hampton Press, 2006: 325-45.

Willard-Traub, Margaret K. "Professionalization and the Politics of Subjectivity." *Rhetoric Review* 21.1 (2002) 61-70.

2 On Mentoring

Winifred Bryan Horner

With my training in linguistics, I always look first to the dictionary when I am writing on a subject and the *Oxford English Dictionary (OED)* never fails to enlighten my understanding of a concept—or more importantly other people's understanding of the many meanings of a word.

The citation for *mentor* is relatively brief and its history equally short. I'm sure the mythological derivation of the word will be covered and explored elsewhere in this book. Odysseus turned to the goddess of Wisdom, Athena, (in all mythologies, Wisdom is depicted as female) to advise and guide his son, Telemachus, in his absence. Athena disguised herself as an Ithacan noble, Mentor, to fulfill her role. The *OED* further notes that "the currency of the word in French and English is derived less from the *Odyssey* than from Fénelon's romance of *Télémaque*, in which the part played by Mentor as a counselor is made more prominent. Its first citation after Fénelon, an eighteenth century author, is in 1750 by Lord Chesterfield in advising his son. Wisdom is embodied in the female, but in my early experience, my first mentors were always men. There are no feminized versions of *mentor* even though *tutor*, often given as a synonym and of much older origin, has three—*totoress*, *tutress* and *tutrix*—as well as a form of the person being tutored as *tutoree*. In my limited research for this article I discovered that mentoring is a hot topic particularly in academe. When I looked up *mentor/academe* on the Internet, there were 191,000 hits as well as a journal, called *Mentor, An Academic Advising Journal.* Looking back on my own experience I suppose I have served as a mentoree, and later as a mentor, and also as a mentoress, and possibly a mentrix.

As an early graduate student teaching freshman composition I was told in effect to "keep my place." My first experience was with the director of freshman composition, a man cut from the old pattern—blustering, and smart—who periodically lumbered down the hall to the coffee room where he sucked on a large cigar and loudly held forth in a cloud of evil-smelling smoke, giving the word to his favorite male graduate students who circled him like a bunch of hungry young wolves. I never saw him as my mentor although I knew he treasured his relationship with the male graduate students, involving them in weekly poker games and other seemly male bonding activities. He kept tight control over the graduate students, allowing for no deviations from the rules which were of his making. I was first impressed by such power, later intimidated, and finally disgusted.

This was in the 1960s and the department was interviewing for new positions. I had been impressed by a particular black female applicant who was turned down. I assumed it was because she was black, but I later learned it was, in fact, because she was a woman. That came as a great revelation to me until I realized with surprise that the department was entirely made up of males and that a woman of whatever color would be an intrusion in the old boy's club. The men in the department were definitely not into mentoring women graduate students.

In the Master's program, I was assigned an advisor who informed me early on that over his dead body would I continue teaching in the program and when I inquired about continuing with a PhD, he told me that advanced degrees caused terrible things to happen to women. His prophecy proved true when he, himself, later married a woman PhD. There were no women mentors at that time simply because there were no senior women in the profession. In those days mentors by default were male. He, like many of my early memorable mentors, is now gone to the academic heaven in the sky where he felt confident that God and his angels would all be male.

When I went to graduate school my first advisor turned out to be immensely helpful in the long run but first I had to prove myself. He tried to guide me to abandon the PhD program but on the advice of a woman mentor I was determined not to settle for anything less than a PhD. When he discovered that I had no trouble with the language requirement and that I was actually a good student he became a dedicated supporter to whom I will always be grateful, guiding me with care and counsel through the minefield of the PhD program. He was my first true mentor. I knew then that there was no way I could immediately repay him, but I determined then to pass on his wise counsel if I ever was in a position to do so.

During my PhD program probably my best mentors were my fellow graduate students. I remember one who tried to give me some help in reading Old English, which my professor told me that I pronounced with a French accent. That night I went to a party celebrating the completion of "O" in the Middle English Dictionary and I was finally admitted to the cadre of graduate students. My fellow students, both male and female, were the ones who led me through the labyrinth surrounding the idiosyncrasies of the professors. We willingly helped each other. As one of the mature graduate students I was assigned the task of getting one of our better students across the campus and into the room to take his qualifying exam—which he had deftly avoided once before by going to a movie instead.

When I returned to my original university as an assistant professor I was helped through the advancement process by a male colleague who largely provided a shoulder to cry on over cups of coffee and martinis after five. One day when I complained that garbage collectors in New York were better paid than professors at the university, he took a long sip of coffee, looked thoughtful and replied that he thought he would rather teach than collect garbage in New York.

I learned early on that the name of the game was research and writing, two occupations that I thoroughly enjoyed. After attaining the rank of professor with a good publishing record, I was offered an Endowed Chair and suddenly I found myself in the position of mentor instead of mentoree. It was a constant surprise that my opinion was now of great value. I had a friend who had recently retired who bemoaned the fact that although she now had all the answers no one asked the questions anymore. However, when I talked at the lunch table the students listened and when I talked in class they took notes. As the first woman endowed chair on the campus, I discovered that I was a model for all women, a role that humbled and challenged me.

I was assigned a graduate student as a research assistant, but I failed at my first position as a model when my assistant dropped out of the PhD program because, she confessed, she didn't want to work as hard as I did. I was amazed because I really loved my work and felt as though teaching, writing, and researching were great fun and much superior to other occupations such as collecting garbage in New York City. I found writing pure joy when it came out right.

Finally I embraced the role of mentor. I realized that I had two things going for me. I had no more promotions to work for, and I was exactly where I wanted to be. I knew then that my future was with my students, whom I hoped would carry on the work that I had started. Since I had started at the very bottom, I felt I did have some answers and they were voracious in asking the questions. I was eager to help but I was humbled by my new status.

I found that I was able to open doors for my students that were hard for them to open themselves. I tried to help them get on panels, urged them to attend conferences, and helped shape their papers into publishable articles. I tried to help them develop a nose for an article and shape an idea into publishable form. At conferences I always tried to introduce them to the people whose work they knew. At one conference a colleague of mine from another large university and I organized a party for our students in the history of rhetoric so that they could get to know each other. We also invited the well-known scholars in the field who responded with the expected grace of real scholars who are always interested in what young researchers are doing. The party was lively, and the conversation sparkled. Friendships were forged and ideas were shared. It was networking at its best and mentoring at its finest.

As a dissertation director I worked hard to get my students past that hurdle and often passed on the advice of one of my professors in graduate school that the best dissertation is finally a "done" dissertation. It is hard to convey the idea to eager graduate students immersed in their research that the dissertation is not their life's work and the best thing is to get on with it and move to other things like a salaried position.

At one time I was reviewing articles for all the major journals in the field and I loved having the opportunity to read the newest and best work being done. I felt as though I were on the cusp of new knowledge. In return I tried to be encouraging and helpful in specific ways.

I have heard of several universities where mentoring has been set up on a formal basis. I don't know how that works but I do know that in order for it to work, there must be questions and the mentor must feel that she or he has answers. That is the basis of the relationship. Most important there must be the questions—a knowledge of those things you know you don't know, and that alone takes a certain amount of wisdom. Finally, the relationship is built on common interests, common goals, and most of all, respect for the other. In the end those mentoring relationships develop into deep and long lasting friendships where knowledge is no longer one-sided and wisdom is shared.

3 Educating Jane

Jenn Fishman and Andrea Lunsford

You cannot step into the same river twice, for fresh waters are ever flowing in upon you.

—Heraclitus

The more things change, the more they stay the same.

—French Proverb attributed to
Jean-Baptiste Alphonse Karr

Women who entered the profession some thirty years ago, as Andrea did, took mentors if and where they found them, though they might not have used the term *mentor* itself.* Almost certainly they would have found no formal arrangements for mentorship, no organized means of becoming initiated into the academy, and precious little if any systematic encouragement. What they did encounter was the "old boy's network" through which men found academic positions and moved often seamlessly into the academy. As a result, such entry could be fraught with special difficulty for women. Women entering the field of rhetoric and composition—Jane Rhetors of an earlier generation—found themselves in a double bind: not only were they at a disadvantage in being women but they were also entering a field whose place in the academy was itself contested.

Today—well, that's another story. While still marginalized in terms of its relationship with literary studies, the field of rhetoric and writing is now firmly established. In fact, if today's Jane Rhetor wishes to explore possibilities for mentoring, she may be close to overwhelmed by upwards of 50 Modern Language Association (MLA) and Comp-Pile citations for works that range from conference talks to books, articles, and doctoral dissertations. Were Jane to make an index to these materials, her subject list would start with access, a category she would subdivide to reflect the extensive efforts that have been made by and for people historically absent or marginalized within higher education, especially women, first-generation students, returning students, and scholars of color. Care and caring would come next, cross-referenced with help(ing), support(ing), and nurture (nurturing). Entries for contrasting terms like collaboration and competition would be followed by feminism, feminist, and feminization, as well as friendship, gender, masculinity and men, and mothering. Under the heading "professionalization," Jane would include references to work on pedagogy, student-teaching, and teacher-training, and she would identify the papers, articles, and discussions of academic mentoring controversies, including Jane Gallop's defense of erotic pedagogy, Jane Tompkins' representation of teaching, and Elaine Showalter's vision for graduate education in the modern languages.

During the last twenty-five years, this body of literature has developed in tandem with mentoring activities that have gained institutional status in numerous departments and professional organizations. Indeed, mentoring has come of age, and Jane, our figure for Everyacademic, appears to be the lucky beneficiary. Certainly, within the Humanities and especially within disciplines affiliated with the MLA, mentoring is now a common component of graduate pedagogy, just as pedagogical training is now a regular, even required part of many graduate curricula. Similarly, mentoring is a customary aspect of professional development, especially for new instructors and probationary faculty. At first glance, these changes seem salutary, evidence that the academy is taking seriously the need not simply to recruit new scholars but to retain them through material mentoring practices. And even at second glance, such changes would seem to bode well for Jane's eventual success, surrounded as she is by opportunities for mentoring. Why, then, are we still deeply ambivalent about mentorship? This question may seem an odd one to ask at the outset of an essay about mentoring, yet we wonder if others who have expressed skepticism in this volume are equally surprised to find themselves focused on how vexed and how vexing mentorship can be. Certainly we were taken aback by our own ambivalent attitudes, not least because we are both strong supporters of mentoring initiatives. In fact, when we responded to Michelle Eble and Lynée Gaillet's call for papers, we were writing an invited talk for a conference panel about rhetoric and mentoring.

And yet, as we turned to this essay, we found ourselves struggling with the assignment. Rather than slipping into our usual routine—two women at two computers writing as though tapped into the same brain—we wrote in fits and false starts, and we shared mostly dead ends and bad ideas. Finally, in a moment of irritation, Andrea declared her utter dislike of the title *mentor*, and her reasons matched some of Jenn's own concerns. As we began to explore the causes of our frustration, we quickly focused on the deeply hierarchical relationships associated with traditional mentorship. As we talked further, we began to identify specific situations in which *mentoring* is simply another word for control. Further, we noted many instances in which academic mentorship not only devalues the work or contributions of the one being mentored but also calls forth the deeply-rooted intellectual prejudices against collaboration and against anything pedagogical. Such attitudes lead colleagues to continue to presume that shared projects are, at best, attenuated junior research assistantships or useful aids for more senior scholars who have run short on ideas or time.

By this time in our process of exploration, we had worked ourselves into a pretty tight spot, one in which we were increasingly uncomfortable writing the kind of essay we had originally intended. Rather than withdrawing our essay, however, we decided we needed to sit down, take several deep breaths, and start all over again, asking ourselves why *mentoring* might (or might not) be the term we would choose for the kinds of mutually sustaining, cooperative work we wanted to acknowledge and endorse. What follows is less a strict answer to that question than an attempt to clarify and explore it.

To begin to do so, we turn first to the past and to an examination of some ancient and early modern antecedents of contemporary mentoring. As historians, we know such a move may plunge us down the proverbial rabbit hole, yet we do so gamely in order to look closely at the complex dynamics of mentorship that present-day students, teachers, and colleagues have inherited. We proceed, too, aware of our own very personal inheritances and the many colleagues in whose presence we embark on this latest escapade. With these challenges in mind, we dedicate our findings as well as this essay to Jane, our archetype for the evolving collegiality we want mentorship to represent. Neither a plain Jane nor a Jane Doe, our Jane is cut from the fabric of rhetoric, with its centuries old teaching traditions, although today Jane might be chair of a French department or a professor of Victorian literature or the director of a newly established writing center. And though we call her Jane, others may know her as John, Juanita, Jens, or Jun. An embodiment of all those who populate the academy, Jane signals the many different figures, forms, and relationships involved in getting and giving an education.

THE FALL

"Well!" thought Alice to herself, "after such a fall as this, I shall think nothing of tumbling down stairs!"

—Alice, *Alice's Adventures in Wonderland*

For Jane, as for many of us, pursuing the history of mentoring can seem like a great, long fall down into a land as rude and strange as the one Alice encountered when she ran after the white rabbit. Certainly, the characters we meet are equally remarkable, starting with mentoring's original pair, Mentor and Telemachus. In Homer's *Odyssey*, Mentor is both a trusted friend of Ulysses and the guardian of his son, Telemachus. The perfect counselor and parent substitute, Mentor stands in metonymically for much of what we know about early Greek education, and their relationship both affirms and idealizes a system in which older and wiser men served younger men as tutors, gurus, and guides. As such, Mentor and Telemachus are models for countless classical counterparts, among them Socrates and Phaedrus. As portrayed by Plato, the elder philosopher and the eager ephebe are exemplary of the intellectually rich course of civic education and personal training that developed in ancient Greece. Surely, their lively dialogue, set on the idyllic banks of the Ilissus, could not be more unlike the dull tome Alice attempted to read, seated on the banks of the Thames at the start of *Alice in Wonderland*. Unlike Alice's bland book, which had "no pictures and no conversations in it," the *Phaedrus* presents a series of vivid interlocutory scenes. At the same time, however, Plato confirms the idea that mentoring must be an extremely patriarchal activity: a veritable sport that combines an athleticism and an eroticism specific to male bodies—all that bursting and sowing—with social relationships that are rigidly structured, exclusionary, and (at least potentially) exploitative.

While this model of mentoring is the product of very specific cultural and historical circumstances, it maps only too well onto subsequent pedagogical arrangements, including leader and disciple, master and apprentice, benefactor and protégé. Perhaps most notably, ancient archetypes inform the modern concept of mentorship that developed in the eighteenth century alongside the Enlightenment revival of the Mentor and Telemachus story. Retold by François de Salignac de la Mothe-Fénelon, Archbishop of Cambray, *Les avantures de Télémaque* was first published in France in 1699, and the earliest English version was sold shortly thereafter. In twelve to twenty-four books (depending on the translation), *The Adventures of Telemachus* combines generic features of the *roman* or romance with an overtly instructional story and style. Set at the end of the Trojan War, Fénelon's didactic tale recasts the title character's search for his long-absent father through a succession of educational exploits. Starting in Ithaca, Telemachus travels from Sicily and Egypt to Crete, Tyre, and Ogygia, each new adventure a lesson in selfhood, citizenship, and survival. Never alone, Telemachus receives constant advising from a series of impromptu teachers. While each man contributes something important to Telemachus's education, the young ruler-to-be receives his primary instruction from Mentor—or really, from Minerva (Pallas Athena), who disguises herself as the elder statesman Mentor in order to oversee the young man's education.

Despite the gender bending at the center of this mentoring arrangement, Jane is hard-pressed to find *The Adventures of Telemachus* a great inspiration. Indeed, eighteenth-century versions of the Mentor-Telemachus story are important because of the pedagogical complexities—some of them not so palatable—on display. In particular, these versions show how mentoring reproduces some of the most challenging aspects of education, including the ways in which schooling encourages not just access but assimilation into normative culture. This message is conveyed consistently throughout *Telemachus*, which was originally dedicated to the Duke of Burgundy as an antidote to the voluptuousness and corruption associated with the young prince's father, Louis XIV. In translation, Mentor's curriculum is consonant with turn-of-the-eighteenth-century Protestant ideology, and Fénelon's unremitting object lessons neatly reinforce the reformation of manners and morals well underway when *The Adventures of Telemachus* first began to circulate. In an English context, Telemachus is an appealing

Everyman, and Mentor is easy to read as a sign as well as a scion of the times. A spokesperson for masculine prudence, self-control, and just rule, Mentor teaches some of the era's most important civic virtues, including "Love of [one's] country" and loyalty to "a Prince, who is at once a King, a Warrior, a Philosopher, and a Legislator" (21).

The pedagogics of modern mentoring are evident from the outset of *The Adventures*, which opens *in medias res* as the nymph Calypso laments the end of Ulysses' enthrallment on her island. A vision of passion, self-indulgence, and excess, Calypso embodies a model of personalized and sexualized education that contrasts sharply with Mentor's more measured and carefully reasoned curriculum. Together, these two figures represent opposite poles of Enlightenment education, and they share little beyond the common misogynist attitude that limits female educators to the roles of helpmeet, seductress, or man-in-disguise. If Telemachus is initially captivated by Calypso's pedagogy of lavish attention and gifts, the outcomes of her instruction are fleeting, while Mentor's teachings have a dramatic and lasting effect. In this episode, as throughout the novel, Mentor begins with the recitation of commonplaces appropriate to the situation: "[A] young man who loves to dress like a Woman, is unworthy of Wisdom and Glory," and "The Heart that knows not how to suffer Pain, and despise Pleasure, is unfit to possess those glorious Advantages" (43-44). Elaborating these general principles, Mentor not only teaches lessons in prudence and self-governance consonant with early modern Protestant ways of thinking; he also reinforces a gendered epistemology that harkens back to classical forms of mentorship. In this spirit, Mentor cautions: "Beware of hearkening to the soft and flattering Words of *Calypso*," and he further warns: "[B]e more afraid of her insinuating Charms than of the Rocks that split your Ship" for "Death and Shipwreck are less dreadful than the Pleasures that attack Virtue" (44).

Mentor's pedagogy does not end with lectures, however. Instead, *Telemachus* balances "Noble Instruction" against "Heroick Examples," and Mentor's formal lessons preface scenes of active learning that require Telemachus to turn theory into practice and to translate Mentor's warnings into concrete and deliberate action. While Jane may notice right away the similarities between this practice and modern day prompts for active learning, she just as quickly notices what Mentor's lessons lack. Although Telemachus is encouraged to assimilate or internalize and apply what he learns, he receives little encouragement to question or explore the fundamental aspects of his curriculum. To the contrary, the opposite appears to be true, and Mentor encourages his charge not to probe his own actions and motives but rather to approximate those of others. In this spirit, Mentor asks Telemachus to compare himself with his father (or really, the ideal of his father) and judge whether his thoughts about Calypso are "the thoughts that ought to possess the Heart of the Son of Ulysses?" By asking this question, Mentor not only personalizes the episode but also naturalizes the moral standards to which Telemachus is learning to adhere—like father, like son. Through this exchange, education takes on the inevitability of legacy and fate, and deliberation becomes a means of reinforcing truth rather than a tool for discovering it. As a consequence, if there is suspense in the scenes that follow, apprehension adheres not to whether but to how Mentor's student will successfully resist Calypso's advances and her contrasting curriculum of constant delights.

What can Jane learn from such episodes and from Telemachus's subsequent adventures? If Jane is looking for examples to emulate, her prospects are definitely not good. Despite Mentor's (and Minerva's) reassurance of advice and unfailing protection, they are less "guides by the side" than a manifestation of the internal judge or "impartial spectator" that Adam Smith describes in *The Theory of Moral Sentiments*. This aspect of mentorship comes to the fore in scenes where Telemachus and Mentor are separated and Telemachus invokes Mentor as though the elder man were an aspect of his own conscience. While each of us can remember approaching a problem by asking ourselves, "What would (someone else) do?" *The Adventures of Telemachus* calls to mind not only the power of imitation and modeling within education but also the striking similarities between Smith's spectator and Jeremy Bentham's panoptic observer. As always, it is a fine line between the critical thinking and self-discipline involved in principled action and the kind of internalized discipline that invites us to participate in our own oppression. The father-son dynamic at work is also problematic, not least because it invokes a psychology of anxiety and influence that places an aggressive and antagonistic logic of substitution at the center of mentoring relationships. For Telemachus, whose ostensible aim is to reclaim his father, success entails establishing a clear line of succession, and the full story ends when the son is able to succeed (and perhaps eventually supercede) the father.

How, Jane wonders, can such a tradition inform our activities both today and tomorrow? Exceptionally male, privileged, and battle-ready, mentorship also seems to be geared toward reiteration and individualism. In this model, women are antithetical to social and political efficacy—unless they are helpmeets or gods willing and able to pass as men—and difference is absent or erased. Although we know better than to toss the baby out with the bathwater—or to relinquish everything from past history—we nonetheless find ourselves alongside Jane wondering exactly what to do.

Once again, then, we turn to history, this time to see what happened two hundred years ago as the idea of mentoring gained currency.

Further Down the Rabbit Hole

Curiouser and curiouser.

—Alice, *Alice's Adventures in Wonderland*

Although modern readers often find eighteenth-century didacticism off-putting, Fénelon's contemporaries greeted *Les adventures de Télémaque* enthusiastically, and European audiences maintained a strong interest throughout the century. According to popular dramatist John Hawkesworth, by 1768 *Telemachus* had "been translated into every language in Europe, Turkish not excepted," and by 1800 the original French text had been Anglicized by 15 different authors, including Hawkesworth himself as well as the novelist Tobias Smollett. The story's success makes sense, given the state of eighteenth-century education. Following mid-seventeenth-century efforts to universalize schooling and a late seventeenth-century surge in population literacy, Britons witnessed the unprecedented popularization of teaching and learning. Throughout the period, official interest in instruction and curricular change was matched by public discussion, which grew exponentially with social mobility, new professional and consumer opportunities, and changing habits of sociability. Even to period observers, the pedagogy phenomenon was noteworthy. As *Telemachus* translator Charles Taylor (writing as Francis Fitzgerald) observed, "Never before was EDUCATION more fashionable" (iii).

Such claims are substantiated by the multitude of pedagogical tracts, conduct books, and instructional texts extant in present-day archives, including multiple versions and editions of *Telemachus*. If, on one hand, the evolution of Fénelon's work suggests the ways in which mentoring opened up different opportunities for advancement to different groups of readers, the English *Telemachus* library indicates how, on the other hand, certain concepts of citizenship and personhood were confirmed along with particular ideas about teaching and learning. Initially, of course, mentoring was a privilege for princes, and *Telemachus* appealed to their counterparts among the aristocracy: the readership most likely to match their sons (and occasionally for their daughters) with actual mentors. At the same time, Fénelon's publishers and translators worked to frame *Telemachus* for a broader audience, including not only a class-aspirant readership eager to emulate the gentry but also a relatively new general reader ready to claim a place among the "middling sort." Appealing to each of these audiences, mid- and late eighteenth-century editions of *Telemachus* included an ever-changing array of introductory essays, advertisements, and explanatory apparatuses. These more accessible versions of the Mentor-Telemachus story joined the bevy of self-help manuals already in print, and taken together they offered contemporary readers an approachable and definitely affordable Mentor: a wise guardian and guide in the form of a book.

The popularization of *Telemachus* centered on translators' and editors' efforts to demonstrate the appeal of both mentoring and the novel to increasingly broad audiences. Thus, while Joseph Addison acknowledged that Fénelon's story "was written for the instruction of a young prince" (373-74), he and other commentators took great pains to show that *Telemachus* was an appropriate story not only for royalty but also for readers destined for other kinds of rule. Early on, then, essayist Andrew Michael Ramsay identified in Fénelon's epic "Heroick and Royal Virtues" that are "proper for all Conditions," including not only monarchs and public men but also "no less every private Man in his Duty" (22). In response, some publishers took the opportunity to turn *Telemachus* into an actual textbook, and in 1742 John Gray released an edition with the English and French text printed *en face*, which he hoped would be "more particularly useful" not at home but "in schools" (np). Whether Gray's edition became required reading, *Telemachus* did become part of the eighteenth-century curriculum, and subsequent translators including William Henry Melmoth could address themselves "to those that have read this work only as an exercise at school" and "them who have learned French in this country," as well as "persons who are wholly unacquainted with the French language" (iii).

Not until the late eighteenth century, however, did mentoring begin to acquire the look and feel of a popular phenomenon, one available to ordinary people. One turning point came in 1770, when publisher Alexander Hogg produced a *Telemachus* poised to compete with the periodical presses. Boasting a new economy of small margins and small print, as well as a new translation, Hogg's distinctive volumes made every effort to appeal to a truly general readership. Identifying the novel as written "to promote the Happiness of Mankind in general," Hogg offers a "great Variety of Notes, Historical, Critical, Explanatory, Scholastic, Political, Moral, Philological, Satirical, and Illustrative [. . .] CALCULATED TO GRATIFY EVERY CLASS OF READERS" (title page). Even more importantly, in the same volume translator Melmoth emphasizes the moral aspects of Fénelon's tale, making them central to the novel's pedagogy and its wide appeal. Describing *Telemachus* as second only to the Bible, he celebrates the works' ability "to do more real service to the world than any that was ever written" (iv). Perhaps for this reason, publisher Hogg envisions *Telemachus* as an apropos mentor for a truly inclusive readership, arguing that the story uniquely "forms our Minds for a King, a Citizen, a Father, a Mother, a Master, a Gentleman, a Tradesman, a Servant, and even a Slave, if such should be our Lot" (title page).

In this boast, Jane immediately recognizes a model of literacy education predicated on the rise of consumer capitalism and Enlightenment individualism. At work is the unique interiorizing of the self associated with both Protestant self-reliance and (silent) reading. These developments, Hogg's title page reminds us, emerged in a culture that still believed in the Great Chain of Being, still figured educated women primarily (or exclusively) as mothers, and still worked to justify slavery. Thus Jane would have to read very hard against the grain to find within *Telemachus* grounds for critique, and she would be equally at a loss to find within Fénelon's story hints or clues about alternative mentoring stories and arrangements, even though such stories were widely available within eighteenth-century life and society. In short, while a genre like the popular novel readily explored alternative mentoring relationships, mainstream mentoring literature stayed relatively fixed on particular masculine relationships and their sustaining ideologies.

BACK ALONG THE RIVER

Begin at the beginning [. . .] and go on till you come to the end:
then stop.

—The King to the White Rabbit,
Alice's Adventures in Wonderland

After this second foray down the rabbit hole, Jane once again surveys the literature on mentoring and tries to account for what she sees today. How has the steady flow of scholarship been informed by (or resisted) the history of mentoring detailed here? Does the current interest in and commitments to mentoring testify to significant changes in the nature and practice of mentoring—or is it one more example of *"Plus ça change, plus c'est la même chose"*?

What stands out to us in reviewing the history of mentorship and the current literature surrounding it is how limited we are in our ability to talk about the experience of mentoring and of being mentored. To a degree, this volume is a case in point, and Jane is right to wonder why it is a collection on *mentoring* and not, for example, telemachery. That is to say, our very language for talking to one another about mentoring practices and relationships promotes a sense of imbalance by virtually erasing mentees. The latter term was coined in the 1960s, although it is still unrecognized by spell check. Awkward at best, it characterizes the act of being mentored as a derivative or passive activity, drawing on Anglo-French legalese, which assigns agency with the suffix "or" and names passive parties using the suffix "ee." Regarded as a novice, a mentee is someone who undergoes an extended process of initiation and assimilation in order to learn duty and obedience alongside the rudiments of a discipline and/or a profession. Construed as an apprentice, a mentee is not only a student or pupil (roles associated more with childhood than with professionalization), but also someone socially as well as intellectually subservient to a master or mentor. At best, it seems, a mentee may rise to the favored status of protégé and be groomed specially for future success, including succession of his or her own teacher.

Against this backdrop, we find it hard to claim (or reclaim) mentoring, either for ourselves or for Jane. Even if treachery occurs only at the extreme fringes of mentorship, we are troubled by other mundane but equally dispiriting problems. In particular, across the wide array of mentoring tales we sampled, we see a consistent lack of reciprocity between teacher and student, mentor and mentee. In our own experiences, this sense is highlighted whenever mentoring is classified as a service activity, as though its practice were *pro bono* work that involves handing things down (or handing them over) and giving them away for free. Missing is a clear sense of the lively exchange, the mutual teaching and learning, that anchors the kinds of relationships we wish to name here.

When we first started drafting this essay, Andrea proposed "colleague" as an alternative to mentor and mentee, a suggestion that sent us both scrambling for a dictionary. From French roots (*col-* together + *legre-* to choose), colleague connotes partnerships created and maintained by choice, and it suggests relationships founded on mutual respect rather than hierarchies of age, gender, or rank. Further, as the examples in the *OED* make clear, colleague belongs to the world of work: a colleague is both someone "who is associated with another (or others)" through election or employment and someone who works or unites with others to accomplish common goals. Colleagues are co-workers, then, as well as confederates or allies, and the term is well suited to accommodate the deeply personal and simultaneously professional aspects of what others might call mentoring. As we thought more about the term "colleague," we found that, without hesitation, we can use this term to describe our relationship. Along with being co-authors as well as great friends, we have been "colleagues" since practically the day Andrea joined the faculty at Stanford, where Jenn was already a graduate student. Perhaps uniquely, we began as co-teachers (rather than teacher and student), as we worked together to revise the English department's pedagogy curriculum; we also shared work in progress—Jenn, an article on teaching eighteenth-century literature and theater; Andrea, an essay on collaboration that she and Lisa Ede were writing. As Andrea began a five-year longitudinal study of writing at Stanford, Jenn joined the project, and Andrea joined Jenn's dissertation committee. With each new collaboration, we learned—and continue to learn—from one another, although that learning is different for each of us and reflects our different knowledge and experience, background and sensibility. If mentoring has come into play, it has been the kind of mentoring we've been striving toward in this essay—the kind that is radically reciprocal, mutually supportive, and characterized both by trust and by risk-taking. And as we've written this essay and spent a good bit of time exploring our own relationships with others, we have found that "colleague" best captures the way we experience working with students and more junior colleagues—certainly it does so much better than the term "mentor."

In spite of the satisfaction we take in experiencing—and trying to describe—this colleague-to-colleague relationship, we recognize that others may continue to see us as mentor and mentee, and they may prefer those terms to ours. It is also true, as Jenn noted recently in a personal e-mail, that mentors and colleagues have many similarities: "Don't colleagues [. . .] attempt regularly to do one another a professional good turn? Don't colleagues share information and experience without needing to frame or understand their interactions as caretaking," an idea that too often imposes paternalistic (or maternalistic and equally problematic) notions of custody and custodianship onto professional relationships? And yet, as Jenn reflected:

> Collegiality and mentoring do not imply the same dynamics or responsibilities. Historically, the mentor's job has been to guide, a task that easily devolves into the work of managing, monitoring, and controlling. Though it's true that collegiality exists within the same hierarchical institutional settings as mentoring, collegiality does not impose or reproduce the institution and its ideas and values in the same way. I would argue that collegiality comes with a different set of expectations as well as a different dynamic [. . .]. In a sense the kind of colleagues I'm describing aren't colleagues at all; they are individuals who form coalitions and colleague together, although the verb has no etymological relationship to the noun.

In this frame of mind and with this professional sensibility, it seems to us that many of mentoring's best intentions—the desire to create access to and new avenues for academic and personal development, to promote strong pedagogy, to foster professionalism, and to enable individuals to set and accomplish new goals—come into better focus as well as closer reach.

Of course, the issues we've raised concern more than nomenclature. To foster collegiality, what should we be doing? Our own experience points to how hard it is to assign or engineer collegiality, which develops not only in classrooms and formal mentoring situations, but also—and perhaps more so—through shared projects and genuine opportunities to work with others on matters of mutual interest and import. Our own experience as colleagues, for example, grew most powerfully out of our intellectual and personal commitment to a large research project, and our work together on that study led us to discover other areas of shared interest.

Recreating such conditions is easier said than done, we recognize, and it is tempting to close with a litany of the ideological and structural changes we would like to see take place to support what is less a plan than a vision for improved education. It is equally tempting to use our last words to sketch a curriculum or, in broad strokes, enumerate principles of inclusivity and active learning that we think can provide the basis for any colleague-building program. We are aware, however, that such plans or visions must be realized in local, particular contexts and that attempts to generalize about them will always fall far short of the desired goal. What we hope our forays into the rabbit hole of mentorship have accomplished is a gesture toward the kind of collegiality we wish to embrace, an invitation to join us in the reciprocal process of learning and teaching ourselves and others how to work most cooperatively and productively together.

* Many thanks to Janet Atwill for inviting us to talk about rhetoric and mentoring at the American Society for the History of Rhetoric Pre-Conference at the 2004 NCA Convention in Chicago.

Works Cited

Addison, Joseph. *The Tatler.* Ed. Donald F. Bond. Vol 2. Oxford: Clarendon P, 1989.

Fénelon, François de Salignac de la Mothe. *The Adventures of Telemachus.* 2 vols. Trans. Littlebury and Boyer. London, 1719. Eighteenth-Century Collections Online. Thomson Gale. Univ. of Tennessee Lib., Knoxville, TN. 8 June 2005 <http://www.gale.com/EighteenthCentury/>. ESTC No. N004302.

Fishman, Jenn. "Re: Two quick things." Private e-mail. 31 March 2006.

Gray, John. Introduction. *The Adventures of Telemachus.* Trans. P. Des Maizeaux. London, 1742. Eighteenth-Century Collections Online. Thomson Gale. Univ. of Tennessee Lib., Knoxville, TN. 1 July 2005 <http://www.gale.com/EighteenthCentury/>. ESTC No. T176637.

Hawkesworth, John, trans. *The Adventures of Telemachus*. London, 1768. Eighteenth-Century Collections Online. Thomson Gale. Univ. of Tennessee Lib., Knoxville, TN. 1 July 2005 <http://www.gale.com/EighteenthCentury/>. ESTC No. T144205.

Hogg, Alexander. Introduction. *The Adventures of Telemachus*. Trans. William Henry Melmoth. London, 1770. Eighteenth-Century Collections Online. Thomson Gale. Univ. of Tennessee Lib., Knoxville, TN. 1 July 2005 <http://www.gale.com/EighteenthCentury/>. ESTC No. T153155.

Ramsay, Andrew Michael. "Discourse on Epick Poetry and the Excellence of the Poem of Telemachus." *The Adventures of Telemachus*. London, 1719. 1-37. Eighteenth-Century Collections Online. Thomson Gale. Univ. of Tennessee Lib., Knoxville, TN. 8 June 2005 <http://www.gale.com/EighteenthCentury/>. ESTC No. N004302.

Taylor, Charles (Francis Fitzgerald). *The General Genteel Preceptor*. Vol. 1. London, 1797. Eighteenth-Century Collections Online. Thomson Gale. Univ. of Tennessee Lib., Knoxville, TN. 2 July 2005 <http://www.gale.com/EighteenthCentury/>. ESTC No. T096661.

4 Their Stories of Mentoring: Multiple Perspectives on Mentoring

Janice Lauer, Michele Comstock, Baotong Gu, William Hart-Davidson, Thomas Moriarty, Tim Peeples, Larissa Reuer, and Michael Zerbe

Mentoring for all of us has offered valuable opportunities for professional and personal development. Over the last eleven years since our time together at Purdue University, we have had the chance to reflect back on those influences and now, through this essay, to share them with others.

Janice Lauer: During my twenty years mentoring graduate students in rhetoric and composition (R/C) at Purdue University, I have had one of the richest teaching opportunities of my forty-nine-year career as a teacher. As a mentor I have also learned a tremendous amount, continuously reshaped my ideas of composition pedagogy, come to understand the importance of different styles of scholarly development, and honed many of my own theoretical views. Recently, I sat down (virtually, of course) with my mentoring class of 1994 and discussed our experiences together. This essay, then, is a collaborative effort among me and seven former graduate students, from a range of countries, of different ages and professional backgrounds: Michelle Comstock (University of Colorado at Denver), Baotong Gu (Georgia State University), Bill Hart-Davidson (Michigan State University), Tom Moriarty (Salisbury University), Tim Peeples (Elon University), Larissa Reuer (Chapel Hill, North Carolina), and Michael Zerbe (York College).

Bill Hart-Davidson: Looking back over the ten years or so since I began the graduate program in rhetoric and composition at Purdue, I can say that Janice's vision for what the program was supposed to do—what it was supposed to produce—is clearer to me now than it ever could have been while I was in the program. To put it simply, the program was producing the field of rhetoric and composition, along with the associated fields of technical and professional writing, computers and writing, among others. As graduate students, we were involved in the making of the field, not simply the object of this making. The faculty in the program were exceptionally dedicated to this vision, providing opportunities to learn alongside them as well as from them. The mentoring experiences at Purdue were equal parts on-the-job training for the professional work of rhetoric and composition scholarship, teaching and administration and, as my colleagues point out, community building. These experiences gave us an understanding of and an appreciation for the hard work of growing a field still in its academic infancy, still discovering and vetting ways of knowing, all the while recognizing its deep historical roots in the rhetorical tradition. We emerged from these experiences, as graduates, with a head start not only on our own professional habits but also with real connections to the future of our field.

Larissa Reuer: I felt the sense of community the minute I stepped off my plane from Russia. Two graduate students from the R/C department picked me up, took me to a grocery store to get some necessities, and fed me a home-cooked meal, while answering my many questions about the program. The people in my group were part of a smaller community.

MENTORING COMPOSITION INSTRUCTION

Janice Lauer: We all first met together on a Monday in August, 1994, the first day of an intensive week of mentoring in preparation for the teaching of introductory composition, 101, the first of a two-semester sequence. The mentoring course met every day all day for an entire week before the start of school and then once a week (for two to three hours) during the semester. Our group consisted of doctoral students with diverse backgrounds of teaching experience; nationalities (e.g., Gu from mainland China and Larissa from Russia); married and single status; and different professional interests (e.g., technology, WPA, historical rhetoric, contrastive rhetoric, rhetoric of science, professional writing, and feminist theory). All had also done MA work in rhetoric and composition in different programs.

The week was devoted to the pedagogy with which they would work during the semester. I briefly reviewed the conceptions of writing on which the pedagogy was based: writing as inquiry, a rhetorical act, a strategic art, a collaborative process, and as cultural critique. During the week, the mentees enacted this pedagogy as they wrote their own papers. During the process they shared their work with a small group and me and received responses. The purpose of the week was to give the mentees a chance to see how the pedagogy worked for them as writers and to anticipate problems their own students might have. As the week progressed, the group also discussed different types of teacher responses and evaluation appropriate for this pedagogy.

Thereafter at weekly meetings, we planned together the remaining writing experiences for the students (the last one being a group paper). During the semester, I periodically examined selected work in their students' portfolios, especially the instructors' responses to their work and visited each class. As I sat in these classes, I was fascinated and impressed as I saw so many effective ways of presenting new strategies, guiding group workshops, stimulating whole group discussion, and motivating students to engage in their own inquiries. This year-long mentoring created a close bond within the mentor group that in many cases has lasted into their professional lives now.

Michelle Comstock: When I arrived at Janice's orientation in 1994, I had already encountered a number of composition theories and practices in several graduate courses and in my experience teaching developmental composition at Indiana University—South Bend. What struck me right away about Janice's approach was its emphasis on writing as inquiry. A line from my orientation notes reads: "This course will give students a chance to raise questions that are important to them (not to us). It will engage them in the kind of writing in which the writer reaches new understanding, and it's this new understanding that is the end, not the text itself."

Janice's emphasis on writing as inquiry forms an integral part of every TA practicum I teach. In fact, I read from her handout last week as I met with a new group of teaching assistants at University of Colorado at Denver. Her claims for writing as inquiry, cultural critique, collaborative, strategic, and rhetorical continue to resonate with professors and students in our undergraduate writing program and MA program in the teaching of writing. In the face of ongoing institutional and legislative pressure toward a pedagogy of correctness, I find myself making Janice's argument over and over again—that writing should be initiated and guided by meaningful student-generated questions, questions arising from their own experiences of cognitive dissonance.

Larissa Reuer: Like several others, I was familiar with the approach to writing instruction practiced at Purdue. Before I came there, I spent two years teaching writing at another university while working towards my Master's degree. Their approach to composition was also writing as a process. New to me was a deeper understanding of writing as inquiry, as a rhetorical and strategic act, and as cultural critique. Professor Lauer's mentoring helped bring everybody on the same wave length regarding composition pedagogy while helping us capitalize on our strengths and overcome weaknesses. Her mentoring and my own teaching of writing helped to hone my ability to think independently and to defend my views in an academic setting, not the kind of skill someone educated in Russia would have. Needless to say, while teaching composition, I was frequently just a few steps ahead of my students when it came to different genres of writing and critique, and I was learning with my students. Professor Lauer's mentoring sessions helped make me a better teacher by making me a better independent thinker.

Baotong Gu: I came into the program with a background different from that of most of my cohorts. On the one hand, I had taught various courses, including graduate courses, at the college level for about eight years. On the other hand, all those eight years of teaching took place in China, and I had never taught any course, much less a composition course, to native speakers of English or in an English-as-native-language setting. Naturally, while I was excited at the prospect of teaching composition to native speakers, I had a lot of apprehension and questions before delving into this brand new phase of my teaching career. Fortunately, the mentoring sessions answered almost every one of my needs and concerns.

For me, two things stood out about the intensive one-week mentoring workshop: flexibility in pedagogical approaches and meticulous guidance on pedagogical details. For experienced TAs, the flexibility in pedagogical approaches Janice encouraged during the workshop allowed them to customize the course to their particular focus and teaching style, with ample room for individual innovation and creativity. For new teachers like me (I considered myself a new teacher considering the subject matter of the course and the cultural setting of the class), Janice provided meticulous instruction and guidance on every aspect. This preparation, coupled with the group sharing and discussion of our teaching and Janice's continued guidance in our ensuing biweekly mentoring sessions throughout the semester, got us (for me at least) off on a much less shaky, and often surprisingly smoother, start of our graduate teaching than it would have otherwise.

Bill Hart-Davidson: It is difficult to explain in the abstract how thoroughly Janice's approach to mentoring composition instruction weaves theory, pedagogy, and day-to-day practices such as classroom management together in ways that are invaluable for both new and experienced teachers. So I will offer an example of something Janice asked us to do, to know, to understand, and yes, even to role play awkwardly during that first week of orientation: making a quality response to someone's text. On the surface, it's a deceptively simple lesson that was presented to us in the same way I now present it to students in all my writing classes. It has three parts. And I usually say something like this:

> When you respond, begin by simply describing what you see. If it helps to get you started, begin by saying 'I see that. . . .' After you have described what you see, then offer an evaluative statement something like: 'I think this is working pretty well. But don't jump to this step first'; and 'Finally, after your evaluative statement, make a suggestion. If you've identified a positive feature, mention how this same strategy might be used elsewhere, or how a change in another part of the text could enhance it. If you've identified something that isn't working well, explain how a revision could make it work better.'

Simple, right? Almost commonsensical. Yet it is very important not to stop with the explanation above. Because while it makes sense, it is not always easy to execute due to the fact that our ways of interacting with people we do not know very well can get in the way. You have to practice! I usually start by modeling it for my students, attempting to show it can become a natural way to structure even the simplest comments. Describe, evaluate, suggest. Theoretically, we have a model that adheres closely to Vygotskian scaffolding. Pedagogically, structuring peer response in this way emphasizes process and revision at the purpose level rather than merely the syntactic level. Socially, well, it just makes things much more productive and pleasant for everybody. But for all of this to work, students have to really adopt it.

Mike Zerbe: One of the best outcomes of the composition instruction mentoring program for us as graduate students was the initial experience we gained reading, analyzing, and critiquing each other's work. I vividly recall the trepidation I felt the first time my comments on a student paper, copied onto a transparency, were placed on the overhead projector for all to see. This occurrence took place with a sample paper even before the semester started, during the week-long "boot camp" (as we called it). Serious, sustained discussion, by my graduate student colleagues and Professor Lauer ensued, on my comments in the margin and text of the paper, on my summary comment, and on the grade I had given the paper. The entire affair was at once profoundly humbling—after all, we all had previous teaching experience in our master's degree programs—and enormously enlightening. Our pedagogical knowledge and skill was enriched.

Tom Moriarty: At the time, I thought it was a real pain in the butt. "You really want us to enact the pedagogy by trying it out for ourselves?" I thought during one of our first mentoring sessions. "Like actually use the heuristics and write a short paper?" Yep, that's what Janice Lauer wanted us to do. And she wanted us to do it quickly— in three days. I managed to produce a mediocre, C/C- paper (in my judgment). I was quite proud of my effort, however, because it was the first introductory composition paper I had ever written. Like many graduate students in English, I had never taken introductory composition, thanks to the AP exam in high school. I had never used heuristics to analyze my readers. I had never pored over my teacher's comments on a first draft, savoring the praise and looking for guidance to improve my essay. In short, I had never been on the business end of a writing pedagogy. The experience taught me an important lesson: what we teach in introductory composition is writing process, and we do it by making process visible to students, by making it accessible and doable for writers who don't have a lot of experience putting words on paper. By the time I wrote my first introductory composition essay under Janice's tutelage, I had internalized many aspects of the process we were preparing to teach, and the experience of actually going through it helped me understand its value. It was more than a pain in the butt.

Tim Peeples: I have a hard time identifying all the ways this mentoring experience has affected who I am, what I value, and how I have worked and now work within academia. I started my PhD studies at Purdue after six years of teaching first-year composition, first for two years as a graduate TA and then for another four years as a full-time faculty member. As someone who had taught over sixty sections of first-year writing but had been minimally active in research the four years prior, I came into my PhD very comfortable as a teacher but uncertain of myself as a student/scholar, so at first I resented anything that I felt was getting in my way of studying the field. What I quickly learned was just how much I was indeed learning about the field—both theory and praxis—through this formal mentoring. Perhaps in a more cunning mentoring move than I could or can ever imagine, Janice invited me to carry on this mentoring experience well beyond what most of my classmates experienced. Beginning the following year and then again for two years after that, I continued my development through formal mentoring, but now in the role of the mentor. As is now cliché, we typically learn more and more deeply when we assume the role and responsibilities of "teacher," and this was definitely so for me. Over the next three years, I had the privilege of being part of three more mentor groups, learning from and forming close relationships with almost thirty more R/C students. In addition to extending my mentoring experience to future classes of students, I also had the kairotic opportunity to become part of a group of eight current or graduated members of the R/C community to co-author a significant revision of *Four Worlds of Writing*, the composition textbook that informed the pedagogy we learned in our first-year mentoring.

My significantly extended mentoring experience has shaped my course objectives and class pedagogy, from first-year courses through

advanced professional writing courses and even into faculty development workshops, evidencing a commitment to writing and rhetoric
as "inquiry and action in context," the subtitle of the revised *Four
Worlds of Writing.* I also bring this commitment directly through the
issues I focus on in my scholarly work, sometimes indirectly through
the lenses I use as a scholar and professional (e.g., textbook reviewer
and professional organization board member), and almost always
through my own processes as a writer/rhetor/scholar (and administrator).

Academic Advising

Janice Lauer: I acted as this group's academic advisor until they selected their dissertation chair. Over the years I learned about the
importance of academic guidance to help students satisfy in a timely
way their course, language, residence, and preliminary exam (prelim) requirements. This advising helped students avoid the side-
tracks and pitfalls that often cost students time and money. As part
of advising I also worked with faculty to create long-range plans for
the scheduling of courses so students could plan for their desired or
required courses, a planning that gave priority to our students' needs
over faculty preferences.

Baotong Gu: Going into a new program is nothing short of a self-
guided adventure, often leaving students on their own to figure out
what program of study best fits their needs and program requirements. Such was not the case when we entered Purdue's program.
In my first meeting with Janice before the start of the semester, she
carefully explained various program requirements and helped me lay
out a multi-year plan with a detailed sequence of courses based on
my personal background and interests. As a result, during my five
years at Purdue I was never confused about what courses to take,
what requirements I had satisfied, what requirements I had yet to
fulfill, and what the next step was for me. What was most valuable
to me was the knowledge and assurance that Janice, or some other
faculty member, would be there to help with whatever academic issues I would encounter.

Mike Zerbe: The academic advising mentoring significantly helped to
ensure that we graduate students would not suffer a fate that be-
falls so many of those who pursue post-baccalaureate education: the

graduate program that has no end. At Purdue, academic advising was viewed by the R/C faculty as an important part of their role as graduate instructors. By planning course schedules far in advance, regularly offering required courses, helping us to select a secondary area, and keeping us apprised of matters such as foreign language requirements and courses, Professor Lauer and the other R/C faculty enabled us to make measurable and timely progress toward our degrees. All seven of us obtained our doctorates within six and a half years, including Larissa whose husband's job took them abroad for several years.

Larissa Reuer: By virtue of circumstance I spent more than half of my PhD program abroad, first in Russia for the second half of my second year and then three more years in France for the last three years. Professor Lauer, my academic advisor and dissertation chair, helped me design a plan of study and research such that would allow me to avoid falling behind my group when I needed to return to Russia for several months. I was also able to defend my dissertation proposal and complete most of my dissertation research before my family's move to France, thus allowing me to avoid separation from my husband and completing the dissertation in a timely manner.

Tom Moriarty: I like to joke that my fondest memory of academic advising with Janice occurred about a month before the first semester started. I sat in Janice's office one hot afternoon as she looked through my file and talked about the courses I should take my first year. "Of course you'll take composition theories in the fall and classical rhetoric in the spring," she said. Since I already had taken those exact courses in my MA program, (or, as I later learned, courses with exactly the same titles), I suggested that maybe I could skip those courses. "No," Janice replied. "I think you need to take them." "Really," I protested, "I took those courses back at my old school. Back in my MA." Janice sighed and opened a drawer in her desk. She pulled out the syllabus for the composition theories course and turned to the reading list. "Have you read this?" she asked, pointing to the first item on the page. "No." "This?" "No." "This?" "Yeah, I read that." "Hmm." Janice looked up for a moment, then back down at the syllabus. "This?" "No." "This?" "No." I paused. "I think I need to take that course." I tell this story not to illustrate how dumb I was in graduate school, but to show you the delicate balance Janice achieved as a mentor, a delicate balance between advisor and supporter, taskmaster and friend.

Tim Peeples: As others have illustrated, good mentoring didn't always mean pats on the back and soothing words. Though there were plenty of times when I wished I would have received a pat on the back instead of the mentoring I needed, I wouldn't ask for things to be any different looking back on the experience. The following anecdote I want to share fits most neatly into the category of academic advising, although it is not about choosing courses and such. It's about being/becoming an academic.

I recall very clearly one instance in my first semester of the program when we were discussing several readings on composition theory and pedagogy from the 1970s. Janice was giving the articles what I thought was an overly generous read and talking about them as if they had had lots to contribute to composition pedagogy and theory. I was bound and determined to analyze and evaluate them through lenses of much more contemporary theories and kept constructing critiques rather than trying to understand the articles on their own grounds. Then came what turned out to be an all too familiar set of motions: the leg Janice had crossed over her other leg began to bounce a bit, one hand calmly lay in her lap and the other slowly reached for her glasses, her glasses were slowly pulled off and one stem was almost invisibly shaken in my direction, her brow furrowed, and her eyes got coldly squinty. 'Tim, you're being anachronistic. First, you must learn to read the arguments in their historical context. Once you are able to do that, then you can try your hand at postmodern critique.'

COLLABORATION FOR PRELIMS (COMPREHENSIVES)

Janice Lauer: After their course work and prior to their dissertation work, our students took preliminary (comprehensive) examinations in rhetoric and composition. Our exam had two parts: a 24-hour take-home examination with five questions based on the core courses and a week-long essay on a choice of subjects co-designed by the examining committee and the students.

Baotong Gu: The prelim study group was tremendously beneficial in my preparation for one of the most grueling parts of the PhD program—the prelim exams. In the few months leading to the exams, we met once a week to discuss the important issues covered in the core courses, to design our own questions and write individual responses, and then to respond to and edit each other's answers. Out of this close interaction developed not only an unusual camaraderie but also valuable knowledge and learning. For me, personally, the most valuable part of this peer study group was not only a chance to get feedback on my essay responses and to share my perspectives on many issues, academic or cultural, but also the opportunity to learn from my peers' insights, and, most important of all, to ask "stupid" questions I was too embarrassed to ask in class.

Mike Zerbe: Undoubtedly one of the most perilous times for a graduate student is the period after coursework has been completed. The community of graduate students suddenly had no schedule to rely on to call the community together. Fortunately for us, we were able to maintain our strong sense of togetherness. Toward the end of our coursework, as we began to stress mightily over our upcoming comprehensive (*i.e.,* "preliminary") exams, Professor Lauer said to us, "Prelim writing is a genre, and you should practice it!" And practice it we did. Armed with at least three prior years of exams, our (anonymous) predecessors' answers to the questions posed on those exams, and an understanding of how the exams were evaluated, we spent the entire summer of 1996 writing answers, getting together, reading and critiquing each other's work, and then doing it all over again a few days later.

Michelle Comstock: In many of our Purdue graduate courses, each student was given responsibility over a particular section, key text, or figure in the field—an approach that prepared us (and encouraged us) to collaborate for the preliminary exams. Everyone who participated in the prelim study group brought his or her reports, notes, practice test responses, and potential questions to add to the pile, creating a diverse, yet comprehensive set of primary and secondary materials. My fellow prelim group members were generous with their resources and ideas—they didn't have to be.

Tim Peeples: I can still spin around in my office chair, reach into a filing cabinet, and put my hands on files that include the many, many documents our mentor group used as we prepared for our prelim exams. For one, I see these documents as textual artifacts that illustrate one kind of disciplinary learning process. The interactive, intertextual exchanges moving from past questions and researched responses to newly created questions and researched responses to peer feedback capture the nature of the ongoing dialogue that defines any discipline or profession, and in this case captures a moment of that disciplinary dialogue in one specific context. I also see these prelim preparation documents as remnants of a scholarly and pedagogical process. Though it might look, from one perspective, like we were simply preparing for a big test, the prelim process represented for me a significant period of mentoring. I learned a great deal about being a learner and teacher and scholar, and about the formation of energetic academic communities. In fact, I would evidence this focus on an academic community in the amount of work we put in to create an electronic library of all the resources we received and produced to pass on to the mentor group that followed us—we consciously approached our prelim study work as a form of academic community building.

Dissertation (Post-Prelim) Groups

Janice Lauer: In the period after the prelims as students recovered, they often faced the problem of losing ground in selecting their dissertation committee and preparing their prospectus for defense. To face this gap, the students decided to meet together to keep each other going. Each week they informally shared their progress and received feedback from the rest of the group. Eventually three groups formed meeting every third week—the newcomers fresh from the prelims, those whose dissertations were in progress, and those going on the job market and finishing their dissertations. In each of these phases, different kinds of mentoring were called for. In the first group, we raised questions about students' initial ideas for a dissertation. We also discussed the nature of the prospectus document and characteristics of an effective one. In the second group, members entered into each other's projects, offering additional readings or other feedback. The third group is discussed below. All of these groups kept students from becoming isolated and enabled them to keep abreast of their peers' research.

Bill Hart-Davidson: The post-prelim study group was one of the best examples of guided, but largely self-organized peer mentoring, but there were many others as well. From these, we learned that our best resource for nearly all challenges—academic, administrative, or pedagogical—was the group of colleagues surrounding us. When it came time for me to make a choice about where I might like to work, something I have done a couple of times now, I used as a criterion the group of colleagues I might work with as the most important single factor.

Baotong Gu: In many PhD programs, it's not uncommon for students to find themselves almost totally on their own at this stage of their program except for less-than-frequent consultations with their dissertation committee chair. The post-prelim group at Purdue's R/C program extended the collaborative relationships among students and fostered a prolonged sense of community. I found the group meetings to be especially conducive to the development of my dissertation ideas. In fact, the very topic of my dissertation came as a direct result of one such meeting. I remember I was interested in doing my study on technology-related issues and was having a hard time deciding on and narrowing down my topic. Janice suggested: "Since there have been some studies on this topic already, why not look at the issue from a different perspective: how cultural contexts shape writing technology development?" As my classmates chimed in to offer their input on the topic, my months of readings and thoughts on the topic suddenly began to make sense, and it dawned on me that few studies had looked at the issue from this unique perspective.

Dissertation Mentoring

Janice Lauer: One of my most challenging, time-consuming, and rewarding mentor roles has been as a dissertation director and committee member: I have chaired fifty-two dissertations, co-chaired six (two are still in progress), and served on thirty-seven other committees (two are still in progress). For me, a director in some sense is a co-author or midwife, coaxing inquiry questions into shape; guiding the research process; pointing out false directions, dead ends, and overly ambitious goals; and suggesting resources. At times, I have helped rescue projects from pits of discouragement or procrastination. Occasionally my prose suggestions have found their way into the discourse. Overall. my experience has been highly rewarding as I have watched with pride impressive texts emerge, often inspired by ideas, readings, and faculty research in our program—texts that have made important contributions to the R/C field. From these close collaborations with students, I have learned immeasurably.

Larissa Reuer: I left the country soon after I defended my proposal. Frequently Professor Lauer, who was my dissertation chair, was my only connection with Purdue. E-mailing and phone calls were a preferred mode of contact. Perhaps if technology were more advanced then, I would have been able to benefit from the dissertation group meetings (although probably not in the celebrations afterwards if only because of the time difference—even the French don't usually drink before lunch).

Mike Zerbe: For two years, several of us met almost every Friday afternoon at a local café. One of us would be the person whose work was being evaluated that day, and that work received a great deal of feedback from the other members of the group. By this point, we had been together for so long that tact and diplomacy were unnecessary. We ripped each other's work apart and helped the writer put it back together again. Then we retired to a local establishment to celebrate the occasion. I had never before been a part of such an intense and rewarding writing group. I have not been since and doubt that I shall see the likes of it again. It remains one of my most cherished memories of my graduate school experience.

Bill Hart-Davidson: I don't think I appreciated just how much I learned from the mentoring I received on the dissertation process until I had the chance to direct a few dissertations myself. What I was somewhat surprised to discover is that I had a sense not only of the genre but also of the important personal and professional motivating factors that characterize the best dissertation projects. One of the most important of these is also a tenet of Janice's approach to all writing instruction: a dissertation must be an act of inquiry, motivated by a genuine and compelling question not only for the field but also for the writer. Another important motivating influence that I try to pass on to dissertation advisees comes from the interactions that one has during the dissertation process, most notably at the prospectus and final defenses, but also throughout in more informal meetings. A common feature of all of these is the chance for the student to be the center of an intellectual conversation. The students' ideas are at issue, and the groups' focus is on the refinement of those ideas.

Tim Peeples: Though our mentor group had already developed into a very close-knit group of colleagues, as well as friends, and had developed a very strong co- or peer-mentoring community, the two years I spent working with my classmates on our dissertations created the most powerful intellectual space I have ever experienced. Not only can I not imagine what writing my dissertation would have been like without our intense, all-afternoon weekly meetings, but I cannot fathom how different my professional life would be without that experience. I learned further about the processes of building and maintaining an intellectual community, something I have applied to my work since in many ways: as a writing program administrator, as a member of a rhet/comp community creating a new writing major and minor, as a coauthor, and as a colleague helping other colleagues work on and complete a variety of publications. I learned an immense amount about areas of rhetoric that I otherwise would not have encountered and gained a much deeper perspective on and appreciation for the field as a whole. I also gained what I am certain will remain a life-long, close, supportive community of colleagues.

THE "JOB-GROUP"

Janice Lauer: Students normally entered the job group the year they were applying for positions. We strongly urged them to wait until they had completed at least two chapters of their dissertations and had the remainder of their research well underway even though they (and their families) were eager to get out of a life of poverty and the student role. We provided lurid stories of the struggles of their predecessors who had left for positions ABD and the problems they faced trying to succeed in their first positions while finishing their dissertations. We warned them that many departments were eager to hire R/C students regardless of the status of their dissertations but were often also traps for lifelong ABDs or revolving doors.

At the beginning of the job group (in late August), we examined samples of effective resumes, teaching portfolios, and application letters. Through September, students exchanged their resumes and letters of application, receiving feedback from the group. In October, we discussed the jobs advertised on the Modern Language Association (MLA) list and other sites, sharing information about positions with which we were familiar. In November, faculty offered guidance on job interviews at the MLA Convention or by phone, using examples of situations (sometimes bizarre) for which they might prepare. In late November or early December, we organized interview commit-tees (faculty in rhetoric and composition, literature, and/or linguis-tics) and held mock interviews, providing feedback right after the interview. During the second semester, we discussed the on-campus interview and then resumed work on the dissertations, describing the dissertation defense scenario and the format requirements that students often underestimated in their planning.

Baotong Gu: Our job group, run by several faculty members, prepared us for our job search in every way possible. To me, one of the most helpful aspects of this preparation was the analysis of the job ads and of the cultures of different programs. As an international grad-uate student, I had little knowledge of the make-ups of different programs and their respective needs. Understanding what some of the programs were looking for and where they came from was very helpful in my interviews with these schools. Another equally help-ful aspect was that my professors also helped me better understand my strengths and weaknesses and helped me identify my particu-lar niche in the market, giving me a special confidence going into the job interviews. The fact that I, an ethnic minority and a for-eign national still on a student visa in this country at that time, got more than a dozen campus interview invitations is a testament to the strong mentoring I received. Ironically, I was one of those few students who left for my first tenure-track position as an ABD. However, it was more a matter of financial circumstances than one of personal choice that prompted me to test the turbulent waters of the job market. Even though I left Purdue a little prematurely, the close monitoring and constant push by faculty members on my dis-sertation committee enabled me to complete a good portion of my dissertation before I left. As a result, I was able to complete my dis-sertation in my first year on the job. This selfless help by Purdue's R/C faculty continued into my first years on my job.

Michelle Comstock: During my last year at Purdue, I remember that the faculty in the job group also helped us situate our work within the larger field. Jim Porter gave us an assignment I hated at the time— the identity statement, asking us to summarize our identity in the field in one sentence and then use that statement to inform our ap-plication letters, descriptions of research, and interview responses.

Given the eclectic nature of my work at Purdue (teaching women's studies and professional writing, mentoring TAs in feminist pedagogy, performing research with community action groups, serving on university task forces), I found the assignment difficult and resisted doing it for some time. However, the identity statement proved to be a pivotal moment in my graduate student experience—it was an opportunity to professionalize my work, to make it coherent and legible to the larger field of English studies. Today, many of my university colleagues are skeptical of these practices of professionalization or of marketing oneself via categories and specializations, fearing it contributes to a corporate model of higher education. I share their fears; however, I also understand the importance of helping a master's student, for example, make her work count (monetarily and socially) in the local school district where she teaches or of helping students become writing consultants in local businesses, as well as in the campus writing center.

Mike Zerbe: In this context, the lessons we learned from critiquing each others' vita and cover letters, from stories of graduate students who had gone before us, and from mock interviews helped us to make the job search a cooperative rather than a competitive experience. It amazed me how willing we were, for example, to share research on institutions that were advertising positions. We also covered each other's classes during campus visits. Although hectic, I remember feeling that I was well prepared for interviews and that I had the full support and confidence of my job group.

Tom Moriarty: I had the unique experience of spending two full years in the job group, first as an unsuccessful ABD with one chapter of my dissertation completed, and then as a very successful, soon-to-be-minted PhD with four of five chapters under my belt. Janice prepared me for a hard job market my first year, telling me that it would be difficult to get a job with so little of my dissertation completed. But I was determined to try. I dutifully put together my resume and cover letter (stretching the meaning of the word "substantial" in the paragraph where I discussed the progress I'd made on my dissertation), and sent out over fifty applications. The interview committee grilled me during my mock interviews and wished me luck when I went off to Toronto for my one MLA interview. That spring, when my one interview didn't pan out, Janice gently raised the possibility of staying at Purdue for another year, making substantial progress on my dissertation, and going back out on the market in the fall. I stayed, I progressed, and I had a very busy job season the next year.

Bill Hart-Davidson: While you can only take a position in one department (if you are lucky!), the job search is a process of introducing yourself to many departments to which you apply. If all goes well, a candidate can have the opportunity to meet and talk to representatives of many departments. These are colleagues who will sit on future conference panels, review articles for journals, recommend students for graduate study, review tenure and promotion cases, and generally be involved in a host of ways with ones' professional life. One lesson I learned from the job group is just how small the field is and how important the relationships you form during the job search can be. By having a mentoring experience focused on what various types of institutions might ask of a new candidate, what kind of professional life we might have in one department vs. another, we were given a valuable sense of the field's diversity.

Conclusion

Bill-Hart Davison: One of the more important lessons I took away from all of the mentoring experiences in the R/C program was simply that mentoring, itself, is valuable. Though it felt at times as if we were merely huddling together for survival, we also knew that the time we set aside to meet and talk about course readings before a graduate seminar, or the time we spent creating practice exam questions and critiquing each others' answers was not ancillary to our learning—it was the way we were learning!

Tim Peeples: As both a professor and administrator, I remain highly influenced by all of these mentoring experiences. One of my primary goals now is to support the development and maintenance of strong intellectual communities. The mentoring experiences at Purdue provided an extremely powerful complement to the more formal instruction I had over the years.

Larissa Reuer: Permeating this article is the sense of community that was a valuable tool of learning and helping us pull through. There were many opportunities to be part of a larger R/C community at Purdue such as through the interdisciplinary lecture series, which featured prominent people in our field. Professor Lauer and other professors organized annual get-togethers to welcome new students and introduce them to other students, faculty, and alumni. I was always amazed at how much work professor Lauer put into community building and maintaining. I can picture a bulletin board outside her office door with all the former graduate students' families' pictures on it. I remember her asking me for a photo of my family and how proud I felt that I was becoming part of such a close community.

Janice Lauer: Thanks for everyone's participation both in mentoring at Purdue and in contributing to this essay. Our community has greatly enriched my life as a mentor and a person.

5 Mentorship, Collegiality, and Friendship: Making Our Mark as Professionals

Ken Baake, Stephen A. Bernhardt, Eva R. Brumberger,
Katherine Durack, Bruce Farmer, Julie Dyke Ford, Thomas
Hager, Robert Kramer, Lorelei Ortiz, and Carolyn Vickrey

This chapter focuses on the shared experiences originating in and extending outward from the PhD Program in Rhetoric and Professional Communication at New Mexico State University (NMSU) during the years 1988-2001. These represent the first classes of students in an innovative program that brought together talented people from a range of backgrounds who were interested in pursuing a PhD that bridged academia and industry. Each of the contributors worked closely with co-author Steve Bernhardt, who was course professor, advisor, and dissertation director to each of us. In various combinations, we worked together on research projects, on funded initiatives, and on training and development projects. We collaborated to build a strong department, to implement classroom technologies, and to develop our teaching portfolios. We presented together at conferences, co-hosted conferences, and co-authored various articles. Each of us has gone on to new positions, finding satisfaction in academic, industrial, and scientific settings. In this chapter, we reflect on our mentoring experiences, both during the PhD program and after. These reflections explore the relationships among an English professor and his graduate students, but we believe the insights are applicable to other situations.

Themes or Best Practices in Mentoring

Certain themes will organize our discussion. Using e-mail, chat, and a discussion board, we have consolidated our impressions to describe best practices in academic mentoring. The following themes capture our shared thinking:

- Mentoring is both explicit and implicit. It entails the direct giving of advice from one person, usually older or more experienced, to another. But it also is indirect, as when the less experienced person learns by watching the actions of the more experienced person in various settings over time. Hence, mentoring guides by words and by examples.

- Mentoring involves the development of professional and personal self-confidence as much as professional knowledge or skills. Subtle encouragement to believe in one's abilities can be as important in a mentoring relationship as more concrete guidance and advice.

- Mentoring relationships vary widely in how they begin, how they evolve, and how they are remembered. Mentoring is an adaptive skill, where mentors and mentees become accustomed to various forms of interaction and grow to be productive in individual ways.

- Mentoring begins in a hierarchical relationship, but can evolve toward a co-equal relationship, where issues of status, authority, or hierarchy are not as important as shared concerns, interests, and pursuits. Mentoring relationships form naturally out of daily interactions that characterize working and studying together, talking, listening, socializing, and building sustaining friendships. Mentoring is a relationship where knowledge, experience, and reflection flow both ways across a permeable boundary.

- Mentoring builds bridges between classroom and theory, between classroom and workplace, between personal and academic pursuits. Mentoring points toward experiences, such as internships or consulting work, that move students outside the classroom. Mentoring is also a path for ideas that range too far afield to be brought back within the academic fold. An open exchange in a mentoring relationship gives students a voice and validates their interests and sense of direction.

- Good academic mentoring leads to significant, concrete outcomes. Mentoring provides an opportunity to carry out projects that are timely to the profession, projects that reflect shared interests and expertise, and projects that result in useful end products. The dissertation is one obvious end product, but there are many others.

An Etymology of the Term

The term *mentor* as a noun describes more than just someone who guides and teaches another. In early uses *mentor* took an initial capital letter. According to the *Oxford English Dictionary* (OED) Online, Mentor was a persona of the goddess Athena in the *Odyssey*. He served as guide and advisor to Telemachus (also spelled *Telemakhos*). The *OED* continues with an exposition of a seventeenth-century French political novel in which a character Mentor is a counselor. The importance of the term *mentor* is reflected in the *OED* note that its fourth-century Greek origins may derive from the word for "mind."

In the *Odyssey,* Mentor offered words of advice and actions of guidance to Telemachus, whose father, Odysseus, has been missing for ten years and whose mother, Penelope, is besieged by lustful suitors. No stronger words of advice can be found than Athena's address to Telemachus as he is bowed prostrate in prayer. Athena in Mentor's voice exhorts Telemachus to live up to the high standards set by his father, the long-lost Odysseus, and to set sail in search of information about Odysseus' whereabouts: "You'll never be fainthearted or a fool, Telemachus, if you have your father's spirit," Mentor (Athena) declares (27).

Mentoring in this classical example is implicitly defined as advising and personally guiding the mentee. As Professor of Classics Susan Ford Wiltshire writes, "this mentoring involves standing nearby on the lookout for the younger person's needs, offering words of encouragement, and—equally important—stepping back when appropriate to allow the younger person to make it through an ordeal on his own" (10). The words of mentoring between a professor and his or her student rarely rise to such level of exhortation as found in the *Odyssey*; nor does the typical academic mentoring situation involve the need to set off on a long sea voyage while suitors remain behind to pester one's mother. Still, reflecting on the term and its rich literary heritage is worthwhile as we move into a discussion of how mentoring should work in an academic setting, and how it has worked in each of our lives.

Mentoring as Advising and Guiding

The concepts of *advising* and *guiding* capture the explicit and implicit acts of mentoring as we have experienced them. Explicit mentoring is obvious, as when Ken walked into Steve's office asking for advice on how to develop a paper on minimalist documentation. Steve handed Ken his copy of John Carroll's book, *The Nurnberg Funnel,* the foundational text that argued for a shift from the philosophy of including every possible contingency in written instructions to including just what is necessary to get the user up and running. "You should read this," Steve said, which was all that needed to be said in that situation. Robb recalls similar succinct advice from Steve, such as "This would be good for you," "Read this, you'll like it," or "You probably shouldn't do that." Casual, thrifty in syllable and emotive content, such advice often yields significant outcomes because it inspires without overwhelming.

Like Ken, Eva went to Steve with a "how to" question. For her, it was how to design a series of quantitative studies for her dissertation. As Eva describes, the advice wasn't quite what she expected, but it proved far more helpful in the long run.

Eva: I went to see Steve, who would, I was sure, be able to tell me exactly what I needed to know; after all, he was "the quantitative guy" in the English department. Imagine my surprise when, instead of telling me what, he told me who—who to go to for help with statistics. This advice came with what I saw as a confession: Steve admitted that, when he did quantitative research, he worked with a consultant who was a statistics expert. Steve taught me that knowing where to look for answers is sometimes more helpful than having the answers themselves.

While Eva knew Steve as "the quantitative guy" in the English department, Carolyn knew him as "the computer guy." Steve was the faculty member most involved with computers in writing and teaching, so when it came time to select committee members for a dissertation focused on collaborative writing using specialized computer software, Carolyn turned to Steve. He suggested English department faculty who would be able to offer good advice even without having extensive

knowledge of computers and writing and also faculty members from
Business and Education with expertise in using electronic communication and computers in classrooms.

Underlying such guidance is a characteristic essential to good
mentoring: the mentor's ability to sift through his own explicit and
tacit knowledge in order to identify the most salient pieces of information or advice. In addition to responding to seemingly straightforward
questions, this involves addressing "the questions a student *doesn't* ask,"
and figuring out exactly what the student really needs.

Implicit mentoring is a kind of showing by doing. All of Steve's
students have observed him balancing multiple tasks—the requests of
students to read a dissertation proposal, a consulting report deadline,
faculty committee meetings, and family life. He does it with a smile,
without ever appearing flustered. Yet, such simple acts that might not
even register in the memory of the mentor can have lasting impact on
a new initiate to the field. Seeing Steve calmly walking around at a
conference unsure of what room he was supposed to be in for the next
presentation, but not panicked, reassured newcomer Ken that the conference world is hectic for everyone, that even experts can get lost, that
some uncertainty is acceptable—even ingratiating.

For Julie, the image of the first time she and Steve met left a lasting impression. On the day before her first doctoral class she needed
his signature on a course override form. Having only read his work
and corresponded with him via e-mail, Julie was intimidated by Steve's
scholarly reputation. When she approached his office, the first thing
she remembers seeing were his feet in Sketchers' sneakers. While it
seems like such a trivial detail, seven years later, Julie remembers it
clearly and classifies it as the moment she realized that while she took
Steve seriously, he didn't take himself too seriously. Such down-to-
earth qualities are invaluable in a mentor.

MENTORING AS SUPPORT

A less tangible aspect of good mentoring involves nurturing students,
not necessarily in overt ways, but through more subtle, spontaneous,
or unprompted forms of encouragement. Nurturing affirms students
as they struggle with issues of professional identity: "What am I doing here? Do I really have what it takes to succeed?" Finally, it entails
nudging students toward developing potential they may not even realize they have, as Lorelei, Eva, and Carolyn reveal in the following
accounts:

Lorelei: As the only Mexican-American in the PhD program, and the first in my family to graduate from college, I came to NMSU with a nagging preoccupation of not being good enough. It didn't help that one of the first students I met there told me that the only reason I had gotten into the PhD program was because I was female and Hispanic! My academic insecurities betrayed me as I sat quietly in class, too self-conscious to contribute. The comments of other students sounded so smart, eloquently expressing thoughts that would never have occurred to me. I felt I was not living up to the standard of a doctoral program, but Steve helped me move beyond that point. He challenged me in ways I needed to be challenged—by bringing me into class discussions and asking me to share impromptu responses to questions that he knew I could answer.

He acknowledged my ethnicity in the way that mattered most to me: not by making things easier for me because I was a minority student but by expecting the same of me as he would any other student. Before too long, we started talking about how my bilingual, bicultural assets could benefit me as a student and strengthen a dissertation. Steve did for me what any truly good mentor must often do—he sought me out because he sensed I didn't have the confidence to come to him. He challenged me because he knew how much I could accomplish, even though I didn't know it at the time. And as a result, I grew in my self-confidence and into my shoes as a doctoral student.

Eva: When I decided to leave my instructorship position to pursue a doctorate, friends and colleagues questioned my sanity. They told me to expect four- plus years of suffering: competition with other students, lack of faculty interest, high stress levels, isolation. My PhD experience could not have been more different. Steve took an active interest in my professional development. Recognizing that I brought with me both industry and teaching experience, he pushed me toward a leadership role, urging me to run for president of the local chapter of the Society for Technical Communication (STC). This was an unfamiliar and uncomfortable role for me, but Steve's ongoing encouragement and affirmation helped me grow into it and recognize my own potential. Similarly, he coached me through my anxiety as I began to develop my dissertation, not by saying "Don't worry, you'll be fine," or through direct advice, but through praise for my writing and organizational skills that in turn bolstered my confidence.

Carolyn: I recall Steve telling me on several occasions that I was always
calm and collected, even during trying times with numerous deadlines facing me. While I like to think that it is true—and most of the
time it probably is—it still helped me to hear it. Steve's words served
as an affirmation or self-fulfilling prophecy when I needed that underlying support and confidence to stay focused and sail through
difficult situations without becoming flustered and distracted.

To return to the Telemachus example, the ship needs to set sail with
fresh wind. The feeling of beginning a new voyage under such a wind
excited all of us in our first class together at New Mexico State—a
proseminar on rhetoric and professional communication. In that class,
we read two selections that allowed us to voice anxieties about our pre-
paredness for the journey and to clear the air. One was the account of
Nate (a.k.a. John Ackerman) as a student entering the PhD program at
Carnegie Mellon University. Nate's is a story of tortured assimilation
and accommodation, his stumbling toward a secure identity as a scholar. The other key reading was a chapter from Stephen Brookfield's
The Successful Teacher. Chapter 4, "Understanding the Tensions and
Emotions of Learning" details the *imposter syndrome*, whereby students in a new program, no matter how talented and bright, often feel
as though some colossal oversight has allowed them into a program or
situation for which they are ill prepared. The two readings allowed us
to begin to process the feelings of inadequacy and uncertainty that can
drain performance if left unattended. We were able to find a common
emotional stake in the program that could undergird our own varied,
intellectual stakes.

Mentoring as Building Relationships

Some of the most fruitful mentoring experiences arise out of simply
working together on a project. One project that lasted for several years
was a National Workplace Literacy Demonstration Project, focused
on training workers at various hospitals across New Mexico. "New
Mexico is a big state and our seventeen hospitals were spread across
hundreds of miles of interstate and two-lane roads, so we had many
road trips, with long, quiet discussions of our project," Steve recalls.
Graduate students and professors worked together to conduct a needs
assessment, create various classes in communication skills for industry
workers, and work with hospital employees to encourage good com-

munication practices. Bruce Farmer brought to this project a wealth of experiences from many years of work as an engineer and manager at TRW, in their space and electronics division at Redondo Beach, California. Bruce was a valued student in the program in part because he had wisdom developed through years of workplace experience, and he had long reflected on the relationship of good communication to good management practices. Bruce emerged as a leader and a mentor to both professors and hospital administrators.

Another site of mentoring was at the intersection of computers and writing. Several of us were interested in teaching composition with computers in our composition classes or in business and technical writing. Many projects evolved, including internal workshops for teachers and students as well as external training seminars (such as STC workshops on Web development and graphic design). Robb recalls his experiences working as a graduate assistant in the NMSU computer classroom that Steve oversaw.

Robb: We had our own team in those days, the Computer Classroom Support Group, with our own logo and help documentation. We were immersed in technology and teaching, both from the student's and teacher's perspective. I remember the sole computer classroom schedule going from mostly empty to completely full in those first few experimental semesters. The timeliness of our interests couldn't have been better, nor was Steve's push to pull technological landscapes into the traditional classroom setting. Steve encouraged me to develop case-based instruction at my site, Glyph, and to run usability studies for my dissertation. He showed me how to connect teaching to research.

Carolyn also was interested in the pedagogical value of the computer, specifically as a tool for teacher training. She and others co-developed various help sheets and training workshops for graduate students and faculty, while preparing them for pitfalls, such as students becoming distracted by the machines in front of them. Working together, Steve and Carolyn built a research protocol to collect transcripts of online peer editing sessions (using a chat facility) and from transcribed voice recordings of face-to-face sessions to compare patterns of interaction with implications for teaching. In each case, Robb and Carolyn were working on the departmental goal of improving teaching with technology. Steve helped them connect those pragmatic interests to useful dissertations.

There was significant overlap in these computers and writing projects. As graduate students, everyone was teaching and some also worked as lab assistants. We were close to the action. Additionally, many of us were in Steve's classes at the same time—classes such as "Research Design and Data Analysis" and "Computers and Writing." So there was close, overlapping integration of our intellectual interests, our teaching, and our assigned workload. It was natural for good projects to develop in such a setting and for productive relationships to deepen, leading to collaborative scholarly publications.

We also deepened relationships by other means: when not hard at work, we were collectively hard at play (or doing both at the same time). There was the time Tom and Steve mapped out Tom's dissertation over a boiling pot of pasta and a bubbling pan of spaghetti sauce at Tom's apartment. The two would also meet in other inspiring settings—visiting a Roman excavation site in Basel or playing golf. Tom recalls how his relationship with Steve—nurtured in such informal settings—proved solid enough to support him through more challenging times.

Tom: Of course, I was full of ideas as I tried to shape my focus around audience analysis in the new IBM business environment of the World Wide Web. In both informal and formal settings, the conversations with Steve were a process of discovery and change with an emergent focus. At times, I was pulled in directions that did not get me the desired result of finishing the chapter outline or shaping the theory of audience analysis in online media; but in the end, I always had more quality than I had started with. The blind alleys shaped my own understanding.

In fact, the mentoring relationship turned into one of personal growth and character building. For example, when I pushed for defending my dissertation and then realized that my committee was not ready to pass my ideas, it became clear that I needed to grow personally before going back to revise what I had written. I needed to learn to accept advice from Steve, who had been extremely supportive during this difficult time. His calm manner and empathy helped me get through this time and my various stages of development: from denial, to blame, to acceptance of suggestions, to finally rethinking and changing my dissertation. There is no doubt in my mind that without Steve's belief in me and the work I was doing, I could not have finished this task.

MENTORING AS HELPING TO DEVELOP
SKILLS AND QUALIFICATIONS

Good mentoring also develops students' skills and qualifications in their field. For us, this development was brought about by the act of us belonging to the same professional associations, such as STC, and attending the same conferences—the Association of Teachers of Technical Writing (ATTW), and the Conference on College Composition and Communication (CCCC). During the act of collectively crafting conference proposals and participating in the planning of papers, good mentoring takes place, mentoring that nurtures students' academic confidence while at the same time builds necessary skills. For us, that occurred every time that we worked with Steve on a conference project. Examples of this include the time that Lorelei and Steve prepared and presented a paper at an international conference in Puebla, Mexico, or the time that Katherine and Steve co-hosted the annual national meeting of the Council for Programs in Technical and Scientific Communication (CPTSC) in Las Cruces. Additionally, several of us were involved in hosting CPTSC in Santa Fe. At conferences, we either presented together or supported each other during individual presentations.

Back at NMSU, we also worked together on various projects that developed skills and qualifications. Steve had a strong belief in internship programs, and in all forms of experiential learning, and he encouraged PhD students to find sites of work for extended internships. Tom first interned at IBM-Tucson, working in information development to develop a new administration manual for hierarchical data storage. After eight months in Tucson, he returned to campus for a semester, and then he did another eight-month internship with IBM-Germany, where he eventually was hired on and has been ever since in a successful managerial career. Lorelei did a nine-month internship in Juarez, Mexico, where she worked in the office of Financial and Economic Development as a bilingual facilitator for Mexican non-profit organizations seeking funding from American foundations. Ken pursued an internship at the Santa Fe Institute, a high-powered think tank where complexity theory and computer modeling were hot topics.

The internships provided a forum for testing the ideas, the readings, and the research—as represented in our rhetoric and professional communication classes—against the practices of businesses and labs. Because students gain credible expertise in a field of practice that can be compared to academic practice, internships cause a change in status and authority relations. Tom's experiences eventually led to a dissertation on what "knowing your audience" means in the context of a large firm's website (IBM's German site). Lorelei's internship led to a dissertation topic (suggested by Steve) that centered on comparative professional communication practices on the US/Mexico border. Ken wrote a book on metaphor in science writing.

Other students in the program interned in various settings and, like Tom, Lorelei, and Ken, all brought back highly useful experiences and enhanced credibility as professional communicators. Robb worked as a graphic artist at IBM-Santa Teresa; his experiences there led to work on text design, integration of visuals, and enriched teaching in technical writing classrooms. These interests in design and visual rhetoric, of course, were well suited to Steve's interests, so it was natural for Steve to direct Robb's dissertation and for them to collaborate on two published articles.

Robb recalls that the mentoring relationship was not trouble free; sometimes he found Steve to be impatient or his advice hard to follow. With the IBM internship, Robb took six years to complete the degree. During that time he observed classmates work through frustrations with their own work, watched a couple of good friends leave the program altogether, saw Steve's career shift and grow, and rode out significant personal events.

Robb: At the time Steve recommended an internship to me, I was frustrated with the degree program on multiple levels, struggling with issues common to first-year students: identity, intimidation, doubts about scholarly direction. I initially saw the internship as a chance to escape. As it turned out, the internship I completed at IBM became the adhesive that bound the theory and practice of visual communication together. Steve's support for my work never wavered, though I know I gave him reasons to doubt me. It was hard for me to ask Steve for advice and input, hard to be on a personal level with him. I was stubborn, intensely private, and that didn't always jive with his more gregarious and matter-of-fact personality. I regret to this day that I was too stressed to enjoy being a PhD student to its fullest extent, but Steve and I made it work through his patience and experience and my willingness to stick it out. My advice to others in mentoring relationships would be this: be aggressive with mentoring; make it happen, take advantage of every moment it offers to build the relationship because it reciprocates for years to come. And find a path that's yours and stick to it.

Julie's internship was with the College of Engineering at NMSU, working with faculty from seven different engineering disciplines to coordinate their self-study materials for an upcoming reaccredidation. As part of this internship, Julie also received valuable experience collaborating with the industrial and civil engineering departments on the research and writing of an economic impact study for a new state highway. Most significantly, this internship led to further collaborations between the English department and the College of Engineering at NMSU. One of these collaborations, still in place today, is the integration of graduate-level technical communication students onto engineering senior design teams. Her dissertation on transfer of learning from composition and technical writing classrooms to senior capstone courses was a natural outgrowth from her work with various facets of engineering education.

Eva spent a semester working as a grant writer for the Waste-Management Education and Research Consortium (WERC), a university consortium focusing on environmental education and technology development. Drawing on her previous experience as a technical writer, she worked with engineers, environmental scientists, and technicians to identify and apply for grants. Eva's time at WERC gave her the opportunity to broaden her professional writing skills.

The internships punctuated our relationships: time together working and studying balanced against time apart working in other organizations and applying our learning. Even Steve went off on an internship of sorts, when he accepted a year-long consulting project with Roche pharmaceuticals in Basel, Switzerland, helping drug development teams map their arguments and coordinate their work across multiple sites. After initial panic that "Steve is leaving," we continued to work together that year, projects continued, and we honed our abilities to work at a distance to write exams, get research plans approved, and draft and revise our scholarship. Our work while Steve was gone continued to be successful—not because we could send e-mail messages with attached drafts of plans and chapters but because before he left we had built a solid mentor-mentee relationship that allowed limited electronic contact to advance our work.

Mentoring as Finding a Path toward Timely Ideas

Mentoring involves not only development of qualifications and skills but also growth as problem-solvers, listeners, and trouble-shooters. Working out a compelling dissertation topic is often a major challenge that the faculty advisor and student face, as the following colloquy between Katherine and Steve indicates:

Katherine: Steve taught me a lot about writing when I was a graduate student, but perhaps the most valuable lesson he taught me was
about listening. When I seemed frustrated with his typically neutral
response to the many ideas I had for a dissertation topic, Steve commented one day about the old household documents I often brought
by to chat about. While I would later write about "'the peculiar set
of cultural blinders' that make it difficult for us to see many of the
ways in which women . . . have contributed to technical communication," until that moment, I still had those blinders on. I never
would have imagined sewing instructions could be an acceptable
subject for serious study, but Steve both observed my interest and
authorized my pursuits.

Steve recollects the development of Katherine's dissertation topic in this way:

Steve: I remember when Katherine came back from packing up her
great aunt's attic in Oklahoma City, after her aunt died. We had
a class that term on computer documentation, and Katherine had
found a manual from the first dial phones. The text showed how to
put a finger in the wheel corresponding to a letter or number, and
then rotate the dial clockwise, stopping at the metal crescent and
removing the finger to let the wheel spin back. We talked about how
it had been necessary to provide user support for the technology as
it moved into the household. Katherine had noticed, too, that there
were scripts provided to show the user how to manage a conversation on the new phone device—what to say, how to take turns, etc.
We laughed about the need for a script but understood the anxiety
of new technologies and the need for hand-holding. We also realized
there was something serious here, the germ of a great idea for research on how technologies are domesticated. Katherine didn't stay
with the phone, but followed her own interests in sewing to explore
the domestication of the sewing machine at a moment when a radi-

cal technological transformation was taking place, moving a serious, expensive, engineered device into the parlor to be operated by a
woman in a house. It was a rich historical transition and a rich topic
for an outstanding dissertation (her work won multiple awards). I
think we felt our way toward this topic through shared curiosity,
guided by our willingness to simply talk about what interested us.

Steve and Katherine's reflections illustrate yet another characteristic of
mentoring at its best: the sense that both mentor and mentee share in
the journey.

CONCLUSION: FROM PAST TO PRESENT

So here we are, years after our time as doctoral students, with Steve
as our mentor—all of us now graduates of the doctoral program, all
of us now professionals, all of us now mentors to a new generation of
students or employees. The lessons we learned, the skills we developed,
and the modeling we observed have eased our transition into new roles
as mentors and professional collaborators, and we continue developing
our relationships as colleagues and friends.

Many of us continue to collaborate on projects, whether pedagogical, practical, or scholarly. Lorelei and Julie are working on long-term
research of organizational communication within a leading airline.
Julie has also done consulting work with Steve. Eva served as program
developer for ATTW when Steve was program chair and has continued her involvement with the organization. Steve wrote the forward to
Ken's book. Tom manages a large business group for IBM-Germany,
and he and Steve get together as they can, on one side of the Atlantic
or the other, typically to golf or enjoy each other's families. Katherine,
Lorelei, and Steve strategize over career moves, discuss department
politics, and help each other make decisions related to professional
growth and career management. Several of us recently celebrated
Bruce's birthday at a distance, with stories and testimonials delivered
via e-mail. We tend to respond to posts on the ATTW listserv in coor-
dinated ways; a post by Robb will be followed by one from Steve, only
to be trumped by Ken. What we don't say on the listserv is that we are
sustained at a distance by our relationships.

Of course, we still meet up at conferences like ATTW in San Francisco in 2005 where some of us presented together, supported each
other's sessions, and went out to a jazz club afterwards to celebrate.

The very fact that we can come together five-to-eight years after working in a mentor/student relationship and collaborate on a piece such as this one is perhaps the best evidence of good mentoring.

We left an important detail of the Mentor legend out of our introduction to afford us a closing. Mentor, it turns out, does more than urge Telemachus to make the journey. The goddess, in Mentor's guise, also *accompanies* the son on the journey: "I'll find a ship for you and help you sail her," Mentor (Athena) promises (27). In small, significant, and various ways, we found ships for each other, and we helped each other set sail.

    * Dedication: We dedicate this essay to Bruce Farmer, who succumbed recently to long-term illness. Bruce was a generous and fiercely intelligent mentor to those with whom he worked and studied.

Works Cited

Berkenkotter, Carol, Thomas N. Huckin, and John Ackerman. "Conventions, Conversations, and the Writer: Case Study of a Student in a Rhetoric PhD Program." *Research in the Teaching of English* 22.1 (1988): 9-44.

Brookfield. Stephen. *The Skillful Teacher*. San Francisco: Jossey-Bass, 1990.

Homer. *The Odyssey*. Trans. Robert Fitzgerald. Vintage: New York, 1990.

Kramer, Robert, and Bernhardt, Stephen A. "Moving Instruction to the Web: Writing as Multi-Tasking." *Technical Communication Quarterly* 8.3 (Summer 1999): 319-36.

Kramer, Robert, and Bernhardt, Stephen A. "Teaching Text Design." *Technical Communication Quarterly* 5.1 (Winter 1996): 35-60.

"Mentor." *The Oxford English Dictionary Online*. 2005. 1 Sept. 2005 <http://dictionary.oed.com/entrance.dtl.>.

Vickrey, Carolyn, and Bernhardt, Stephen A. "Supporting Faculty Development in Computers and Technical Communication." *Computers And Technical Communication: Pedagogical and Programmatic Perspectives*. Ed. Stuart A. Selber. Greenwich, CT: Ablex Press, 1997, 331-52.

Wiltshire, Susan Ford. *Athena's Disguises: Mentors in Everyday Life*. Louisville, KY: Westminster John Knox Press, 1998.

6 Wendy Bishop's Legacy: A Tradition of Mentoring, a Call to Collaboration

Anna Leahy, Stephanie Vanderslice, Kelli L. Custer, Jennifer Wells, Carol Ellis, Meredith Kate Brown, Dorinda Fox, and Amy Hodges Hamilton

Wendy Bishop—author and editor of books about pedagogy and the profession—died in November 2003 while battling cancer. Even after becoming ill, she actively mentored students at Florida State University and encouraged scholars and teachers across the country. In addition to her loving husband and their children, she leaves behind a legacy with those she mentored.

This essay by a few who were mentored by Bishop documents influences that Bishop's work has had on us as individuals as well as on the larger field we practice. Bishop widely advocated an open exchange of ideas about our professional lives and espoused collaboration. We build here upon and continue to be mentored by Bishop's work as a writer and role model.

WENDY BISHOP, MENTORING, AND COLLABORATION

Anna Leahy: I never met Wendy Bishop and saw her speak just once but knew her work long before we corresponded. My immediate mentors in creative writing were superb at guiding me as a poet but assumed I'd become a teacher by osmosis, observing their deft coordination of workshops in which I was a student. Though I sensed that her work was not universally lauded or well known among creative writers, I happened upon it, as many do. Her books became guides for those of us steeped in composition pedagogy by graduate programs but embarking on careers as creative writing professors. Later, when I began a collection to address this lack, I contacted Bishop to see whether she would contribute. While a few contributors to *Power and Identity in the Creative Writing Classroom: The Authority Project* are well published, Bishop is the so-called big name.

I was impressed that Bishop agreed to contribute but more impressed that she answered every message promptly, with encouragement for the project and with companionship for me, a stranger. When I asked contributors to revise their essays to make the volume more cohesive, Wendy, even though she had the most cachet and, therefore, the least pressure to change a word, produced a more significantly revised essay more quickly than any other author. Shortly before her death in November 2003, I asked contributors to update their biographical statements, noting in a message to Wendy that she needn't respond if she didn't feel up to it. She answered: "i'm just back from the hospital but would like to edit this for some inaccuracies. hope i'm in time. thanks for doing so much for me, best, wendy" (14 Nov. 2003). I did something—did *much*—for *her?*

Long before Bishop's work gave me validation, I became enamored with collaboration. In eighth grade, the smart kids helped the struggling kids with homework. In college, a peer and I decided to work together on a Shakespeare paper. We each chose our own topic, we each took control of our own ideas, but we brainstormed and revised together. I corrected his grammar and reeled in his unwieldy ideas; he read quotes aloud and made leaps to unexpected connections. Together, we each learned more about our interpretations than we could have separately.

Since these early collaborations, I've learned better ways to collaborate productively with an art historian, a computer scientist, and others. Bishop has been a wonderful guide and generous encourager in these endeavors through her vast work as an editor devoted to bringing together various perspectives and voices in dialogue. One of her projects, *Acts of Revision,* ends with a piece authored with her longtime collaborator Hans Ostrum; the title "Thank You, Thank You Very Much: Coauthors on Collaborative Revision" advocates that teachers, scholars, and writers can benefit from working together—and the final product, too, might be more complex as a result. In her introduction to *Teaching Lives,* she writes, "I need to put myself in dialogue with others. By sharing published teaching stories I learned how to have a voice and a place" (viii).

Yet, in conversations with colleagues, my collaboration has been questioned: What does a co-author do? If you are the trained writer—or the lead author—aren't you the *real* author? In addition, the academy confers less value on editing and on pedagogy scholarship than it does on textual or scientific research. Bishop ignored or plowed through such concerns. She advocated collaboration, through practice and advice, wherever it might benefit others and generously dismissed the desire to divvy up credit or create hierarchies: "In writing about our own teaching lives, we figure out our classrooms, we speak to others, and we compose ourselves in beneficial ways" (*Teaching Lives* viii). Bishop resisted easy consensus, recognized that readers would argue with her ideas, but spoke to those of us "who care to share stories together" (*Teaching Lives* x). She helped me trust that we can and should work together to understand and improve our work as teachers, scholars, writers—whatever professional roles we assume.

I have been shaped both by Bishop's writings and by her modeling of a mentoring relationship. Her published writing and her encouragement via e-mail validated my commitment to collaboration that underpins this essay. When Wendy died, several of us agreed that continuing collaborations could encourage us and others to rethink the traditions that have shaped us, to mentor as peers, to work in tandem and offer each other support as Bishop had.

Bulldozing the Pyramid, Wendy Bishop's "Story," and the Rise of Creative Writing Pedagogy in America

Stephanie Vanderslice: In his history of creative writing, D.G. Myers reports that creative writing programs in the post-Iowa era were "created by a kind of institutional proselytism,"(164) and that, as Donald Justice reflected, "those who went through Iowa went out and took part in other writing programs—a kind of pyramid scheme" (qtd. in Myers 164). Whether entirely comfortable or vaguely troubled by what David Starkey calls the rather "cushy" (qtd. in Bizarro 300) terms of their employment, few writers protested. It took Wendy Bishop's discontent with her own education to lift the curtain on creative writing in America near the end of the twentieth century and to reveal the wizard at the machine. She let in the light for all of us who would follow in challenging the status quo, in challenging the myths of creative writing, of teaching, and of mentoring.

Patrick Bizarro underscores what many of us now teaching know by heart: Bishop's ground-breaking work suggests that "academic creative writing ha[d] not been responsive enough to theoretical and pedagogical changes" (qtd. in Bizarro 298) sweeping through academia in the last century. Bishop laid the foundation that supports our continued efforts to critically examine the pedagogies from which we have emerged and upon which we thrive.

Let us consider why Bishop's work resonates with many of us who identify themselves as the second generation who wish to re-make what it means to be both a teacher *and* a writer in America. The narrative Bishop invokes as she begins her critique of the status quo, her *story*, stirs something deeply in us—because her story *is* our story. By telling it, she mentors scores of people she never even met.

In *Teaching Lives,* Bishop asserts that the "the good and the bad (or indifferent or spotty or dramatic or quiet) teaching I experienced as a student still informs me. It must be critiqued, assimilated, accommodated, transcended, reprocessed" (219). Her narrative continually refers to the displacement she felt as a woman and outsider in the academic world and insists that it is the "miseducational part[s] of that experience that drive me to improve instruction" (236). Indeed, she wonders aloud if others shared her displacement. We scribble "Yes!" in the margin.

Bishop describes work with "master teachers," who did not "teach" her and her fellow students, who returned "no annotated texts, gave no tests, shared no grading standards, kept to no schedule or syllabus, designed no curriculum" because, she assumed, "[w]e were not ready, worthy or worth it" (240-41). We read her words and remember our own encounters with master teachers, our own deferment to whatever scraps of enlightenment we could garner. We read Bishop's epiphany that she could not "teach the way [she] had been taught" (243) and recognize that what we have suspected all along may be possible: we may not have to.

This narrative helped to ignite the revolution in instruction and theory that continues to burn after Bishop is no longer physically among us. In "On Learning to Like Teaching Creative Writing," Bishop issues what can now be seen as the clarion call for a "deep revision of what it means to teach and learn creative writing, a re-prioritization of products and processes, a curriculum that investigates itself, that denounces old premises, topples myths, renames and reaffirms" (*Teaching Lives* 248). Her call for rethinking helps to underpin new investigations such as our collection *Can It Really Be Taught? Resisting Lore in Creative Writing*. As she continued to answer and question in numerous volumes and journals, legions of writer-teachers who eagerly consumed Bishop's work began to chart their own paths, to answer that call in the myriad ways we do today. We honor our mentor's powerful narratives by proffering our own.

Finding a Heart of Gold in My Inbox

Kelli L. Custer: During my first year of my PhD, I became caught in that end-of-the-semester panic, staring at a blank computer screen and wishing for a way to make another paper appear. It was a very hot and humid April night; every movement seemed slowed. I was feeling what I imagine many first-year doctoral students feel: What have I done? Can I really do this? Do I really want to?

Looking for possible sources, I turned to an essay by Wendy Bishop, "Heart of Gold." In it, Wendy describes her experiences as a doctoral student at the same university as I and her journey into the field of rhetoric and composition. As I read names of my own professors and that the "heat deadened the small town of Indiana, Pennsylvania" (34), I began to feel slightly less alone in this place we shared as graduate students separated in time, and even less alone when she described her graduate work much as I was feeling then: "exhausting, draining, scary" (34). She explains at the end of the essay that she loves the field of rhetoric and composition because "it is the blue-collar, sleeves-rolled-up, why-the-hell-not frontier of English studies [. . .] a place where I welcome an e-mail from San Bernardino" (36). The e-mail was a note she had received from a graduate student she didn't know, asking for help. And, so, because I grew up in the frontiers of the West and understood what she meant about composition, later that night, in what would be my first-ever fan letter, I tracked down Wendy's e-mail address and sent her a note, thanking her for being not just an academic source of inspiration, but a personal one as well. I didn't really expect an answer, but it arrived before 6:30 a.m. Wendy assured me that she had felt much of what I was feeling and that I would find a way through. She wrote, "i do hope here by morning's light that a way into and out of your paper presents itself [. . .]. i hope you'll be on your way into the dissertation before long. let me know how it all goes" (18 Apr. 2002).

This commitment to mentoring appears in many of Wendy's published works. In "Learning Our Own Ways to Situate Composition and Feminist Studies in the English Department," she claims, "Since graduate students clearly represent great potential for English departments, we should explore public and private channels for teaching these soon-to-be-peers critical consciousness [. . .]. These students have the potential to make the changes within the house of English studies we have sometimes despaired of making" (Teaching Lives 133). There, she writes about the difficulties of being a woman in the academy, often not taken seriously, and I again felt a chord striking in me.

When I was trying to write an article for publication, to add my voice to the academic conversation, I struggled with overcoming fear of entering that world. I turned again to Wendy. Who better to ask than someone as prolific as she? The ideal at Indiana University of Pennsylvania was to be like our alumna, Wendy—send everything for possible publication. She even published her comprehensive exam answers.

So, I e-mailed her again. With her usual warmth and modesty, she extended herself and her experience to me. She told me why she loved writing and publishing:

> because i love the learning it affords me and i am too ornery not to think that somewhere one or two overlooked teachers will maybe benefit from it. i actually visualize, i think, the working teacher i was 20 years ago as a part-time instructor and think about how i'd like to be in dialogue with that person, who, like me, most of us, is really not in a huge program that is supporting them. it's a lifeline—for those on either end—writer and reader. i like participating in that compact—if i don't hazard publication, i can't. (7 May 2003)

That didn't mean she didn't feel fear, she said, nor that she didn't feel hurt when she was attacked in print for ideas she'd written. But she urged me to go with my ideas and "to just kick off from the edge and try to enjoy it" (7 May 2003).

Whenever possible, Wendy mentored students—even anonymous ones who called to her from other places. Her academic achievements were significant, but she didn't just write; she engaged in dialogue. She reached out to readers on the other side of the page. For me, as for others, she was a brief, and now deeply missed, mentor, but she remains a continuing role model.

FROM MICROFICHE TO MENTORING

Jennifer Wells: The first time I met Wendy Bishop, I was in a remote corner of the San Francisco State Library, squinting through the glare of fluorescent lighting at what would become a career-altering piece of microfiche. That piece of plastic contained her article "Suddenly Sexy: Creative Nonfiction Rear-ends Composition," and after reading it, I realized with relief and exhilaration that it was not insane, in supposedly post-expressivist 2003, to argue for a composition pedagogy that included, and even encouraged, this controversial genre and its reliance on the personal voice. In addition, not a composition code-talker, Bishop wrote directly, eloquently, sincerely, with humor and incisive wit, ripping open disciplinary clichés and offering a place for me and many others.

Shortly after that day in the library, I set aside a Bishop book budget in my graduate-student-sized checking account to buy one of her publications each month. It was through text that Wendy first mentored me. I breathed in her essays. In those words were reminders of who I wanted to be, once, what I wanted to become before the inevitable onslaught of papers and interdepartmental politicians and a life outside of academia desperate to be lived. Wendy brought me back to that place that made me want to teach writing and showed that the teaching life most of us wish for was, in fact, possible.

In May 2003, I wrote an e-mail to Wendy, telling her how much I liked her work and asking if she thought there was room for further study in the confluence of creative nonfiction and composition. It was the first time I had written to a big name of composition. I expected little, perhaps no, response, for we are all busy, overwhelmed with messages from our students (and families and friends). Wendy wrote back the next morning: a *long* e-mail that detailed her belief in "this confusing productive nexus between fact/fiction, creative writing and composition and literary studies [. . .] all that makes it a bit hard to hold still and study and define but also very exciting" (3 May 2003). That first response sparked an ongoing correspondence that continued until three weeks before her death. She had told me she had cancer, but I wouldn't find out until after she died that she had been writing even though chemotherapy had left her nearly blind.

I never did meet Wendy in person, and, so, we didn't have the traditional mentoring relationship. However, in publishing partially because she wanted to reach out to others who felt adrift in this strange sea of academia, and in responding with enthusiasm to letters from strangers, Wendy mentored me and many, many others. She continues to mentor us still.

MENTORING FREELY, MENTORING FREEDOM

Carol Ellis: The spring after she died, I taught and lived Wendy Bishop's *Teaching Lives* in a graduate seminar where the classroom walls seemed prison walls in an unwelcoming curriculum unable to envision the journey through creative writing into creative composition and ultimately into creative nonfiction, a "suddenly sexy" genre relationship that Bishop recognizes as evidence that all writing is creative, and all writing uses the personal to deconstruct then reconstruct the text.

The appearance of the creative personal and the writer's freedom to be on the page—using the page to liberate a voice containing gender, culture, politics, and aesthetics—is an invitation to join the revolution in which composition's creativity deconstructs authority and reconstructs texts and courses into spaces that liberate language and empower the writer to be creative. The creative risks liberating stories and styles in which new voices coexist with the canon. The disorder of the personal, of individual experience, slams into the order of authority to challenge its persistent demands for power. Creativity is disorder, and to recognize the presence of creative writing in composition is to recognize that composition methodology studies the art of composing, an imperfect action of revolution treasured by Bishop.

Teaching promises learning on freedom's open space of a page. As her writing mentored me, Bishop taught that freedom is a necessary companion of creativity and sensuality. My imagination expanded in the conversation occurring in the interpretive circle of writer, text, and reader. The elation I felt as my own writing fell into creative nonfiction transmitted itself to the students whose surprise to learn that they mattered in the texts they wrote and read created an investment in the personal pronoun *I*. They felt an obligation to think deeply, to work at writing well, to tell a good story, and to know the way freedom invites the possible. For Bishop, for so many of us, to write is to live. Moreover, to write freely is to live freely: it *teaches* us to live freely, to refuse the cultures of fear and patriarchy by walking on to the space that is ours to write and read as we wish. When we question the authority of the writer, the text, and the reader, we create a narrative of liberation plunging us into the uncertainty of freedom.

In that composition class, we wrote and read our creative displacement: who is the writer, what is the text, who is the reader? We could not necessarily reply with only one answer and, instead, found that every written page contained a multiplicity of writers, texts, and readers. What we at first perceived as chaotic revealed itself as the actions of freedom in the arena of intellect and body. We began the semester by knowing all the answers; we ended the semester in a morass of questioning that caused us to examine our writing and wonder who wrote it.

In our discomfort, we sought to change our writing into the creative writing that Bishop claims all writing is, because by now she was in the classroom with us. She beckoned. She distracted me, and the students saw that I was distracted and overwhelmed with her presence. My distraction freed me to free the students and to recognize our concealed alternative selves and their voices.

After class, I drove home listening to a B.B. King concert at San Quentin prison. "Glory in your spot," he says between songs, and I thought how Bishop would continue the riff: glory who we are and where we are by creating those spaces in writing. Remember, first there was the word, then there was the world filling with words, then there are your words telling your story. My story includes a semester in which an absent woman became present to the teacher teaching her ideas about teaching, learning, reading, and writing as kinds of freedom that she wanted us to notice as much as we noticed ourselves being free. Bishop mentored my own voice into freedom.

THE LEGACY OF ETHNOGRAPHY AND CHANGING THE RULES

Meredith Kate Brown: When I stepped into Wendy Bishop's class my first semester as a graduate student, I knew it would be different than any of my previous academic experiences. Upon her insistence, I had to work at calling her "Wendy," though her multitude of publications merited "Dr. Bishop." She was more humble than she could have been and always spoke to me as a colleague. In her class, I felt that my opinions and experiences, as well as those of my classmates, were valuable and that sharing these in the classroom environment contributed to my overall learning.

The following semester, I enrolled in Wendy's research methods course, where I was introduced to her book *Ethnographic Writing Research: Writing it Down, Writing it Up, and Reading it.* When I began to read, I could see why ethnographic research appealed so strongly to Wendy. Ethnography privileges the researcher's personal experience within a unique environment, and these voices of experience and learning are the voices that Wendy privileged in her classroom. Wendy's choice to write an ethnographic dissertation largely resulted from her desire to reveal the value of personal experience in a genre that sometimes pretends to be objective. She recognized that, in even a meticulously controlled study, the experiences and goals of researchers shape outcomes. Moreover, the regulated atmosphere of controlled studies cannot capture writers' real writing environments and behaviors. Wendy persistently asserted that ethnographic methods are "not *in service of* but are *equal to*" (*Ethnographic* 5) quantitative and other methodologies, an argument supported by more scholars now than ten years ago.

When Wendy wrote her dissertation, she understood that the necessity to justify her method choices and to address common criticisms of ethnographic research was largely due to her graduate-student status, which made experimental and subversive research risky. For ethnography to be successful, not only must it break from positivist methodologies but also positivist conventions of style, which are often required by rigid dissertation guidelines. Wendy addresses the contradiction these guidelines expose in "I-Witnessing in Composition": "The novice is usually told, 'prove you belong' not prove you have 'strong beliefs, ideas, feelings, and an admirable character.' Yet feelings, beliefs, character—all are hallmarks of the convincing I-witnessing styles of Geertz and Elbow and Rose" (153).

Without a narrative style highlighting the researcher's rhetorical position, graduate students are likely to create an underdeveloped ethnography, only contributing to the criticism of their method choice.

With her research methods class, Wendy shared her experience struggling to write her dissertation. She wanted us to understand why it was important for her to write a textbook she wished she had had as a graduate student. She emphasized the complexity of ethnographic research as a combination of rigorous data collection, data interpretation, rhetorical awareness, and effective writing style. She offered graduate-student teachers a strategy to articulate what is going on in classrooms and to liberate them from the artificiality of controlled research studies. And, most important, she showed us that as ethnographic researchers we undergo "practical and engaging changes because the researcher discovers how to read and write and think better, to sharpen his or her latent skills of perceptions, and to humanize sites of literacy" (*Ethnographic* 181). Wendy's mentoring philosophy grew out of, in part, a keen awareness of what her own needs had been as a young scholar and teacher. By addressing those needs with future scholars and teachers, she encourages us to tackle new questions and to build upon her work.

TEETERING ON A GOLDEN MEAN

Dorinda Fox: When he wrote "The Speech the Graduates Didn't Hear," Jacob Neusner may have been having a bad day or perhaps a student was rude to him and he needed to vent. Sometimes we like each other, and sometimes we wear on each other's nerves. Neusner tells graduates, "Try not to act toward your coworkers and bosses as you have acted toward us."

I thought, *what a curmudgeon—how awful to publish something with such a nasty tone.* Then I remembered something in the conference panel from which this collaborative essay grew and now pull a Dr. Neusner myself. Wendy Bishop was a rather famous and infamous scholar in creative writing, rhetoric, and composition. Sometimes we wore on each other's nerves. Or I wore on hers. I realized years after that I had acted badly toward this mentor. And then she died.

In December 2003, I meet with an overscheduled graduate student about what I consider to be reasonable demands—due dates, collaborative discussion with much student-defined rather than teacher-defined content—placed upon her in our online professional writing course. The student is tired. Contempt drips from the words she utters. She explains her very full life, including many important professional and family activities that must trump assignments. While she vents, I talk to myself in my head: *Be calm. Don't get angry.* It doesn't work.

I tell the graduate student that taking multiple courses while working full-time and raising children is not only stressful but perhaps impossible to do without much emotional distress due to fatigue. Her answer to relieving that stress involves changing the course's demands to meet her circumstances. I tell her that won't happen. She just needs to do less in her limited time; what she does will then be accomplished better. This is not what the student wants to hear. She leaves angrier than when we began talking. When the student mercifully leaves (if only to file a complaint in the graduate office), I think, *That was me ten years ago when I was talking to Wendy Bishop. I was one self-involved bitch. I should say I'm sorry.*

This meeting is not good for our young graduate program. In addition, I am new to teaching in it. My supervisor will lose a weekend to reviewing the course and the student's work in order to defend me to the graduate coordinator. I will feel guilty about that. My supervisor will say little, but it will strain our relationship from then on.

I go home and check e-mail while making spaghetti for my family. Carrie Leverenz has posted that Wendy Bishop has died from complications of leukemia. I so want to say, *I'm sorry. You taught me so much and continue to teach my students so much. I'm sorry I was so awful.* That won't happen. I make my sauce feeling intense regret. I have another glass of wine.

A mentor is one who influences a student during one semester or program of study as well as, or more so, years later when that student has time to reflect. Bishop summarizes what I learned as her graduate student, as well as from her voluminous published work about teaching, in an article about creative nonfiction: "Trying to work toward emotional, spiritual, familial, intellectual, professional, political, and the big ETC. of truths is not just part of, but is the process of writing, of composing nonfiction. It is the golden mean, too, of a version of academic life that many of us might choose" ("Suddenly Sexy 265"). I read this article because I wanted to know Bishop's thoughts on a subject that I would be teaching. Time and again, I return to her work for guidance—much more often than while in graduate school when she herself was available. This article was not her best or most influential. There are many more.

Bishop's emphasis on the "emotional, spiritual, familial, intellectual, professional, political, and the big ETC. of truths" and the "golden mean" of those truths mirrors the work and rhetorical strategies of ancient Sophistic rhetoricians I present in advanced composition classrooms. Bishop did not seem interested in determining what was wrong or right about the process of producing student writing or even the content of student writing. Instead, she, like most good rhetoricians, asks that we examine how pedagogical and personal truths were and continue to be achieved. Such an examination, for instance, can involve the study of fractured narratives or double-voicing in Bishop's *Elements of Alternate Style* to bring alive ancient ideas such as *dissoi logoi* to students living literally thousands of years later.

Bishop continues a tradition of direct and indirect mentoring. She was a better mentor than I knew at the time and that I let her know, but the best mentoring extends beyond itself.

Mentoring, Learning, and Relearning from Each Other

Amy Hodges Hamilton: When I first learned that my mentor and major professor, Wendy Bishop, was very ill, I didn't know how to respond. I was scared to go visit her in the hospital. I wanted to see her, but I was afraid I wasn't close enough. I'll never forget walking toward her room in critical ICU that steamy August afternoon—I was shaking with fear to see the strongest person in my life weak.

Wendy welcomed me into her room, held my hand, and comforted *me*, and I was just a student. After only minutes, Wendy began to ask me questions about my dissertation research. As I talked about my findings, she insisted on engaging in the conversation by removing her oxygen mask and whispering ideas and places to look for further research. At that moment, I realized Wendy's strength as a person and mentor was ongoing, and I was convinced she would fight the cancer. But what most astounds me now, as I sit and reflect on Wendy's mentoring life, is that she was always teaching, always.

I first walked into Wendy's classroom as an undergraduate English major. From that first day in Wendy's writing workshop, I was intrigued by her openness. She wrote with us and always entered into writing exchanges as our equal. Wendy reflects on this practice in "Traveling Through the Dark: Teachers and Student Reading and Writing Together": "writing teachers must also be writers and engage in the writing process with students, and through this journey, students will begin to know that we write and understand the process firsthand" (106). Much of Wendy's scholarship focuses on the importance of the teacher and the student engaging in dialogue about writing and the writing process. Her practice defines a mentor as a guide.

Because of the impact of Wendy's mentorship for me as an undergraduate writer, I chose to pursue a PhD at Florida State University, in order to study with her again. Wendy always shared her grapplings with the readings and her ideas in graduate seminars. One semester, she wrote a practice-to-theory essay with us, in which she questioned how various theories of composition informed her teaching life:

> I do not believe I can have a smorgasbord pedagogy, but I do feel entitled to range widely, as a teaching generalist, as a writing specialist. I am obliged to define, refine, name and explain my practice and to build new knowledge from which to set out again. It is the building and the appreciating and the setting out strongly that matters to me. Writing teachers who get up each day and do their work are doing their work; they do not have to apologize for having values and beliefs, for coming from one section of a field and for moving— perhaps—to another section—from one understanding of instruction to another understanding of it—as long as they are willing to talk, to share, to travel on in company. ("Dragged a Comb" 14)

Wendy was always "willing to talk, to share, to travel on in company." In fact, she insisted on it.

Her mentorship was especially strong outside the classroom. She often invited students to collaborate at conferences and in publications. When I thanked her for including me in *The Subject is Writing*, she responded: "this is actually fun and exciting and i want you to see the entire book production process if you're interested—part of my lifelong mentoring goals of showing you how the whole system works, w" (6 Nov. 2002). Wendy modeled effective mentoring by talking and working with her students at all levels—undergraduate and graduate—inside and outside the classroom, even beside her hospital bed.

Through stories such as these—both published and unpublished—Wendy Bishop is still teaching us, as a field and as individuals, how to become effective teachers and mentors. Wendy's conclusion in *Teaching Lives* best captures her ideas on how to lead a mentoring life:

I believe in teaching. Because I relearn my life as my students explore theirs (320).

WORKS CITED

Bishop, Wendy, ed. *Acts of Revision: A Guide for Writers.* Portsmouth, NH: Boynton/Cook, 2004.

—. "Dragged a Comb Across my Head." Essay Draft from Composition Theory and Practice Course. Florida State University, Tallahassee, FL. Fall 2001.

—, ed. *Elements of Alternate Style: Essays on Writing and Revision.* Portsmouth, NH: Boynton/Cook Heinemann, 1997.

—. *Ethnographic Writing Research: Writing it down, Writing It up, and Reading It.* Portsmouth: Boynton/Cook, 1999.

—. "Heart of Gold." *Living Rhetoric and Composition: Stories of the Discipline.* Ed. Duane H. Roen, Stuart C. Brown, and Theresa Enos. Mahwah, NJ: Erlbaum, 1999. 25-36.

—. "I-Witnessing in Composition: Turning Ethnographic Data into Narratives." *Rhetoric Review* 11.1 (1992): 147-58.

—. "re: bio update, if you want." E-mail to the author. 14 November 2003.

—. "re: CNF and Comp." E-mail to the author. 3 May 2003.

—. "Re: Identity and fear." E-mail to the author. 7 May 2003.

—. "Re: Thank you." E-mail to the author. 18 Apr. 2002.

—. *Released into Language: Options for Teaching Creative Writing.* Urbana, IL: National Council of Teachers of English, 1991.

—. "The Subject is Writing, third ed." E-mail to the author. 06 November 2002.

—. "Suddenly Sexy: Creative Nonfiction Rear-ends Composition." *College English* 65 (January 2003): 257-76.

—. *The Subject is Writing*, 3rd ed. Portsmouth, NH: Boynton/Cook, 2003.

—. *Teaching Lives: Essays and Stories.* Logan, UT: Utah State UP, 1997.

Bizarro, Patrick. "Research and Reflection in English Studies: The Special Case of Creative Writing." College English 66:3 (January 2004): 294-309.

King, B. B. *Live At San Quentin.* MCA Records, 1990.

Leahy, Anna, ed. *Power and Identity in the Creative Writing Classroom: The Authority Project.* North Somerset, UK, 2005.

Myers, D.G. *The Elephants Teach: Creative Writing Since 1880.* Englewood Cliffs, NJ: Prentice Hall, 1996.

Neusner, Jacob. "The Commencement Speech You'll Never Hear." *The Price of Excellence: Universities in Conflict During the Cold War Era.* Lanham, MD: University Press of America, 1995. 199-202. Also available at Google Book Search < http://tinyurl.com/4u7c2l>.

Ritter, Kelly and Stephanie Vanderslice. Can It Really Be Taught? *Resisting Lore in Creative Writing.* Portsmouth, NH: Heinemann, 2007.

7 Mentoring Friendships and the "Reweaving of Authority"

Diana Ashe and Elizabeth Ervin

Meet the Authors

Diana: When I met Betsy, I was in the middle of interviewing for jobs. It's hard for anyone to stand out in the blur that is the academic job search, but Betsy did. She seemed to hold so much that I, as a rookie academic, was seeking: a great job at an excellent university where she taught courses I dreamed of, a stellar publishing record, a wicked sense of humor, a supportive husband who is truly a partner, and great hair. I chose the job at University of North Carolina Wilmington (UNCW) in part because I identified with so many of the department members, like Betsy, and felt I could find a place for myself here.

That part happened quickly, because I had an unusual hiring situation and served on five committees that first year. To start the program I was hired to help create, I held or sat in on meeting after meeting, many of which featured Betsy among the participants. Betsy modeled for me how these processes work, how to handle them, and sometimes filled me in on institutional history to help it all make sense. I definitely had a place at UNCW right away. It was exciting and overwhelming, and I was pretty sure that I had landed a job at Utopia University, where everyone is supportive and helpful. I now realize that Betsy's contributions to smoothing my way helped me to form that impression.

Since that first year, I've come to realize that Utopia University doesn't exist, and that's a good thing. During my second year, I worked through extended illness for much of the term, then ran afoul of a senior colleague more than once. Betsy not only guided me through it all, but she argued on my behalf and even formally protested the handling of the situation. I am still astounded by her generosity and fearlessness. Hers is a daunting act to follow: I have been watching for five years now as she votes her conscience in every instance, prepares scrupulously for classes and meetings, balances openness and respect for confidentiality, shows awe-inspiring creativity at work and at home, and is truly committed to helping her students learn and think.

I'm afraid I'll wear out the tiles between her office and mine, since I pop in there so often. I head to Betsy's office (conveniently located right next door to mine) for a hundred reasons: to get her view of the potential fallout from a decision I'm contemplating; to understand the departmental mood on an issue; to ask what she would do in my position; to seek guidance on dealing with a particular course, student, or situation; to vent; and to deepen my understanding of, well, anything. Lately, I also head to Betsy's office to ask pregnancy-related questions and look for reassurance that, yes, it is possible to be an involved parent and a successful academic. After all, Betsy is doing it, so maybe I can, too.

Elizabeth: Wow, Diana sounds like a handful, doesn't she? She's actually not, although when she first came to UNCW, I confess that I was a little disappointed, not by the fact that she was *here*, but by my initial impression that she was going to be a man's woman—that is, a woman who cultivated friendships and loyalties with men rather than women. Within weeks of arriving, she was hosting football-watching parties and feeding the scruffy MFA students who lived downstairs from her, and for these sorts of gestures she was immediately and virtually unanimously adored. And for good reason, for the fact is that while Diana *is* a man's woman, she's also a woman's woman, a children's woman, a dog's woman . . . that is, an utterly dependable and considerate friend to just about anyone on two or four legs. Need someone to serve on the committee that's interviewing new office assistants? Ask Diana. Out sick and and need someone to take your class for a few days? Diana. Last-minute babysitter, dog-walker, lunch companion? Diana, Diana, Diana. She is always the first volunteer for any ad hoc responsibility, the first to stop by with a Ziploc full of "extra" cookies, the go-to person for anyone mulling the vagaries of personal and professional comportment. And it's not just that Diana is handy; she's also smart. She's the only person in the department who can teach every course in the Professional Writing option of our major (and more than a few literature and English education courses as well).

But if it sounds like Diana is a pushover, that would be wrong, too, for she also communicates her boundaries, standards, and allegiances with remarkable clarity, an ability which has justifiably earned the admiration of students and colleagues alike. Last year, for example, a graduate student whose thesis I was (ostensibly) directing wrote to Diana for advice on his project; his request took the form of an e-mail spanning several screens, wholly lacking in paragraphs or capital letters, and addressed to a different professor. Diana managed to offer generous and substantive advice to this student even as she reminded him that she was neither Dr. Sweeney nor a member of his committee and schooled him on e-mail etiquette. I marvel constantly at her rhetorical skills.

Fortunately for me, I'm Diana's mentor, which means that I have ready access to the stores of candy and baked goods, Hello Kitty office supplies, sound advice, and untold favors and kindnesses that Diana regularly offers and that serve as the foundations for friendship and collegiality. Whenever I lose perspective, brought low by the world of academe or the world in general, I go to someone who invariably has it: Diana.

If the tone of this essay sounds less like an academic argument and more like the minutes of the Mutual Admiration Society, there's a reason: we're friends, and we think that's the key to our successful mentoring relationship. To its collective credit, academe has during the past decade recognized the need to diminish the ethos of coercion and domination that has traditionally undergirded mentoring relationships and to infuse these relationships instead with the nurturing, altruistic qualities that Janice M. Lauer associates with an "ethics of care" (234). While we applaud any effort to make humane what is widely acknowledged as an important, even fundamental, relationship, in our view Lauer's vision represents a shift more of degree than of kind, suggesting a kinder, gentler execution of the same relationship rather than a critical restructuring of the relationship itself. Most significantly for our purposes, the notion of an attentive and sympathetic hierarchy seems to reaffirm a unidirectional flow of influence initiated primarily by the mentor's sense of obligation or benevolence, which is in turn largely a result of the mentor's available time and sense of professional satisfaction. While we agree that this model of mentoring can yield positive results, we also believe that it takes a short-sighted view of mentoring by conforming to the familiar dyadic relationship of mentor and mentee but paying little attention to the networks of affiliation that support long-term commitment to the academic enterprise.

We advocate a longer view of the mentoring relationship, beginning with two related assumptions: first, that one's professional and personal needs don't end (that is, one does not become autonomous) when employment is proffered or tenure granted; and second, that unequal relationships do not magically become equal when the employment status of one member of the relationship is officially elevated. If we accept these assumptions, then we must likewise accept that junior colleagues (including graduate students, though our primary focus here is faculty) are not empty vessels awaiting the assistance, empowerment, or goodwill of their mentors and must instead be recognized as already fully functioning ethical and professional agents. As such, their needs may be most effectively met by working with senior colleagues who consciously acknowledge the unsettledness of their own personal and professional trajectories: the goals, challenges, and accomplishments that mark any career or life. Our point is that junior colleagues and senior colleagues, mentees and mentors, young adults and older ones typically appreciate and thrive within the same kinds of relationships, namely, those that are multifarious, mutual, and generative. In this essay we argue that such relationships—in a word, *friendships*—offer a potent model for mentoring, one that not only echoes but also enlivens the principles of critical pedagogy that influence so much of our academic work.

Private Circles: Mentoring and the Problem of Exclusivity

The emotional intimacy inherent to friendships has historically played a significant role in mentoring relationships. The ancient pederastic relationship, for example, cast the mentor and mentee as lovers, complete with swooning, jealousy, terms of endearment, and sexual favors; though strictly hierarchical, its purpose was to educate a young man in the obligations of citizenship and usher him into respectable manhood—a community of equals (see Ervin). In the more familiar context of academe, mentoring is generally regarded as a professional relationship requiring the mentor's career advice, letters of recommendation, thesis direction, and the like. The intellectual intimacies that emerge from these relationships so frequently morph into emotional and physical intimacies that affairs and marriages between junior and senior colleagues or between graduate students and their faculty mentors barely raise eyebrows anymore. And yet such intimacies can be so fraught with perils that they are generally dismissed as anomalous to the "ideal" mentoring relationship rather than (in many cases) constitutive.

There are good reasons for this, of course, one of which is that intimate mentoring relationships frequently evolve into exclusive relationships. We see at least three problems with this exclusivity. First and most innocuously, it is limiting. After all, no single mentor offers a complete set of resources and perspectives that a mentee needs for the five or six years of the official relationship, much less for an entire career: a longtime member of a department may know much about institutional history but little about securing large grants; an excellent mentor in teaching may have little guidance to offer a mentee regarding electronic publishing; and so on. Exclusive (and exclusionary) mentoring relationships also run the risk of creating what Barbara Couture describes as "a closed and singular identity, a private circle of like minds" (5) and in the process stifle the development of junior and senior faculty alike.

The "private circle" that Couture describes often leads to a second problem with exclusive mentoring relationships: distorted understandings of proprietary boundaries. In our experience, mentors and their assigned mentees are so relentlessly encouraged to identify with and advocate for each other's interests that their relationships often narrow into a kind of insularity or clannishness, isolating them from other colleagues whose support would likely be beneficial. Within such relationships, mentees may be directly or indirectly discouraged from seeking advice or feedback from colleagues other than the assigned mentor or, more perniciously, deployed as pawns in departmental politicking or interpersonal feuds. The mentor may feel justified in claiming credit for the mentee's successes and responsibility for his or her failures, regardless of whether he or she has been directly involved in the mentee's work. Our university's recently devised Graduate Mentor Award illustrates how such behaviors can be institutionalized as good mentoring: designed to affirm the importance of the mentoring relationship, the award pits mentors against one another in a competition for recognition, one whose outcome is based at least as much on the mentee's accomplishments as the mentor's actions or initiative. Although Lauer's ethics of care requires the mentor "to be present to the one cared-for rather than to identify with one's possessions (scholarly possessions)" (234), we see little evidence that the mentee, however "cared-for," is so neatly differentiated from the mentor's scholarly possessions. Indeed, as Jacques Derrida suggests in his treatise *Politics of Friendship*, such differentiations are impossible within the zero-sum "friend/enemy distinction" (127). In short, without radical restructuring of the relationship, to the mentor go the (mentee's) spoils.

The reduction of people and their complex interactions to a potential professional "yield" is made possible by an economy that values products over processes, and this is the third problem of exclusive mentoring relationships that we wish to highlight here. Donald E. Hall argues in *The Academic Self: An Owner's Manual* that as "academics, we should approach with enthusiasm the processes, as well as value highly the products, of our work" (44), and of course many of us do just this, particularly in our pedagogies. Such enthusiasm can be difficult to sustain in traditional mentoring relationships, however, in part because they come with a built-in expiration date—usually tenure, a threshold beyond which mentoring is believed to be unnecessary or superfluous. The policy on mentoring approved by our Faculty Senate exemplifies this mentality:

> The hiring of each faculty member is an investment in the university's future. The university hires promising faculty in the hope and expectation that they will successfully complete a probationary period, achieve tenure, and provide the university with years of estimable service. Accordingly, it is in the university's interest that each academic department provide continuous mentoring of its junior faculty from the time of hiring until a tenure decision is made. Typically, junior faculty are assigned one or more senior faculty mentors to advise them and guide their professional development in teaching and research.

Here, the achievement of tenure and promotion represents the indisputable beginning, end, and purpose of the mentoring relationship; the mentor's role is to "advise" and "guide" junior faculty, with no expectation of reciprocity or enduring personal or professional commitment. Such policies leave little room for more expansive enactments of mentoring and thus tacitly endorse the "private circle."

Hall reminds us of the danger inherent in this approach to professional development, a danger many of us have either witnessed or experienced: "If we tie our senses of professional payoff only to a desired reception of the end product of a process, then we are setting ourselves up for disappointment, perhaps even a state of bitterness or burnout" (46). Examples of this are not hard to find in mentoring relationships. In worst-case scenarios, the relationship ends abruptly and often painfully, leaving the mentee adrift and vulnerable to a mentor who withdraws support or is actively punitive or vindictive: the paradigmatic "tor-mentor." More typically, the relationship simply dissolves (in the mistaken belief that it is no longer relevant) or becomes antagonistic (in the equally mistaken belief that relationships between professional "equals" are fundamentally different from those between junior and senior colleagues). Some mentors and mentees, however, form trusting, generative relationships that allow them to adjust almost effortlessly to a post-tenure mentoring relationship. Such relationships explicitly challenge the model of exclusive, proprietary, finite mentoring that dominates academe, and they can best be characterized as friendships.

THE "VIRTUOUS CIRCLE" OF MENTORING FRIENDSHIPS

As with so many subjects, Aristotle informs our theoretical understandings of friendship. He proposes three categories in *Nicomachean Ethics*: friendships of utility, which are based upon what the participants can do for one another; friendships of pleasure, which are based upon how the participants can make one another feel; and perfect friendships, which are based upon participants wishing the best for one another (210-12). Though influential, Aristotle's categories are not without critics. Derrida, for example, takes issue with the stipulation that perfect friendships must be limited to "men of equal status," asking "What can such equality in virtue be? What can it be measured against?" (23). He prefers "symmetry," without which mentoring relationships cannot achieve equality. Dianne Rothleder, moreover, questions Aristotle's emphasis on individuals. In response, she proposes a fourth category: friendships of play, which are "more truly concerned about the emotional well-being both of the group as a whole and each individual in the group" (124). Traditional, product-oriented academic mentoring relationships can generally be characterized as friendships of utility, with some evolving into friendships of pleasure as well; most are institutionally defined as relationships between "unequals" and are therefore precluded from developing into perfect friendships. Friendships of play, on the other hand, offer the potential for a different vision of friendship—and thus, we argue, of mentoring—because they encourage openness and risk-taking, seek to counter the "hyper-individualism" of exclusive relationships (with its attendant product orientation) by valuing broader networks of influence, and are concerned with infusing group interactions with democratic principles.

Rothleder suggests that friendships of play bring out the best in people because they "make space for stories to be told, for people to feel connected," and for "secrets [to] be revealed without fear of ridicule" (127, 133). Tiziana Casciaro and Miguel Sousa Lobo make a similar point in the context of business. The authors argue that not only do personal feelings play an important role in forming and maintaining professional relationships, but they are "even more important than evaluations of competence" and function as a "gating" influence—that is, determine whether or not we will work productively with our colleagues (94). Partly this is because working with amiable colleagues is simply more pleasant and less of a hassle; partly it is because we may feel more comfortable revealing our vulnerabilities without fear that the colleague will use them to negatively influence our reputations, a conclusion that echoes Rothleder. Simply put, they say, working

> with people who seem to like us [. . .] can produce a
> virtuous circle in which everyone is more open to new
> ideas, more willing to help, and more trusting than
> would typically be the case. A similarly positive envi-
> ronment can be created if you work with someone who
> has an attractive personality—someone who is empa-
> thetic, for example, or generous. You know that you'll
> have liberal access to her intellectual resources, how-
> ever abundant or modest they may be, and are likely
> to reciprocate by freely sharing your own knowledge.
> (95-96)

The "virtuous circle" described by Casciaro and Lobo—candid, generous, dynamic—stands in sharp contrast to the "private circle" typical of exclusive mentoring relationships. Such relationships might develop spontaneously, but according to Casciaro and Lobo they can also be actively promoted: through "intense cooperative experience[s]" that require colleagues to depend on people other than their official mentors; by positioning likeable people in "affective hubs" that allow them to foster collaborations among people who might not otherwise interact; and by rewarding those who create and maintain productive work relationships over the long term (97-99).

Hall reiterates the importance of establishing strong collegial relationships that are not dominated by the mentor-mentee dyad: those "micro-support networks that both nurture and challenge [us] professionally [. . . and] enrich us in many ways" (64). For Hall, those networks include groups "of departmental colleagues, of like-minded professionals on e-mail lists, of friends at conferences and nearby institutions [. . .] those colleagues who help us overcome obstacles and who also enliven our collective professional existences" (64). Hall's rendering of valuable professional interaction differs profoundly from the exclusive relationship described in our own university's official mentoring policies. Thus it is perhaps unsurprising that in his book, a guide to personal development from an academic perspective, the word *mentor* arises only once, when he reminds readers to take personal responsibility for their careers, since "a mentor's work can only go so far" (56). Obviously, Hall does not identify the structured mentoring relationship as critical to the personal and professional development of the academic individual. We can infer, however, that what he describes as the *effects* of mentoring (personal and professional success facilitated by others) may be best accomplished through a relationship similar to what Rothleder calls friendships of play. Because such relationships are based upon expectations of mutuality and reciprocity—Derrida's symmetry and Casciaro and Lobo's virtuous circle—they are more likely to outlast changes in status among participants, even if they require ongoing "work."

Although friendship can smooth the way for amicable social interactions and may be enriched by personal feelings, it is most constructively understood as a form of critical practice, one that requires one to exercise judgment "without the ease, comfort, and simplicity of *a priori* categories" (Rothleder 118). In this way, Rothleder likens

the work of friendship to the work of democracy: "[l]istening to others, allowing them to join," and extending to everyone, not just those
whom we consider our "friends" in the narrowest sense, access to the
resources that can provide "a basic sense of inclusion" (116-18). Couture articulates a complementary view, observing that "[a] democracy
thrives by allowing an ever-widening public circle of possible friends to
develop and prosper" and "supports the reciprocal, equal participation
of all in dialogue toward public truth, a circle of possible truth" (8).
As the critical practice of democracy, friendship thus offers a model of
mentoring that not only expands the "public circle" but also negotiates
the ambiguous boundaries between the public and the private.

MENTORING AT THE PUBLIC/PRIVATE BOUNDARY

If indeed friendship and mentoring are to be conceived as reciprocal, democratically structured exchanges of influence, then the question becomes how such relationships are to be enacted. As we have
explained, ours is a "public" relationship (i.e., one that is administratively documented and construed by the university as supporting the
"greater good") composed of private actions (e.g., shared meals, mile-
stones, and celebrations; supportive conversations; collaborative projects). It's tempting to think of such actions collectively as an optional
bonus to the public mentoring relationship—as in, "Wow, you're so
lucky to get along with your mentor/mentee." However, we suggest
that such interactions both constitute and proceed organically from
mentoring friendships and, moreover, foreground one of the most important and least acknowledged roles of mentors: assisting junior colleagues in framing private actions and decisions within "ever-widening
public circles." On one level, then, mentoring friendships represent a
way to settle privately a public understanding of academic life, honoring the process in addition to the product of academic endeavor. More
broadly, though, they offer "a potent political tool" (Rothleder 136),
not only for new faculty members, but for anyone negotiating the pub-
lic/private boundaries that organize (invisibly and often confusingly)
the academic landscape.

Although exceptions abound, most departments want people
to stay. The expense of hiring new faculty as well as the benefits of
high morale and continuity of mission mean that low faculty turn-
over is generally regarded as a welcome sign of departmental stability.
Of course, when colleagues work together long enough and closely

enough to know well (if discreetly) the details of one another's private lives, "stability" can be as stifling as it is reassuring. And yet, while no one wants to be surrounded by busybodies, surely senior faculty members can be forgiven for taking a special interest in the personal lives of their junior colleagues. After all, once the "public" decision to join the faculty has been made, there are few guarantees that a new colleague is committed to the long-term health of a department or institution; it makes sense, in this context, that their "private," personal decisions would be attentively monitored for what they might reveal about the strength of that commitment. However aware they are of these unofficial investigations—and however eager they are to gain the confidence and trust of their colleagues—junior faculty may seek the guidance of mentors as they consider whether and how to disclose personal information, and feedback on how such disclosures are likely to be received.

In our own experience, the public/private boundary is fluid but holds the potential for significant political fallout. Our circumstances, of course, differ, but key decisions in our private lives have affected the perception of our public roles as department members, sometimes calling for tricky negotiation and other times offering our colleagues the very reassurance they seek. For example, when Betsy joined the English department at UNCW, her husband Don did the same. More specifically, the department struck a bargain to hire two tenure-track faculty in rhetoric and composition instead of the single position that had been advertised—an unexpected windfall for everyone concerned. Betsy and Don immediately reciprocated these good-faith efforts on their behalf by reassuring the department that they were committed to being in Wilmington: they bought a house near the university and began hosting departmental social gatherings, taught their classes and served on committees with energy and enthusiasm, and in general immersed themselves in the life of the department. A few years after they were both tenured, colleagues were delighted when Betsy and Don announced that they were having a baby. Showers and date-and-weight contests followed, and the process was so communal that, as one colleague confided to Betsy at the time, "It feels like the department is having a baby." After twelve years, the "private" (personal) and "public" (academic-institutional) lives of Betsy and Don are so fully integrated that neither would be quite the same without the other.

None of this was too surprising. Everyone knew, in other words, that Betsy and Don would be foolish to look a spousal-hire horse in the mouth, and the fact of the matter is that they appreciated (and continue to enjoy) the intimacy of their department friendships. Diana's situation was different: not only was she hired in a particularly competitive field (technical writing) but she was single. Members of the department fretted—Can we keep her? Will she stay?—and were thrilled when she bought a house, then got married. Naturally, we were fond of Diana and glad for her personal happiness, but more to the point here, Diana's "private" decisions signaled publicly that she was settling down in Wilmington. In other words, while her decision to take a position at UNCW demonstrated a "public" (official, contractual) commitment, the subsequent changes in her "private" life signaled much-desired reciprocations of our commitment to her.

Pregnancy perhaps epitomizes the kind of private decision that is believed to hold very public implications within an academic department. Buying a house and finding a local partner indicate a firm commitment to the place and thus, in most cases, to the university. Having a baby, though, opens itself to multiple interpretations (which are often dependent on the faculty member's junior or senior status) and must be negotiated carefully. For example, the task of arranging maternity leave may or may not be administratively or procedurally clear, creating a need for mentoring. And while useful guidance on such issues could emerge from within a traditional mentoring relationship, the need to reassure colleagues that this significant personal decision does not represent a turning away from professional commitment may call for more: more perspectives, more ideas, more creativity, and a more reciprocal exchange.

Diana sought advice from all directions: fellow junior faculty who had given birth since their hires, the director of the campus Women's Resource Center, senior faculty women who had negotiated this situation and senior faculty men who had not. She turned to Betsy first, though, with excitement and trepidation. It was a long and constructive meeting over coffee, a meeting in which Betsy was serious and supportive of Diana's professional concerns while conveying genuine happiness for her personally. In so doing, Betsy's mentoring practice adhered to Lauer's ethics of care, whereby a mentor sympathetically "act[s] in concrete situations [. . .] to make responsible moral decisions in particular human relationships rather than on abstract principles, to step out of one's personal frame of reference into the other's, to be present to the one cared-for" (234). Significantly, during the course of the meeting Betsy encouraged many of the contacts Diana eventually sought out, acknowledged that her own way of handling the situation was just one of many possibilities, and asked questions—lots of questions. We worked together to determine what might be the most appropriate time to "go public" with the pregnancy and who should be told privately before any public airing.

Combining the acceptance, listening, and sharing of stories characteristic of a friendship of play with the ability to frame the stories in terms of their immediate public context meant that this exchange worked its way from friendly mentoring to a mentoring friendship. It also meant that Diana could feel comfortable consulting a range of other mentor-friends, gathering multiple stories and ideas from different levels of the university hierarchy and in the process making her choices truly her own. This model of mentoring enables junior faculty to handle situations just as a senior faculty member would: by consulting and sharing experiences with whichever colleagues seem most appropriate for the situation at hand.

SOME IMPLICATIONS

It's unreasonable to assume that everyone in a department will be buddies, deeply invested in the successes of colleagues.; we know that. Similarly, it is the rare mentor whose ego is so healthy that it can withstand the mentee's need for second and third opinions. In short, mentoring friendships can only succeed if mentors experience them as integral to their own professional (and perhaps personal) development. We see this happening in several significant ways. For one thing, encouraging "an ever-widening public circle of possible friends" relieves the mentor of the pressure to assume sole responsibility for "good advice" or its consequences. Imagine, for instance, what might have happened if Betsy had been the only person counseling Diana on how to handle the professional implications of her pregnancy and that her advice had proven unfeasible. Without a doubt, Diana's chances for effectively navigating the situation would have been compromised. By offering not only feedback but additional mentoring resources, Betsy satisfied her obligations to Diana without holding herself accountable for a decision that was ultimately not hers to make. In the process, she enacted her investment in cultivating a certain kind of colleague—one who makes informed critical judgments about professional issues—and enhanced the possibility that a wider network of colleagues would likewise invest in Diana's success.

Finally, mentoring friendships can assist all faculty in our efforts to make our professional interactions consistent with our most deeply held convictions about knowledge, teaching, and the democratizing effects of education. Such an effort is worthwhile, not only to serve the narrow interests of departmental harmony but for intellectual and political reasons as well. Chan et al., for example, argue that "To gain experience in [. . .] a faculty role that emphasizes not separation but connection, dialog, and a reweaving of relationships of authority is, in itself, a new kind of privilege" (340). Such relationships can contribute to what Chan and his four coauthors describe as an "academically rich" environment (340), one that we believe allows its members to bring themselves fully to their professional endeavors as well as benefit from them in multiple, unexpected ways.

After a long battle with cancer, Betsy died August 22, 2008 at age 43. She touched the minds and hearts of students and colleagues alike, and through her prolific scholarship Betsy's legacy will certainly live on.

WORKS CITED

Aristotle. *Nicomachean Ethics*. Trans. Christopher Rowe. New York: Oxford UP, 2002.

Casciaro, Tiziana, and Miguel Sousa Lobo. "Competent Jerks, Lovable Fools, and the Formation of Social Networks." *Harvard Business Review* (June 2005): 92-99.

Chan, James R., Michael V. Fortunato, Alan Mandell, Susan Oaks, and Duncan Ryan Mann. "Reconceptualizing the Faculty Role: Alternative Models." *Reinventing Ourselves: Interdisciplinary Education, Collaborative Learning, and Experimentation in Higher Education*. Ed. Barbara Leigh Smith and John McCann. Bolton, MA; Anker, 2001. 328-40.

Couture, Barbara. "Reconciling Private Lives and Public Rhetoric: What's at Stake?" *The Private, the Public, and the Published: Reconciling Private Lives and Public Rhetoric*. Ed. Barbara Couture and Thomas Kent. Logan, UT: Utah State UP, 2004.

Derrida, Jacques. *Politics of Friendship*. Trans. George Collins. London: Verso, 1997.

Ervin, Elizabeth. "Plato the Pederast: Rhetoric and Cultural Procreation in the Dialogues." *Pre/Text: A Journal of Rhetorical Theory* 14 (Spring-Summer 1993): 73-98.

"Faculty Senate Minutes, 16 March 2004." University of North Carolina at Wilmington. 2004. 9 August 2005 <http://www.uncw.edu/facsen/minutes/2003-2004/Mar04.htm>.

Hall, Donald E. *The Academic Self: An Owner's Manual.* Columbus: Ohio State UP, 2002.

Lauer, Janice M. "Graduate Students as Active Members of the Profession: Some Questions for Mentoring." *Publishing in Rhetoric and Composition.* Ed. Gary A. Olson and Todd W. Taylor. Albany, NY: SUNY P, 1997. 229-36.

Rothleder, Dianne. *The Work of Friendship: Rorty, His Critics, and the Project of Solidarity.* Albany, NY: SUNY P, 1999.

8 "Mentor, May I Mother?"

*Catherine Gabor, Stacia Dunn Neeley, and
Carrie Shively Leverenz*

In the Association of American Colleges and Universities' (AACU's) forum "On Campus with Women," Beth Burmester argues that it is important for women academics with children to tell their stories. As Burmester points out, stories about academic mothering tend "to glorify a few successful women without offering any solutions for "average" women still unsatisfied with unbalanced work and family lives." In this essay, we offer three stories from average women academics still struggling to balance work and family. We also tell our stories as mentees and now mentors who strive to replicate positive mentoring while also working to enact institutional change. Theorizing our experiences in the context of scholarship on academic mothering and mentoring has led us to four conclusions: 1) Pregnancy, childbirth, and childrearing can deter academic success. 2) The structure of academic life exacerbates family-work conflict. 3) Academic culture is resistant to changes that would foster a better family-work balance. 4) Effective mentoring contributes to academic success, especially for women with dependent children.

As studies have shown, academic women who have babies are less likely to complete their degrees, take positions at research universities, receive tenure, and achieve the success of women without children or of men with children (Mason and Goulden, August and Waltman). Mary Ann Mason and Marc Goulden report in "Do Babies Matter? The Effect of Family Formation on the Lifelong Careers of Academic Men and Women," that although the percentage of female doctoral recipients has increased—from 12 percent in 1966 to 42 percent in 2002—there has not been a parallel increase in women's academic success. Relying on data from the National Center for Education Statistics, Mason and Goulden found that the gap between the number of male and female faculty with tenure has remained steady, in spite of the increased number of women holding doctorates, and salary discrepancies between men and women have actually increased. Mason and Goulden believe that "the unbending nature of the American workplace, configured around a male career model established in the nineteenth century . . . forces women to make choices between work and family."

That none of this is news testifies to the difficulty of the problem. The American Association of University Professors (AAUP) 2001 "Statement of Principles on Family Responsibilities and Academic Work" recommends that institutions should offer "significantly greater support for faculty members and other academic professionals with family responsibilities" through such policies as extended leave for child-rearing, active service with modified duties, adjustments in the tenure clock, flexible schedules, and better access to child care. This statement, initiated by the AAUP's Committee on the Status of Women in the Academic Profession, reiterated recommendations made in 1974. As further evidence of the intransigence of the problem, an entire 2004 issue of the AAUP publication *Academe* was devoted to "Balancing Faculty Careers and Family Work," demonstrating empirically and experientially that the university is not a family-friendly employer. In March 2005, the American Council on Education reported in "An Agenda for Excellence: Creating Flexibility in Tenure-Track Faculty Careers," that "an increasing number of new PhDs are leaving academia or opting for careers outside the traditional tenure-track path" (Hassan). The report notes that "especially women find themselves in adjunct and non-tenure-track positions—despite low pay, minimal or no benefits, and lack of potential job security—for a better balance between personal/family life and professional life" (Hassan).

Given the difficulties women academics face when they choose to have children, mentoring can play an important role in their success. Louise August and Jean Waltman note that finding mentors can be more difficult for women than for men, yet mentors are an oft-cited factor when measuring career satisfaction (180). Elizabeth Ervin's "Power, Frustration, and 'Fierce Negotiation' in Mentoring Relationships: Four Women Tell Their Stores" makes clear the personal costs to women who fail to receive effective mentoring. As Ervin relates, mentors who are unable or unwilling to meet the needs of mentees can have detrimental effects on mentees' academic identities, even driving them out of academic careers. In "Mentoring and Women in Academia: Reevaluating the Traditional Model," Christie Chandler surveys the scholarship on mentoring women academics and concludes that "there is substantial evidence that mentors can be beneficial to women's careers, yet the most helpful qualities of the relationship have not been thoroughly identified" (83). As Chandler notes, mentoring has both a "career-enhancing" and a "psychosocial" function; mentors help advance their mentees' careers while also helping them gain "a sense of personal identity and competence" (81). Chandler also finds a dearth of data regarding the mentoring of women from marginalized groups (80), though existing research emphasizes that social support is key to these women's success (87). Although not necessarily marginalized by race, class, or sexual orientation, pregnant women and women with children do represent a different cultural norm than that of the university, and they, too, need support from those who have "made it" in similar circumstances.

The fact that mentees tend to seek out mentors with similar life circumstances can pose difficulties when a limited number of such mentors exists. Given that mentoring is typically under-rewarded, the pressure to mentor others can especially threaten the careers of those who already face challenges due to their "outsider" status (Chandler 87), for example the lone faculty member of color who is sought out by a steady stream of students of color. Faculty women with children can be similarly in demand as mentors to those who want both children and an academic career. In an open letter to female graduate students in *Profession 2000*, Cindy Moore describes the balancing act required of female faculty under pressure to meet the demands of tenure and of mentoring. Moore laments that as faculty look at their growing list of responsibilities, "doors close" to students: "As a senior woman in our department put it, 'Every day, I have to make a conscious decision between doing something for myself and doing something for someone else'" (151). Fortunately for us, we had mentors who did not close those doors. Although mentoring can be motivated by altruism, the mentoring we received and now attempt to give is also motivated by the larger goal of changing institutional norms. Research has shown that those who have been mentored well are more likely to mentor others (Chandler 82); mentoring with the goal of changing the academy thus increases the potential for change exponentially.

CARRIE'S STORY: "I GUESS I JUST DECIDED I'LL NEVER BE ANDREA LUNSFORD"

I remember the day in 1990 when I told my mentor I was pregnant. I was a first year PhD student, and my mentor had recently asked me to serve as the Director of the Writing Center. I hated to give up that opportunity, but at 30, I had been married 6 years, and being on fellowship had given me the flexibility to manage a pregnancy. Yet, no one had to tell me that having a baby and being an academic were incompatible. Growing up in a working-class community, I hadn't known a single woman with a college degree. Women had babies, and a few of them had jobs, but none had careers that they worked at around the clock. Similarly, I had yet to meet a woman academic with small children.

Lucky for me, instead of a position directing the writing center, Andrea offered to make me her research assistant. I was able to job-share with another assistant in her office, working extra hours right up until the week I was due and then later making up the time I missed. It wasn't until my son was born that I fully realized my good fortune. Had I been teaching and due to deliver in the middle of the quarter, I likely would have lost my funding for the entire term.

Soon after I became pregnant, I remember thinking, "I guess I just decided I'll never be Andrea Lunsford," but Andrea herself never expressed doubt about my academic future. When I returned to work, she told my officemate (who had two small children) and me that we needed to write about managing babies and academic life because so little had been written about it. This recognition that personal experience and intellectual work ought to be connected has shaped my scholarly career and my mentoring of other women who long for that connection. Although research suggests that "mentors overwhelmingly see their most successful protégé as those whose careers were essentially identical to their own" (Chandler 84), the fact that my mentor did not have children did not prevent her from being supportive of me or others in the department who became pregnant. She could support us, in part, because she did not keep her own family life separate from her work. But effective mentoring also requires mentors to respect life choices that are different by becoming conscious of assumptions that mentees should want the careers their mentors have. It may mean responding positively to the desire to live close to family or to not upset a spouse's career. At the same time, mentors should push mentees not to second-guess themselves. Andrea encouraged me to apply for jobs I was afraid to apply for, even as she respected my ruling out locations where my husband would have difficulty finding a job.

As Chandler notes, mentoring provides both career support and psychosocial support. For academic women with children, psychosocial support can extend beyond convincing a mentee that she's smart enough to be successful; it can also involve giving advice about childcare, dealing with unsupportive partners, and managing guilt when she puts her own work ahead of her family's needs. I remember suggesting to Stacia that her husband take their toddler son to visit his family for Thanksgiving, so she could get a dissertation chapter written. Though I later felt guilty for intruding, she did what I suggested, and it became a strategy for writing subsequent chapters. I similarly advised Cathy to arrange full-time childcare even though her husband thought they could manage with part-time care. I rarely give such personal advice to other advisees, but as a woman with children, I knew Stacia and Cathy needed urging to put themselves first, just for a little while.

At the same time, it is important for mentors not just to help individual women, but to work to change the university. Mason and Goulden's survey of ladder-rank faculty in the University of California system found that "[w]omen between thirty and fifty with children clock over a hundred hours each week on caregiving, housework, and professional responsibilities, compared with more than eighty-five for men with children. This model is not very attractive for women who hope to succeed in academia" ("Do Babies Matter? Part II"). And yet no one talks about this disparity. It's as though acknowledging that family responsibilities can interfere with work is a sign of individual weakness. As one faculty member with small children commented, "It just doesn't feel like there's enough hours in the day. Part of that's my own personal time management inabilities, but part of it is because there are so many things that I would want to do and it all takes so much time" (Ward and Wolf-Wendel 245). The individualism that characterizes academic culture makes it difficult to see that the challenges women with children face result from oppressive cultural norms rather than individual failure.

When I decided at 37 and in my second year in a tenure-track position to have another child, I knew that my academic future was at stake. I remember saying to my husband: "If I have to choose between my job and having a baby, I choose the baby. I can always get another job." I do not know any male academics who have expressed such a thought, nor have my female friends who work in corporate settings. Even in institutions that allow people to stop their tenure clock or take a maternity leave, research has shown that many faculty are reluctant to do so (Sullivan, Hollenshead, and Smith; Ward and Wolf-Wendel, "Fear Factor"). Policies may not be well publicized, pregnant faculty may fear the perception of not working as hard as others, or there may be subtle discouragement from peers and supervisors. When I decided to get pregnant, I knew that a colleague had established the precedent of a tenure clock stoppage. Nevertheless, when I discussed the option with my chair, a woman with one teenage daughter, she said that confidentially, if it were her, she wouldn't do it because it might be perceived negatively. So I didn't.

Ironically, both the colleague who had delayed her tenure clock and I, who hadn't, were denied tenure the same year. This fact highlights the importance not only of supporting academic women who choose to have babies but of working against the cultural norms that make having babies in academe so difficult. As Mason and Goulden conclude, "Achieving gender equity in terms of careers and families in the academy requires a restructuring of the workplace." Such restructuring "depend[s] on a collective will to change the campus culture. Passive and active resistance on the part of men (and even many women) poses a serious roadblock to cultural change" (Mason and Goulden, "Do Babies Matter? Part II"). When I was denied tenure, I remember telling Andrea that "in the corporate world, people have their positions eliminated all the time," only to hear Andrea say "but we should be better than that." In Mason and Goulden's words, "The academic world [. . .] in its role as the purveyor of enlightened ideals, is in a position to provide a new model for the successful balance of work and family" (Do Babies Matter?). Mentors are clearly an important part of that model.

CATHY'S STORY: CELEBRATING COMPETENCE, EMBRACING INCOMPETENCE

In the scholarship on mentoring, many studies mention competence as a quality of a mentor or as something to be gained in a mentoring relationship (Chandler; Knox and McGovern; Traschel). As Elizabeth Bell puts it, "Competence, in professional roles, is a constant battle for women in the academy, and is part and parcel of the 'psychosocial support' provided by the effective feminist mentor" (307). Here, I want to offer "psychosocial support" by reclaiming competence for female academics who choose to get pregnant. I will tell my own story that runs against the seemingly dominant narrative that pregnancies are the result of incompetence. In addition to recognizing that many pregnancies are the result of competent planning, I also want to carve out some space for the role that the feeling of incompetence plays in a mentoring relationship.

In the academy, pregnancy is often viewed as incompetent. I'm not simply referring to the old idea that pregnancy addles our brains—or the converse, that too much study will render us infertile. Rather, I mean more modern, unspoken versions that women who get pregnant while in graduate school (or as assistant professors) are incompetent—they cannot plan well—or they have let their sexual desires instead of their intellects rule their lives. When my husband and I began talking about having a second child, I told him I did not want to start trying until I had passed my qualifying exams. Using knowledge gained from my first pregnancy, I did not want to risk having morning sickness or back pain during my exams. My husband saw my logic and agreed that we should wait. I passed my exams with honors, and we began trying. In other words, I made a very competent decision about when to get pregnant. (Good thing we did wait until after my exams because I was on bed rest for three months during my pregnancy).

I wouldn't choose a gynecologist without a vagina or a pediatrician without kids, so, as a child-bearing graduate student, I found a parenting faculty mentor: Carrie. On several occasions, she helped me advance professionally and served as an advocate for me, two characteristics cited in the literature on academic mentoring (Ervin; Flint, Manas, and Serra; Knox and McGovern). First, she asked me to present on a panel with her at a prestigious conference in our field. At the time, I had not yet told her that I was pregnant. Once I did, she wasn't deterred. She told me to write my proposal, and if I could not go, she'd find someone to read my paper for me. I would not have that line on my CV if Carrie hadn't shown me a viable way to be both professionally active and pregnant/child-bearing.

A few months later, I met with the Director of Graduate Studies (a man with no children) to ask for a (maternity) leave for one semester. I looked at my funding contract and understood "four years" of funding to be synonymous with eight semesters. He explained that my funding was only promised for four consecutive years. I tried to make him see that saving a funded spot for me was not a risk. I was not leaving school to "find myself"; I was leaving to give birth, and then I would be back to finish the dissertation. He said that he would appeal to the Dean, but that there were no guarantees. When I told Carrie about the meeting, she replied, "If the academy wants to have smart women on the faculty, then the academy is going to have to make pregnancies and maternity leave possible." Not only did I get the funding, I also got a vote of confidence from my mentor. She had been my advocate, and I respected her by setting reasonable dissertation goals and meeting them, so as not to waste her time—a valuable commodity for child-rearing mentors.

With clear memories of Carrie's words and actions, I have aspired to be a supportive faculty mentor. Thus far, I've had the chance to mentor two students on the issue of pregnancy. One student was newly married to a man who wanted children right away. She and I had several "How did you do it?" lunches. Instead of glossing over the obstacles, I helped her strategize. I see her as a competent planner, someone who uses her intellect to achieve the equally valid and demanding goals of school and parenting. Another graduate student started my theories of composition class twice, only to withdraw once and take an incomplete the second time. She had valid reasons both times—the latter being her pregnancy. She missed a class for morning sickness, which I told her would soon pass. The next time I heard from her, she was being hospitalized for dehydration. After consulting with her doctor, she asked for an incomplete. I gladly granted it, assuring her that graduate school would be here when she was ready to return.

While I was drafting this manuscript, I asked the student to write a paragraph from her perspective as a pregnant mentee. On the date she was to have her paragraph to me, I got the following e-mail instead:

> I really appreciate the time and effort you have spent trying to make this incomplete work. Unfortunately, I just don't see how I am going to finish the remaining assignments this month. [. . .] I have decided to just take a failing grade in the class. [. . .] I keep thinking about the story about your [Director of Graduate Studies] and how he [made you feel that] pregnant women were setting themselves up for failure and incompetence—I hate that I am proving him right.
>
> [. . .] I am so sorry for letting you down, Cathy.

I could have agreed that she was incompetent, perhaps too incompetent to rejoin the academy after her pregnancy. I could have told her that she's totally competent and simply willed her to believe that. But I chose a third option. As a mentor, I chose to point to both her competence and her (perceived) incompetence and welcome both; we are working though her options now.

University of Iowa professor Mary Trachsel makes a similar point in her story of moving from mentee to mentor. She lauds her mentor Maxine Hairston and other ground-breaking female scholars for their mentoring, but then goes on to complicate that rosy portrait with the realities of her sometimes incompetent life. She writes that female graduate students sought her out as a mentor: "They knew I had babies and a little girl; they knew I was a tenure track assistant professor; they wanted to know how I did it. 'I do it badly,' I usually replied" (163). Here Trachsel acknowledges and even embraces the idea that feeling incompetent is a real part of pregnant and parenting academic women's lives. As male and female mentors, we need to demand recognition for the competent pregnancy planning that many women do, at the same time that we embrace the complexities of incompetence that surround birthing and raising children in academia.

STACIA'S STORY

"Scrambling, sleep deprived mother who just wants to finish one thing she starts without being interrupted"—Those words do not appear on my vita, but they are a real part of who I am as an assistant professor going up for tenure this year while mothering a three-year-old and an infant. I simply would not have both the job and the children I love if I had not had the active mentoring of those who had gone before me in managing the dual roles of academic and parent.

The PhD program I entered in 1996 had a certain way of thinking about itself: its professors, and thus its students, idealized the solitary scholar who cleared away the clutter of life and focused on the life of the mind. Other assumptions came with that territory—that a low teaching-load, research university position was the reward we graduate students should seek. I remember feeling out of place as a young woman with a rural working-class background who had already been married for four years at age twenty-six. By the time I completed the PhD in 2003, the topography had changed; the department had hired four younger faculty members, including one who brought with her a keen sense of mentoring with a focus on the practical, the ethical, and the equitable. After I had been "handed off" by two senior professors who weren't quite sure what to do with me or my dissertation topic (feminist critical pedagogy), Carrie welcomed me as her assistant in writing program administration, gave me the motivation I needed to finish what turned out to be a rewarding dissertation project, and respected my choice of location and family over impressive job. A long string of mentoring blessings ensued. Two female graduate students with small children entered the program a few years after me, and I found hope in those role models. I started to believe that I could have both a family and a life as a professor. In the late fall of 2000, Jeanette Harris, another mentor who had made a career-end move "home" in her last few years before retirement, saw a late posting in the *Chronicle* for a tenure-track position at a small university nearby. Actively mentoring me, she invited me to lunch, pushed the cut-out ad across the table, and said, "I think you should apply for this job. It is tenure track and will give you a local option. I know you're not finished with your dissertation yet, but I think you might be the perfect fit for this job, and if they will interview you, they'll know that."

After a phone interview, a campus visit, a job talk, and three meetings with the dean to figure out how I would be labeled, I accepted the position and told Carrie that I had somehow landed a local tenure-track job (probationary with the requirement that I complete the PhD during my first year). At this point, Carrie became an active mentor to me—I believe because she knew I could find momentum with her and a job-keeping purpose on my side. Building from my own experience of being mentored effectively, I offer the following five characteristics of effective mentors to women in the academy: 1) they create an ethos of activism by taking workplace inequities seriously and by posing the hard questions to the powers that be; 2) they show the personal as well as the professional in their lives, modeling the "how" of their own day-to-day struggles with balancing work and non-academic responsibilities; 3) they appreciate that their mentees' choices may differ from theirs, breaking the pattern of mentor-protégé similarity, welcoming diversity in academic career paths, and refusing to perpetuate the implicit values of the campus culture; 4) they put those they mentor on the spot, urging graduate students to get busy doing the academic work that will complete the PhD and land them the job they want or to think seriously about doing something else; and 5) they develop a persistent long-term presence, continuing to influence those they mentor after they enter their first position.

Two of the strengths that benefited me the most were my graduate mentor's ability to see past the path she would have drawn for me to the path that I could be happy with and the fact that she has remained a part of my life, inviting me to be on conference panels and showing an interest in my family and my work. Another mentor for whom I worked as a research assistant also enacts a persistent mentoring; she recently mailed me an article she published for which I had done research in its early stages four years ago. The mentoring accomplished through such simple remembering gives those of us who feel the schizophrenia of diapers and briefcases a way to have a moment in a mental space of our own.

I am happy today with the choices I have made, but I can write these words because positive mentoring continued for me in the family-friendly culture I entered with my first position. A family-friendly campus culture can recruit and retain women who want to balance teaching and professional development as well as working and parenting. The president of my university played major league baseball, has more than one terminal degree, and has three children. My provost once passed his cell phone around a faculty assembly meeting to show off a photo of his 1-day-old granddaughter. My dean, a woman, has five children, a JD, and a PhD. My department chair has three children and a work ethic that inspires her colleagues campus wide. Add to this faculty culture the average undergraduate student's age of 29, and you can picture a campus where strollers and children are seen regularly.

After four years of infertility in grad school, I became pregnant exactly seven days after signing my contract at this family-friendly campus. When I showed up five months pregnant for my first year on the job, knowing that the university had taken a risk on hiring an ABD with only two dissertation chapters written, I felt I had something to prove. I chafed at the thought of someone covering my classes, so I decided to take the farmer's daughter's approach, having no idea what parenting a helpless newborn was like. Thankfully, my department chair, Beth Battles, took an active mentoring role from day one, knowing what I needed when I didn't. I had the baby, returned to teaching, finished the dissertation, had a second baby during Christmas break two years later, and went back to a new semester when my second son was three weeks old.

On the edges of this "success" story are the fault lines that call for continued activism on the part of mentors. The reality is that I came back to work against medical advice eight days after natural childbirth and a third-degree laceration. I remember a voice whispering inside me as I stood, leaking breast milk and feeling stitches, lecturing to students about the rhetorical situation: "You can't even sit down, and your one-week-old baby is out in the hallway with your husband who had to take off work so that you could be here. Are you crazy?" Like Laura Skandera Trombley, "I was feeling trapped between the imperative[s] of biological necessity, which I could not deny [. . .], and the gender-based pressure on me to demonstrate at every turn that motherhood would not 'interfere' with my professionalism" (2). As I look back on my experience and think, "How did I do that?" I also answer "No one should have to, want to, or feel obligated to choose to." I fell into Ward and Wolf-Wendel's third category of women who enact bias-avoidance strategies, "including not having a baby at all, timing the baby during summer break, or coming back to work as soon after the birth as physically possible without missing any (or very little) work" (4). My own use of the most stubborn "bias-avoidance strategy," in fact, did nothing to help pave the way for change. While once I was so proud of willing myself to perform with no maternity leave, I am now disappointed in my embracing of the superwoman narrative, a narrative of consent to and collaboration with the very assumptions that objectify women and women's experiences.

Conclusions

Hearing more women's stories will enable us to initiate social change in the workplace by advocating for healthy lives inside and outside campus walls. Ward and Wolf-Wendel explain,

> Biological and tenure clocks have the unfortunate tendency to tick loudly, clearly, and at the same time. [. . .]
> As more women enter the academic profession as assistant professors, more of them are choosing to combine work and family while on the tenure track. This trend does not mean that women professors are not serious about their careers. What it does mean, however, is

that the landscape and the nuances of the academic
labor force are changing. (2)

The first step toward responding to this change is to increase the
number of women who can share positive experiences of parenting in
the academy. The second step is to establish written policies that offer
more choices for parents in academia. As Beth Sullivan and her co-authors report, "Making policies official increases goodwill among faculty. [. . .] Formalization increases the family-friendliness of an institution by acknowledging that most faculty members will have a family
need to manage at some point over their career, whether to care for
young children, a dying parent, or an ill spouse or partner" (Sullivan,
Hollenshead, and Smith 4). We shape the culture in which we work;
as pregnant faculty and as mothers, we can choose to enact the superwoman narrative of "no special treatment needed," or instead advocate
by mouth and policy-making a just and equitable belief that faculty
who give life to and care for children deserve "special treatment" that
will benefit the entire campus in the long run. Setting up the tenure
track as a path to success for faculty who parent will come more easily
when we work first for changes in cultural perception and a commitment to diverse choices. As John Curtis argues, "The change required
is as much cultural as it is structural. And it is change in which faculty
[as mentors] must take a leading role" (4). As mother-mentors, we can
tell our stories, share concerns about the limited options for women
who mother on the tenure track, and look out for those who deserve to
pursue balanced lives, which is ultimately, all of us.

Works Cited

American Association of University Professors, "Statement of Principles on
    Family Responsibilities and Academic Work." 2001. 6 September 2005
    <http://www.aaup.org/AAUP/pubsres/policydocs/contents/workfam-
    stmt.htm>.
—. Special Issue of *Academe*: Balancing Faculty Careers and Family
    Work. 2004. 21 June 2008   <http://www.aaup.org/AAUP/pubsres/aca-
    deme/2004/ND/>.
Armenti, Carmen. "May Babies and Post-tenure Babies: Maternal Decisions
    of Women Professors." *Review of Higher Education* 27.2 (Winter 2004):
    211-34.
August, Louise, and Jean Waltman. "Culture, Climate and Contribution:
    Career Satisfaction among Female Faculty." *Research in Higher Education*
    45.2 (2004): 177-92.

Bell, Elizabeth. "'Orchids in the Arctic': Women's Autobiographical Performances as Mentoring." *Voices Made Flesh: Performing Women's Autobiography.* Ed. Lynn C. Miller, Jacqueline Taylor, and M. Heather Carver. Madison: U of Wisconsin P, 2003. 301-18.

Burmester, Beth. "In the Kitchen with an Academic Feminist-Mother: A Feminist Narrative." *On Campus with Women* 33.2 (2004). Association of American Colleges and Universities. 2004. 19 Aug. 2005 <http://www. aacu.org/ocww/volume33_2/fromwhereisit.cfm?section=1>.

Chandler, Christy. "Mentoring and Women in Academia: Reevaluating the Traditional Model." *NWSA Journal* 8.3 (1996): 79-101.

Curtis, John W. "Balancing Work and Family for Faculty: Why It's Important." *Academe Online* 90.6 (Nov.-Dec. 2004). 14 Aug. 2005 <http:// www.aaup.org/AAUP/pubsres/academe/2004/ND/Feat/04ndcurt.htm>.

Ervin, Elizabeth. "Power, Frustration, and 'Fierce Negotiation' in Mentoring Relations: Four Women Tell Their Stories." *Women's Studies* 24 (1995): 447-82.

Flint, Charley B., Rita Mamas, and Neddie Serra. "Writing as Mentoring and Empowerment." *Transformations* 7 (Mar. 2001): 71-76.

Hassan, Paul. "Creating Flexibility in Tenure-Track Faculty Careers Focus of New Report from American Council on Education." American Council of Education. 2005. 18 September 2005 <http://www.acenet.edu>.

Knox, Pamela L, and Thomas V. McGovern. "Mentoring Women in Academia." *Teaching of Psychology* 15.1 (1988): 39-41.

Mason, Mary Ann, and Marc Goulden. "Do Babies Matter?: The Effect of Family Formation on the Lifelong Careers of Academic Men and Women." *Academe Online* 88.6 (2002). American Association of University Professors. 2002. 14 Aug. 2005 < http://www.aaup.org/AAUP/pubsres/academe/2002/ND/Feat/Maso.htm >.

—. "Do Babies Matter (Part II)?: Closing the Baby Gap." *Academe Online* 90.6 (2004). American Association of University Professors. 14 August 2005 <http://www.aaup.org/AAUP/pubsres/academe/2004/ND/Feat/04ndmaso.htm>.

Moore, Cindy. "Letter to Women Graduate Students on Mentoring." *Profession* (2000): 149-58.

Sullivan, Beth, Carol Hollenshead, and Gilia Smith. "Developing and Implementing Work-Family Policies for Faculty." *Academe Online* 90.6 (Nov.-Dec. 2004). 14 Aug. 2005 < http://www.aaup.org/AAUP/pubsres/academe/2004/ND/Feat/04ndsulli.htm>

Trachsel, Mary. "The Give and Take of Mentoring." *Against the Grain: A Volume in Honor of Maxine Hairston.* Ed. David Jolliffe, Michael Keene, Mary Trachsel, and Ralph Voss. Cresskill, NJ: Hampton, 2002. 159-72.

Trombley, Laura E. Skandera. "The Facts of Life for an Administrator and a Mother." *Chronicle of Higher Education* 50.2 (5 Sept. 2003): B12.

Ward, Kelly, and Lisa Wolf-Wendel. "Academic Motherhood: Managing Complex Roles in Research Universities." *The Review of Higher Education* 27.2 (Winter 2004): 233-57.

—. "Fear Factor: How Safe Is It to Make Time for Family?" *Academe Online* 90.6 (Nov.-Dec.2004). 14 August 2005 < http://www.aaup.org/AAUP/pubsres/academe/2004/ND/Feat/ndwar.htm>.

Wilson, Robin. "For Women with Tenure and Families, Moving up the Ranks Is Challenging."*Chronicle of Higher of Education* 48.11 (9 Nov. 2001): A11.

9 The Minutia of Mentorships: Reflections about Professional Development

Katherine S. Miles and Rebecca E. Burnett

Katherine S. Miles (hereafter KSM): January, 2nd year in PhD program; beginning of administrative internship.

"I don't need a mentor: someone who will teach me the so-called right way to think and act!" These were my notions about student-teacher relationships when I entered the PhD program. I'd heard horror stories about academic life: (a) professors who submitted students' work and grant proposals as their own, (b) students who had been brainwashed so they couldn't return to civilian life, and (c) students who were prohibited from graduating because their professors had left the country. Now I realize that the horror stories were, in fact, urban legends, which explains, in part, why I'm here, beginning a mentoring relationship.

Rebecca E. Burnett (hereafter REB): Reflective Comment

I remember her caution. At that early point, I wasn't sure whether our relationship would be limited to a four-month internship or whether it would develop into a long-term mentorship. My own very positive experiences—as a mentee during my undergraduate years, in graduate school, and throughout my early professional years in two separate careers—have remarkably enriched my life. I have gained immensely as a mentee and now gain even more as a mentor. I enjoy the process of working with graduate students as they develop their professional personae. By the time they're ready to graduate, I know I'll miss them enormously, but I know that I'll have them as colleagues forever.

The urban legends to which Katherine refers suggest why mentorships are difficult to establish and maintain; such relationships take extraordinary trust, time, and reflection both from mentees and mentors. We have been intrigued by ways to characterize mentoring that capture its fundamental features. We want to reify the parts of our experience that relate to equality, professional development, and reflective practice by closely examining our own mentorship in ways that could be valuable to colleagues in other humanities graduate programs.

We argue for contextualizing mentorships; viewing them out of context can obscure the synergy and distort interpretations (Chao; Kram, "Phases"). For example, the multiple layers that comprise some mentorships may develop at different periods. Mentoring requires diligence, foresight, reflection, and reshaping; thus, decontextualized slices do not adequately represent the multi-layered relationship.

In this chapter, we are interested in the experiences of individual mentors and mentees—regardless of discipline. We focus on qualitative, longitudinal data from worklogs collected over more than two years and on reflections from our own mentorship in order to chronicle its growth and to demonstrate its evolution. Worklogs and reflections suggest that our productive relationship changed over time and resulted in discernible professional development.

Defining and Characterizing Mentorship

We begin by describing the initiation of our mentorship. We then define the ways in which we envision and use the term mentorship and its value in professional development. During the events described in this chapter, we were both at the same Midwestern, land-grant university.

Initiating Mentorship

We examine professional development and reflection as they play out in a relationship that started when Katherine was selected as a PhD intern to work with the Director of Advanced Communication, Rebecca. Two years later, Katherine was invited by Rebecca and the Chair of the Department of English to assume the role of Acting Director of Advanced Communication when Rebecca was on leave for six months. During this six-month period, we talked on the phone, emailed, and video conferenced regularly. Our mentorship extended into a third year while Katherine wrote her dissertation and went on the job market.

Our analysis draws on Katherine's worklog, which recorded her private observations, reactions, frustrations, and questions as she made the transition from graduate student to colleague and administrator. Her worklog was unavailable to Rebecca until we started working on this chapter—when Katherine felt comfortable sharing her entries. Her worklog reflects her growth by describing her experiences and her reflections, thus characterizing the difficulties that many graduate students encounter as they move into professional roles.

Defining Mentorship

We want our story to move beyond the hundreds of print and on-line "how to" guides and manuals about mentoring. Only a portion of the literature is relevant to academic settings, especially mentoring between faculty and graduate students, and even more particularly in the humanities. And only a portion of that literature addresses professional development.

Given the institutionalized relationship between graduate students and their major professors, mentorships are often formally rather than informally developed. Georgia Chao, Pat Waltz, and Philip Gardner use the initiation phase to distinguish between formal and informal mentorships: "Informal mentorships are not managed, structured, nor formally recognized by the organization [. . .] In contrast, formal mentorships are programs that are managed and sanctioned by the organization" (620). Our mentorship began as a formal, institutional relationship—although we have occasionally engaged in social activities together, both formal and informal.

Of particular interest to us, is Kathy Kram's four-phase model of mentoring: *initiation* (the relationship begins), *cultivation* (functions of the relationship continue to grow until capacity), *separation* (relationship is severely altered, such as mentees leaving for their first faculty positions), and *redefinition* (altered relationship takes a significantly different form) ("Phases" 614). While Katherine was in graduate school, our mentorship did not progress beyond Kram's second phase. However, our study extends current work with descriptions of mentorship growth. Furthermore, while Kram's model of mentorship focuses on business environments, we apply this model to graduate education in the humanities.

In addition to Kram, we found Cindy Buell's multiple models of mentoring helpful. Buell identifies four models articulated by participants in her study: In the *cloning model*, mentors seek to duplicate themselves. In the *nurturing model*, the mentors create a "safe, open environment in which mentees can both learn and try [new] things" (65). In the *friendship model*, the mentoring is "viewed as much more collaborative and co-constructed" (67). In the *apprenticeship model*, the mentors provide opportunities for learning "'through that person's eyes'. . . [in order to] become a valued member of the profession" (70). We place ourselves at an intersection of the nurturing, friendship, and apprenticeship models—though on any given day we might change the mix.

According to Buell, mentees prefer nurturing/friendship models, and mentors reported that they practiced these models; however, mentees reported "judgment and intimidation" (71) in their interactions with mentors, behaviors more closely associated with the cloning model. Buell suggests that inconsistencies between mentor-mentee perceptions and practices may be caused by "power relations that can never entirely disappear" (71).

Hierarchy is always present in mentoring; however, the mentor and mentee can use hierarchy as a supportive rather than a debilitating framework. In our effort to represent a productive hierarchy, we address Buell's recommendation to study "mentoring pairs to understand better how these four models are translated into practice" (71). Our systematic, longitudinal observations show that the definitive boundaries of models are fuzzier and messier than theory suggests. In our attempts to navigate the messy boundaries of our mentorship, we found that a sense of mutuality enabled us to more easily adapt to and move among the three models that characterize our mentorship.

Mutuality. We define mentorships broadly, beginning with three critical elements of mutuality that we consider foundational:

• Sharing a common vision of mentorship. We believe that long-term mentoring involves treating the graduate student as a future colleague who is working to develop a professional identity.

- Operationalizing equality. The mentor and mentee have a sense of equality—not in role, rank, or expert knowledge, but in respect, human dignity, and human rights. They operationalize equality by showing respect and mutual concern for each other and by being open-minded and sharing responsibility for the success of their mentorship.
- Acknowledging personal and professional boundaries. Boundaries exist. And they shift on a macro-level as the mentor and mentee move through stages (Waldeck et al.; Kram, "Phases"). However, mentorships also shift on a micro-level between various professional or personal roles, sometimes within a few conversational turns.

Mutality is constantly in flux—partly because relationships regularly evolve and partly because of the distinction between personal and professional personae. Such distinctions are an ongoing theme in Katherine's worklogs, which are fraught with questions and insecurities about defining, respecting, and negotiating these boundaries.

Roles and Boundaries. Some mentoring relationships focus on clearly defined professional roles; others involve people who have multiple roles with fuzzy boundaries. Maintaining a successful and long-lasting mentorship involves continually redefining and rebalancing these roles and boundaries. For example, when faced with an unfamiliar and uncomfortable situation—for example, reviewing her teaching evaluations with Rebecca—Katherine firmly separated her personal and professional personae. She shaped an emotionally distant professional persona, unconnected to what she saw as her personal life. Her worklog captures the essence of her "deeply personal" dilemma, as she tried to segregate teaching and administration, which caused discomfort and confusion—and provoked considerable reflection. She discovered that completely integrating her personal and professional personae didn't work, nor did completely segregating them. This theme of multiple personae occupies many of Katherine's worklogs, and we spend considerable time together reflecting about negotiating and integrating personae.

Katherine's comfort in allowing personal reactions in professional situations evolved as her confidence in her professional persona gradually increased. Accompanying her newfound confidence was a willingness to blur personal and professional boundaries. Once she felt comfortable with her professional persona, Katherine was better equipped to navigate the mentorship's personal and professional boundaries, whose fluidity and flexibility allowed the navigation to become transparent.

Reviewing Professional Development

Professional development includes a number of functions discussed in mentoring literature—phases of mentorship (Buell; Scandura and Williams; Kram, "Phases"), roles of the mentor (Dixon-Reeves; Scandura; Noe; Schockett and Haring-Hidore), and outcomes (Fagenson; Riley and Wrench). For example, literature affirms that mentoring can have a critical effect on professional development and associates it with mentee outcomes; in other words, professional development is often measured and defined in terms of mentees' promotion rates (Scandura; Dreher and Ash), income levels (Chao, Walz, and Gardner; Dreher and Ash), career satisfaction (Mullen; Fagenson), and career mobility (Scandura). Quantitative outcomes from mentorships have prompted some organizations to establish formal mentorships (Chao; Noe). However, available studies draw little attention to the minutia of mentee professional development—for example, the effects of modeling e-mail correspondences or conduct in administrative meetings.

Our ongoing reflection informs our view of professional development as a process that incorporates three primary factors: *socioemotional help*, including respect, encouragement, and empathy; *instrumental help*, including departmental politics, task completion, primary authorship, and communicative skills; and *networking help*, including professional opportunities and introductions (Tenenbaum, Crosby, and Gliner; Scandura; Kram, "Mentoring").

While we agree with many of the functions discussed in the literature about mentoring, we add our own experiences and separate functions into six strategic areas that often function synergistically: academic, administrative, career, communicative, pedagogical, and research development, which are neither mutually exclusive nor prioritized. These strategic areas of professional development are the ultimate goals of most mentorships though most mentorships are selective in their focus—shaped by the experience of the mentor, the needs of the mentee, and the combined interests of both.

Professional Development in a Mentorship

Mentorships involve both mentees and mentors in professional development. But development in mentees is usually more dramatic and occurs at a faster rate than in mentors. Not only are changes dramatic, but benefits are substantial; thus, in this chapter, we focus on the mentee's professional development. Examples from Katherine's experiences and our mutual reflections illustrate growth over time in administrative and communicative development. We selected these areas since they comprise a considerable portion of Katherine's worklog. Other areas are equally important, but they did not receive as much attention during her internship.

Administrative Strategies

Administrative decision-making is often a mystery to graduate students, something they don't have many opportunities to participate in until they are asked to assume some administrative role after they are hired as assistant professors. Katherine, however, had the opportunity to do an administrative internship during her second spring semester in the PhD program, an opportunity to be an inside observer and participant.

During Katherine's internship, one of her major tasks—revising the *Advanced Communication Manual* designed for everyone teaching advanced communication—involved extended collaboration with a subcommittee comprised of herself and two advanced communication committee members, who were, incidentally, Katherine's peers, two other PhD students. As Katherine's worklog entry below illustrates, her lack of confidence in coordinating a collaborative project was her largest disadvantage. She was, in Rebecca's opinion, sufficiently knowledgeable (in a range of areas including rhetorical theory, teaching, and information design) to assume responsibility for this activity, as were the other subcommittee members. However, the worklog below details Katherine's initial reluctance to assume responsibility for major changes in the manual—even though substantively revising the manual was the goal. Katherine's response was to have the subcommittee make only surface-level changes for consistency and to correct local-level errors.

KSM: Spring of 2nd year in PhD program, 3rd week of administrative
   internship

[The two subcommittee members] are working with me on the manual revisions, but I don't even have a clear idea of what needs to be done. In a sense, this project is working out great because the three of us are able to brainstorm ideas; it feels as if I should be more organized, but I don't know the level or degree of revisions the manual needs. I'm also not comfortable in an authoritative role with my peers. I wonder if this will affect my effectiveness (and desire) to do administrative work in the future.

REB: Reflective Comment

I think Katherine knew what needed to be changed in the manual. Why? We talked about possible changes, ones that were well within her knowledge and ability. Unquestionably, such changes would have been dramatic because no substantive changes had been made for years. I probably should have been more explicit about the relationship between her subcommittee's recommendations and the whole committee's acceptance of those recommendations—so credit goes to the subcommittee, but responsibility belongs to the entire committee.

Discussions about this situation led us to believe that Katherine's reluctance to make substantive changes to the manual had less to do with her content knowledge than with her lack of confidence in recommending changes to a program-wide resource affecting more than 40 instructors and more than 3,000 undergraduates. Even though Katherine and her colleagues had the authority to recommend major changes to strengthen the manual, she (and they) opted not to. What beyond lack of confidence played into her reluctance? A realistic constraint was time; substantively revising a 50-page manual was a big task.

Perhaps more important was Katherine's lack of ownership of the project and her ongoing concern with boundaries. How could she change a manual that had existed as a programmatic resource for years? How could she change a document for instructors when she herself was a TA? By most accounts, the manual was incomplete and theoretically inconsistent. Even though recommended changes would have been reviewed and perhaps further modified both by the advanced communication committee (with wide representation of tenured faculty, lecturers, and TAs) and by Rebecca, the Director of Advanced

Communication, Katherine did not push for major revisions. At that time, she perceived the risks to be greater than the benefits.

Two years later, Katherine had gained the necessary confidence and understood the role of engaging other instructors in collaborative processes. She proposed and carried out a project much larger in scope and impact than the manual revision project. This new project—construction of an extensive *Survival Kit* for new instructors of advanced communication—represented a substantial addition of curricular resources for teaching business communication. The *Survival Kit* included a detailed syllabus with daily lesson plans for the entire semester, assignment sheets and evaluation criteria for each major unit, numerous examples that new instructors could use throughout the course, and several in-class/in-lab exercises. In addition, Katherine expanded the scope so that the final resource included not only written communication, but also oral, visual, and electronic communication, which brought the business communication curriculum in line with the university's new communication-across-the-curriculum initiative.

Like the manual project from two years before, the *Survival Kit* project was a collaborative endeavor; this time Katherine initiated the project and solicited help from the advanced communication committee, which garnered committed responses from two lecturers. As the following worklog entry suggests, Katherine had no qualms about initiating the design and development of a major curricular resource.

KSM: Spring of 4th year in PhD program; 6th week as Acting Director of Advanced Communication

I'm motivated [to create the Survival Kit] because I remember what it's like to be a new instructor teaching a new topic. I don't intend the Kit to be prescriptive; I just want new instructors to have a common starting point. The process, so far, is actually fun. I can't believe how much I'm learning from [the two lecturers working on the project]. Even though I set the meetings and construct the agenda and outcomes, their experiences are really driving the daily planning. So, it really doesn't feel like I'm in charge, or like I'm in a bona fide administrative role—it feels like a genuine collaboration.

REB: Reflective Comment

Katherine's negative image of administration was changed by her experiences of initiating and working on the Survival Kit—thank goodness! She discovered that good administrators provide opportunities and participate in equitable relationships. She discovered that administrators don't have to know everything to be responsible and respected. They regularly learn things from their colleagues. In fact, Katherine is beginning to see that university administrators are really in service to students' successes, to colleagues' performances, to programmatic resources. She and her subcommittee did good work that filled a definite need.

The worklog indicates that Katherine's previous administrative experiences and her broader disciplinary knowledge increased her confidence in proposing, developing, and completing substantial curricular resources.

Katherine's confidence wasn't the only thing that increased; she also developed better time-management skills that enabled her to take on additional responsibilities. While acting director, Katherine also worked as a communication coordinator for the human computer interaction graduate program. In effect, her responsibilities had more than doubled since her internship (she was also preparing for her preliminary examinations and planning her dissertation study); yet, as the worklog below explains, she had an easier time negotiating her often- competing tasks and personae.

KSM: Spring of 4th year in PhD program; 6th week as Acting Director of Advanced Communication

Negotiating my multiple identities (student, colleague, administrator) this time around is much more fluid: it's a hurdle I jumped over two years ago. It's also much easier to balance my responsibilities. In addition to all the responsibilities in the first internship, I'm also balancing my work at HCI, which is a challenge in and of itself. So, in essence, this semester, I'm balancing more identities and responsibilities, but it's much easier than it was two years ago.

REB: Reflective Comment

What provoked this change? I think it had less to do with Katherine developing new skills than encouraging her to take advantage of opportunities. I never said "Develop these skills"; instead I said "Here are opportunities that promise good experiences." In the process of those experiences her skills and confidence developed. I also encouraged her to take risks. For example, when Katherine mentioned an interest in applying for the HCI open-call, I encouraged her. When she asked about taking a graduate statistics course, I encouraged her (even though during the course she often regretted that encouragement).

Katherine's increasing experience with difficult and unfamiliar tasks enabled her to make a smoother transition to more complex situations. Current research suggests that experiential learning—in this case, Katherine's ability to transfer experiential skills to new contexts—is a productive method of instruction (Harrison, Lawson and Wortley; Ford). John Brown, Allan Collins and Paul Duguid argue that the learning activity and the context within which that activity takes place are inseparable. Learning and context work synergistically to create "indexical representations" of knowledge: representations that can be utilized in future contexts (38). Thus, by the time Katherine became acting director of advanced communication, she had amassed two years of experiential learning—juggling multiple and competing responsibilities with her HCI research assistantship and her English teaching assistantship—that prepared her to engage in newer, more complex situations.

Adapting previous experiences to more complex problems, illustrated by Katherine's ongoing professional development, is also recognizable in the multiple communication strategies Katherine employed as an administrator. The following section illustrates the synergy between her negotiated personae, professional development, and communicative strategies.

Communicative Strategies

The transition from graduate student to professional colleague involves adjustments in the content and tone of communication. Initial forays into a professional conversation can be fraught with insecurity, self-consciousness, and hesitation. Near the beginning of her internship, Katherine knew about the importance of composing letters and e-mail directed to students, instructors, support staff, administrators, and external audiences. She knew that this correspondence needed to be accurate, clear, brief, politically aware, and professionally courteous. In fact, she already had considerable experience with professional correspondence from work as a technical writer for a local social movement organization—a position that required attention to the competing positions of domestic abuse survivors and public policies.

We discussed administrative contexts for professional correspondence and examined examples. Rebecca modeled the process, doing think-aloud protocols and identifying conventional moves. After Katherine watched Rebecca compose various letters and e-mail messages, she recorded her frustration about the excessive time she took to compose short and seemingly straightforward correspondence.

KSM: Spring of 2nd year in PhD program; 4th week in administrative internship

I'm still spending too much time on these e-mails. I realize that these are incredibly important (since they are a reflection of myself AND ACC [Advanced Communication Committee]), but it just takes so much time. I need to spend LESS time composing messages...What am I afraid of – it won't be perfect?

REB: Reflective Comment

Until I'd read Katherine's log entry, I hadn't been sufficiently reflective about the strategies I use for composing correspondence. What appeared to Katherine to be something I could "just do" was actually a set of strategies acquired over a long period. Her log reminded me that I need to remember that certain strategies take considerable time to develop.

Following two years of professional experience, Katherine extended her communicative competence. But this competence wasn't developed by practice alone. She spent time herself—and we spent time together—reflecting on her processes and practices. But even with the following worklog reflection, Katherine's growth was sometimes transparent to her.

KSM: Spring of 4th year in PhD program; 5th week as Acting Director of Advanced Communication

I didn't recognize the difference in my correspondence until an academic advisor questioned whether Rebecca had provided a model for me to follow [in an important letter concerning program policies]. She hadn't. I'm amazed that other people recognize my progress, yet offended that they automatically assume I had help.

REB: Reflective Comment

When I returned from a six-month leave, several colleagues, including the department chair and associate chair, commented that Katherine had done a fine, professional job. When I told her about their positive assessment of her performance, she was surprised. She is still developing her ability to accurately self-assess her own performance.

A necessary by-product of reflective practice is self-assessment (Yancey). Thus, the ability to self-assess is a learned skill that includes political awareness. Reflective practice includes the messiness of situating oneself within the political organization of a particular workplace or community (Lave and Wenger). We argue that accurate self-assessment includes one's ability to map and negotiate a position within a larger community of practice.

Another component of communicative professional development has to do with oral communication in professional meetings. In the following worklog entry from early in her internship, Katherine chastises herself for not being more comfortable and confident in committee meetings, which resulted in her reluctance to participate.

KSM: Spring of 2nd year in PhD program; 2nd week in administrative internship

I'm an adult and perfectly capable of (and ultimately responsible for) determining my behavior. But I am completely outside my comfort zone in these meetings and can't do anything about it. If I had something to say, I have no doubt that I would say it. But who wants to hear me ramble on, especially since everybody knows I don't know what I'm talking about?

REB: Reflective Comment

I remember the particular meeting. More than halfway through the meeting, I leaned over and privately whispered, "You HAVE to talk." When Katherine finally spoke, her comment was something, like "Yeah, that's a good idea," Since I knew she had interesting, smart ideas, I was surprised that she had so little confidence in them. Her self-assessment and her confidence in her capabilities needed to be strengthened.

The tension Katherine felt could be attributed to what she perceived as a paradox. On the one hand, her student persona necessitated that she learn from the experience. On the other hand, her administrative persona necessitated contributions to ongoing, administrative conversations to which she could add substantive information.

The learning curve for meeting strategies can be steep, especially for graduate students who have minimal experience in faculty committee work. However, two years later, Katherine had developed considerable experience not only in actively participating in meetings but also in running them. When Rebecca was on leave and Katherine was serving as acting director of advanced communication, Katherine was also invited to sit in on the department's administrative committee, composed entirely of faculty. Her worklog reflects a remarkable development in her confidence and competence.

KSM: Spring of 4th year in PhD program; 13th week as Acting Director of Advanced Communication

During the Administrative Committee meeting, when I realized that no one was articulating the underlying implications, I decided to speak. I realized that it takes multiple perspectives to get an accurate read on a current, complex situation and to determine future actions—and that the committee needed my voice as much as I needed its approval. I wanted to be relevant, but I also recognized that I have a unique perspective to contribute.

REB: Reflective Comment

I was sure that Katherine would be a productive participant on the department's administrative committee. We had talked about the committee's responsibilities—to review and recommend department policy and to act in an advisory capacity to the department's chair. I knew she would be prepared and tactful. By serving on this committee, Katherine had a unique window into administrative operations, including the complexities of politics, funding, university mission, faculty personalities, and programmatic evolution.

Because of our mentoring relationship, Katherine had opportunities to engage in professional discourse with faculty and contribute to decision-making. She was able to peek behind the administrative curtain, which strengthened her ability to communicate with other administrators.

CONCLUSION

Our goal for this chapter has been to extend current research about mentoring to include the minutia of mentorship development, particularly the effects of mentoring on a mentee's professional development. Katherine's experiences in an administrative internship and then as acting director allows us a unique, situated perspective. While we value quantitative data, we believe that our longitudinal qualitative inquiry adds to our understanding of mentorships.

Additionally, as we consider the synergy and growth of our mentorship as it is represented in this chapter, we are sensitive to the important areas we have not explored—discussion of all six strategic areas: academic, administrative, career, communicative, pedagogical, and research development; discussion of mentoring benefits to the mentor; the nature of same-gender mentoring; the initial struggle to engage in independent action; and the critical role of reflection in the development of a mentorship. While we are intrigued by the ongoing evolution of our mentorship, we also recognize that such evolution is, perhaps, only possible by applying systematic reflection to each component—and to both members—of the mentorship. As such, we are committed to further developing a picture of the unique attributes and future phases of our mentorship.

Works Cited

Brown, John Seely, Allan Collins, and Paul Duguid. "Situated Learning and the Culture of Learning." *Education Researcher* 18.1 (1989): 32-42.

Buell, Cindy. "Models of Mentoring in Communication." *Communication Education* 53.1 (2004): 56-73.

Chao, Georgia T. "Mentoring Phases and Outcomes." *Journal of Vocational Behavior* 51 (1997): 15-28.

Chao, Georgia T., Pat M. Waltz, and Philip D. Gardner. "Formal and Informal mentorships: A Comparison on Mentoring Functions and Contrast with Nonmentored Counterparts." *Personnel Psychology* 45 (1992): 619-36.

Dixon-Reeves, Regina. "Mentoring as a Precursor to Incorporation: An Assessment of the Mentoring Experience of Recently Minted PhDs." *Journal of Black Studies* 34.1 (2003): 12-27.

Dreher, George F., and Ronald Ash. "A Comparative Study of Mentoring among Men and Women in Managerial, Professional, and Technical Positions." *Journal of Applied Psychology* 75 (1990): 539-46.

Fagenson, Ellen A. "The Mentor Advantage: Perceived Career/Job Experiences of Protégés versus Nonprotégés." *Journal of Organizational Behavior* 10 (1989): 309-20.

Harrison, Jennifer, Tony Lawson, and Angela Wortley. "Mentoring the Beginning Teacher: Developing Professional Autonomy through Critical Reflection on Practice." *Reflective Practice* 6.3 (August 2005): 419-42.

Kram, Kathy E. "Phases of the Mentor Relationship." *Academy of Management Journal* 26.4 (1983): 608-25.

—. *Mentoring at Work: Developmental Relationships in Organizational Life.* Lanham, MD: University Press of America, 1988.

Lave, Jean, and Etienne Wenger. *Situated Learning: Legitimate Peripheral Participation.* Cambridge, UK: Cambridge UP, 1991.

Mullen, Edward J. "Framing the Mentoring Relationship as an Information Exchange." *Human Resource Management Review* 4.3 (1994): 257-81.

Noe, Raymond A. "An Investigation of the Determinants of Successful Assigned Mentoring Relationships." *Personnel Psychology* 41 (1988): 457-79.

Riley, Sandra, and David Wrench. "Mentoring among Women Lawyers." *Journal of Applied Social Psychology* 15 (1985): 374-86.

Scandura, Terri A. "Mentorship and Career Mobility: An Empirical Investigation." *Journal of Organizational Behavior* 13 (1992): 169-74.

Scandura, Terri A., and Ethlyn A. Williams. "An Investigation of the Moderating Effects of Gender on the Relationships between Mentorship Initiation and Protégé Perceptions of Mentoring Functions." *Journal of Vocational Behavior* 59 (2001): 342-63.

Schockett, Melanie R., and Marilyn Haring-Hidore. "Factor Analytic Support for Psychosocial and Vocational Mentoring functions." *Psychological Reports* 47 (1985): 627-30.

Tenenbaum, Harriet R., Faye J. Crosby, and Melissa D. Gliner. "Mentoring Relationships in Graduate School." *Journal of Vocational Behavior* 59 (2001): 326-41.

Waldeck, Jennifer H., Victoria O. Orrego, Timothy G. Plax, and Patricia Kearney. "Graduate Student/Faculty Mentoring Relationships: Who Gets Mentored, How It Happens, and To What End." *Communication Quarterly* 45 (1997): 93-109.

Yancey, Kathleen Blake. "Getting Beyond Exhaustion: Reflection, Self-Assessment, and Learning." *The Clearing House* 72.1 (Sept-Oct 1998): 13-18.

10 Performing Professionalism: On Mentoring and Being Mentored

Wendy Sharer, Jessica Enoch, and Cheryl Glenn

The student is infinitely more important than the subject matter.

—Nel Noddings

Within our discipline of rhetoric and composition, the feature of mentoring most frequently discussed connects with preparing new teachers of writing—and we have a wealth of theoretical, pedagogical, and administrative publications to show for it. Less frequently addressed, however is the mentoring necessary for becoming a well-rounded professional, for knowing how to juggle those myriad responsibilities and expectations that accompany a faculty position. Being a professional includes teaching, of course, but it also includes scholarly publishing, administering writing programs, becoming active in professional organizations, establishing connections with scholars at other institutions, securing funding for research and pedagogical programs, and mentoring future scholars in rhetoric and composition.

How can mentoring relationships in rhetoric and composition best cultivate these professional successes? The three of us focus on this question here by exploring how we—Jess and Wendy as graduate students and Cheryl as a mentor—experienced and envision highly rewarding mentoring relationships. We have divided our experiences and advice into three larger categories: "Models of Mentoring," "The Mentoring Experience," and "The Fabric of Mentoring." Within this first category, Cheryl describes her approaches to mentoring, explaining how her experiences of being mentored influenced how she constructed herself as a mentor to Jess and Wendy. Within the second category, Wendy and Jess discuss several mentoring configurations that enabled the two of them to complete their degree programs success- fully and to construct a solid foundation for their professional success as junior faculty members. Our third section, written by all three of us, explores how the mentoring process benefits from larger, cross- institutional, collaborative efforts by experienced scholars to mentor newcomers to the field. In an effort to reflect the dialogic nature of our mentoring relationships—the continual interchange and collaborative development of ideas—we alternate viewpoints from that of mentor (Cheryl) to that of mentees (Wendy and Jess) and finally to that of all three of us. We hope that this variety of perspectives on the mentoring process will prove useful for current and future mentors.

MODELS OF MENTORING—CHERYL

Men were the only models we had.

—Carolyn Heilbrun

Thinking about writing this essay has been a pleasure—probably be- cause it transports me back to The Ohio State University, where I did my graduate work nearly twenty years ago. Like most women of my generation, I had mostly male models of academic accomplishment, men whose pedagogy, leadership, and scholarship helped to shape me professionally. The men I remember with both affection and admira- tion still influence me as I continually try to balance the demands of academic life. Although they were all different, they all had one thing in common: they cared about the student, maybe not infinitely more than they cared about their subject matter, but they cared. And their influence still holds. I think of Dan Barnes, who modeled how to treat students with respect and kindness; Morris (Murray) Beja, who mod- eled department leadership with energetic vision tempered by a gentle wit; and Rolf Soellner and Stanley Kahrl, whose modeling, though uneven, has remained influential.

I remember Edward P. J. Corbett the best of all the male models, for, given his prominence in rhetoric and composition, Mr. Corbett was the professor I wanted most to please. I over-determined every syl- lable I spoke in his presence and every sentence I wrote for his class. I wanted to be perfect. When I was not perfect, I thought Mr. Cor- bett was the hardest-to-please teacher I'd ever had, and sometimes I felt angry with him for his nitpicking—the only healthy response I could have to a professor who demanded clean, clear, thoughtful and "felicitous" (his term) papers. Like the professors Carolyn Heilbrun describes in *When Men Were the Only Models We Had*, Corbett "annotated each paper, making comments in the margin, as no other paper I wrote in graduate school was ever marked, perhaps ever read. The respect [he] showed for us was invigorating, and full of the promise of what an academic life might afford" (10).

I strived to write with felicity, to be sure, but I didn't always, and when I didn't, I was frustrated with myself and with him. I found an early seminar paper in which he nudges me toward clearer sentence structures: "Here, it probably would be better to keep your subject and predicate together by shifting the participial phrase ("explaining . . . preaching") to a position right after the introductory phrase and by turning the participial phrase into a gerund phrase . . . ." A page later, he finds a sentence that I've executed just right: "This is much neater—and more readable—phrasing than the split construction that I called your attention to on the previous page."

Mr. Corbett modeled many positive attributes of the profession, one of the most important being that to be a successful academic was to be a successful writer. Heilbrun received the same lesson from her male models, writing that "to be highly intelligent, persuasive, and knowledgeable as a thinker and writer, it was essential to write readable, clear, elegant prose and to avoid jargon" (12).

On those occasions that I wrote well, I was grateful for Mr. Corbett's reward of taking me seriously by preparing me for a life in the profession. By the time I was working on a dissertation proposal, he wrote:

> This weekend I got a chance to read the first draft of your prospectus for your dissertation, tentatively titled "Muted Voices: Women in the History of Rhetoric." [. . .] Not only have you discovered that there is a "do-able" subject here for your dissertation, but have also discovered that other contemporaries have begun to work in this field and that you already have a list of candidates for the position of "female rhetorician." This is definitely a subject waiting to be done, and you seem to be the ideal person to do the study. It strikes me that your study, with some slight modification out of the dissertation style, would be instantly publishable.

He closes his two-page, single-spaced response by wondering whether I'll base my career on establishing female rhetoricians (theorists) or rhetors (speakers), writing, "Secretly, I am hoping that you will be able to discover that at least one or two of the women on your present roster could be regarded as a theoretician of rhetoric, in the same sense that we speak of men like Aristotle, Cicero, and Quintilian as being rhetoricians." As usual, he signed off, "Sincerely yours, Edward P. J. Corbett." Ed Corbett was one of the finest male models, but men were not the only models I had.

When Andrea Lunsford joined the faculty, she immediately regendered the professional landscape. I never took any coursework from her, but I learned more about being in the profession from her than any of the men. Maybe I learned so much because I paid such careful attention to the ways she negotiated her presence in the department. I worked long hours as her research assistant, doing everything from unpacking and setting up her office in the beginning to team-teaching with her and collaborating on conference presentations, published essays, textbook projects, and conferences.

We shared an office for the first couple of years, so I was able to watch Andrea perform her professionalism on a daily basis. Whether she was planning new courses; preparing for class; meeting with students; mapping out a workshop; discussing departmental politics with colleagues; or handling sticky departmental, personal, and professional matters, she did so with determination, generosity, and, most often, success. She arrived at Ohio State, having just been elected assistant chair of the Conference on College Composition and Communication, so during that first year she had the conference to plan, on top of everything else she was doing.

When Andrea began planning "her" CCCC conference, she immediately launched a collaborative activity, with me as her main collaborator. It was fun to work on the conference, exciting to read *all* the proposals (that is how the conference was put together back in the 1980s), and truly interesting to correspond with established figures in the field. CCCC has a reputation for being an inviting group, and I found the invitation invigorating. I never felt closed out of anything that was going on, whether on the national or local professional scene or in her life. I felt absolutely trusted—and part of the profession, early on.

When I started my first job as an assistant professor, I felt I had a pretty good idea of how to fulfill my quotidian obligations. What I needed to remember were the bigger lessons I'd learned from my mentoring professors—how to live in a department, how to treat people, how to play well with others, and the harder-to-learn lessons of how to negotiate, hold my tongue, strategize, and work hard (nearly) every damn day! I'm still learning those lessons.

Andrea tells me that she was never my mentor (that she always felt more like a big sister to me), but I think most folks who know us would say that she has and continues to mentor me in many ways. Over the years, I have learned so many things from Andrea, whose productivity remains unmatchable. But what I learned the most, I think, was the pleasure of thinking, teaching, and writing as a woman (maybe I also learned how to mentor like a big sister?).

Yet even though (or because—I've yet to untangle this) I admired Andrea and wanted to be like her, I found myself consciously resisting being compared to her. At a time when she was riding the crest of collaboration and composition studies, I staked my claim in rhetorical history, working hard to establish my expertise in the ancients. Over the years, our research agendas have run parallel and intersected, but whatever our current projects, we remain linked by our long friendship and our mutual interest in the teaching of writing, the preparation of new teachers, issues of inclusivity and diversity, and rhetorical histories. It is hard for me to know if our scholarly connection is based on her mentoring/modeling/big sistering or because of our biographies. I flatter myself by thinking that Andrea and I are alike in a number of psychological ways: we're both eldest children (and big sisters); we've both suffered from remarkably similar personal losses; and we're both cushioned by our resilience.

As this compressed introduction demonstrates, there is no statute of limitations on mentoring. I remain grateful for the mentoring I received as a graduate student and continue to receive. Although Rolf, Stanley, and Ed are gone, their inspiration is not. Dan and Murray are retired, but I still track them down when I need solid advice. Andrea, on the other hand, remains figuratively on speed dial. Their significance for me will always be that they "spoke to me of the qualities of my ambitions, if not of their possibility" (Heilbrun 146). I was just as important as the work.

My challenge as a professor, then, has been to treat graduate students the way I was treated—as just as important as the work. Over the years, I've worked with a number of impressive graduate students—up close and personal. Wendy and Jess are the furthest along professionally and are among the most impressive of the group (their publication records are already putting mine to shame!). They have invited me to coauthor this essay with them. They claim that I served explicitly as their mentor. In many ways, I mentored them as I was mentored.

The Mentoring Experience—Jess and Wendy

The opportunities for feminist work are endless.

—Cheryl Glenn

As the two of us collaborated on this section of the essay, and as we read through Cheryl's introduction, we were amazed at how coherently and meaningfully all of our mentoring experiences fit together. Indeed, Cheryl did mentor the two of us in much the same ways that she had been mentored, and, because we are the inheritors of much of their concern and rigor, we are extremely grateful to the mentors Cheryl describes above. In fact, one of the first things Wendy did as Cheryl's graduate assistant—as Cheryl had done years before with Andrea—was to help set up her office at Penn State. While, to an outsider, this task might seem onerous, it most certainly was not. The experience of seeing all of the files that Cheryl kept (the article drafts, the conference papers, the grant proposals, the minutes and agendas from national, regional, and departmental committee work, the countless scholarly articles photocopied and meticulously organized) was a wonderful introduction to the field of composition and rhetoric. Cheryl, in another gesture of mentoring that she had witnessed at Ohio State, also gave both of us keys to her office and provided us with our own desk in that office. She did not begrudge her privacy, but followed (literally) an "open door policy" so that we could work with her and access our collaborative work at just about any time of the day or night.

Before we describe our mentoring experiences, we want to acknowledge how important it was that these experiences were supported within the structure of the graduate program at Penn State because, for mentoring to succeed, there must be a programmatic foundation for mentoring efforts. Opportunities to participate in a wide variety of professional development activities and to form a bond with a faculty mentor were built into the assistantship structure for PhD students. Otherwise, there simply would not have been enough time to fulfill the duties of an assistantship and develop a close working relationship with a faculty mentor. Within this supportive framework, we collaborated with Cheryl to develop meaningful projects and to identify ways in which to enable our transition into the academic workplace.

CO-TEACHING AS MENTORING

One of the most beneficial opportunities afforded to us was the chance to co-teach upper-level undergraduate and graduate courses in composition and rhetoric. Jess team-taught two upper-division courses with Cheryl: "Women's Rhetorics and Feminist Pedagogies" and "Histories of Women's Writing Practices," and Wendy collaborated with Cheryl in teaching "Histories of Feminist Rhetorics and Writing Practices," a graduate class that focused on women in this history of rhetoric and feminist historiography in rhetoric and composition. While the opportunity to serve as a teaching assistant for advanced courses was intimidating because of our relative newness to the field, the shared responsibility for instruction in these advanced courses proved to be very productive because it gave both of us experience that many of our peers at the other 64 institutions granting PhDs in rhetoric and composition did not have (Brown, Jackson, and Enos).

The opportunity to teach upper-level undergraduate and graduate courses was a great opportunity in itself, but it was in the ways in which we collaborated with Cheryl that we gained a rich and rewarding pedagogical experience. In each course that we co-taught with Cheryl, we shared the responsibility for preparing for class, leading class discussion, and holding office hours. While many teaching assistantships position graduate students as graders or supplemental discussion leaders, Cheryl volunteered to be the grader and asked us, instead, to serve as part of a teaching team, to be collaboratively responsible for the pace, direction, and atmosphere of the course. The graduate course that Wendy co-taught with Cheryl, for instance, involved the collaborative design and implementation of an innovative course that linked graduate students from Penn State, Ohio State, and the University of Oklahoma. In addition to helping with class preparation, Wendy was responsible for coordinating online, synchronous discussions that involved students from all three schools and for helping to organize a face-to-face conference of students and faculty from all three schools.

Within the structures of shared, but productively differentiated, teaching responsibilities, the two of us gained classroom experience and pedagogical confidence within upper-level rhetoric and composition courses. Furthermore, these co-teaching experiences enabled us to address some of the issues that face feminist teachers and scholars when they bring women's rhetorics into the classroom. These teaching assistantships became the means by which we could collaborate with Cheryl to address what Joy Ritchie and Kate Ronald call the "tangled relations among feminist theory, feminist pedagogy, the canon of rhetoric, and emergent women's rhetorics" (218). More specifically, through these co-teaching experiences, we were able to confront many of the complicated questions that Ritchie and Ronald raise about the feminist teacher of rhetorical history:

> Why and how should teachers teach rhetorical history, which excludes or at best marginalizes women? How can teachers counter that tradition by teaching the history and practice of women's rhetorics? Can there be women's rhetorics without traditional rhetoric? How can a feminist pedagogy help avoid essentializing women or reproducing existing power relations, whether it addresses traditional rhetorical history or women's rhetorical choices? (218)

These are important and difficult questions for all feminist rhetoricians and teachers to ask. We had the opportunity to raise them for ourselves as graduate students and to collaborate with Cheryl on what we thought our answers might be. Our tentative answers invigorated our teaching practices and enabled us to consider the exciting connections between feminist scholarship and teaching. At the same time, co-teaching as a mentoring structure allowed us to draw on Cheryl's expertise as we sought out opportunities to integrate our feminist research interests into the courses we taught.

An added benefit of co-teaching was the opportunity to increase the depth of our reading and thinking about scholarly perspectives on feminism(s) and rhetoric(s)—a deepening of perspective that enriched our emerging dissertation projects and also served as groundwork for our research into the rhetorical practices of, in Wendy's case, postsuffrage women's organizations and, in Jess's case, female teachers and rhetorical education. Our co-teaching experiences (including course preparation) were integrated into our larger doctoral progress, helping us as we prepared for comprehensive examinations and planned our dissertation projects.

SHARED ADMINISTRATION AS MENTORING

A PhD in rhetoric and composition all but guarantees work as a writing program administrator (WPA). For this reason, most PhD programs in rhetoric and composition provide coursework and/or experience in WPA work. Jess and Cheryl integrated WPA experience into the mentoring relationship by collaborating on new-teacher preparation at Penn State. This preparation for new lecturers as well as incoming TAs included planning and running a summer orientation; creating a basic syllabus for all first-year composition students and an annotated syllabus to support new teachers through every day of their first year in the classroom; and co-teaching a year-long practicum for new teachers. Cheryl and Jess worked together to build the framework of the course and then divided up specific tasks: creating the course pack for new teachers, planning theoretical and pedagogical topics for weekly meetings, choosing course textbooks, and mentoring the new teachers.

Participation in this WPA project provided Jess with invaluable experience in running a teacher-preparation program, administering a first-year writing program, and developing an administrative attitude that ensures smooth sailing. She was introduced to a number of critical decisions required of a WPA, such as determining the appropriate length and content of an orientation for teaching assistants and locating enough funding for ongoing teacher development. Further, she witnessed first-hand the kinds of mentoring and other professional support that new TAs need. Through this experience, Jess learned both how to run an effective teacher-training program and how to make professionally sound decisions concerning a range of programmatic issues. And because of Cheryl's mentorship, she was not making these decisions on her own; instead, she engaged in these projects while still being guided and supported.

The most labor-intensive—and the most professionally rewarding—administrative collaboration between Wendy and Cheryl involved planning the 1999 Penn State Summer Conference on Rhetoric and Composition. As the Conference Assistant, Wendy had the opportunity to participate in many of the same invigorating activities that Cheryl had done as Andrea's assistant in planning the CCCC conference in the 1980s: she participated in blind review of conference proposals; set up a conference website and schedule; corresponded with featured speakers; and helped to organize social events. In addition, after the conclusion of the conference, she worked with Cheryl to edit a collection of essays centered on the conference theme (*Rhetorical Education in America*). Wendy's experience of co-planning a conference introduced her to a valuable set of skills for an academic career: planning an event budget, learning to locate and tap funding sources within the university structure, and working with other units (such as the conferences and institutes division) within the university.

Perhaps more importantly, as a co-planner with Cheryl, Wendy was able to observe her mentor and in this way learn some of the more subtle, but essential, practices of negotiation involved in organizing a gathering of scholars. Co-planning a conference allowed Wendy to learn some of the lessons that Cheryl gleaned from her mentoring experiences with Andrea: "how to treat people, how to play well with others and the harder-to-learn lessons of how to negotiate, [and] hold my tongue." Watching Cheryl provided the opportunity to learn how to work collaboratively, administrate diplomatically, delegate jobs fairly, and negotiate time constraints effectively.

Our co-teaching and co-administrative experiences with Cheryl were extremely valuable in our careers after Penn State. A common question we faced in job interviews and campus visits asked us to discuss upper-division courses we would like to teach. In response, we could talk in detail about the challenges and opportunities of teaching specific upper-division courses in rhetoric or writing. Hiring departments also found our administrative experiences appealing, knowing that we could lead their writing programs, if not immediately, then at some point in the near future. Those departments were also interested in faculty who can organize conferences and bring visiting scholars to campus.

And later, our diverse teaching and administrative experiences helped us to meet the challenges of being assistant professors. Since we have graduated from Penn State (Wendy in 2001 and Jess in 2002), we have taught, between the two of us, a total of 10 different graduate courses and five different upper-division undergraduate courses. We have both helped to run the teacher preparation programs at our respective schools, and we both assumed WPA positions. Thanks largely to our mentoring experiences; we have both found the transition from graduate student to faculty member a relatively easy one.

DIRECTING THE DISSERTATION AS MENTORING

Learning how to be a teacher, an administrator, and a good colleague are all important components of the PhD process, but the dissertation is an *essential* component and therefore the most intimidating. Again, a mentor has tremendous influence. F.Y. Faghihi found a significantly faster rate of completion among graduate students who felt positively toward their advisors than those who felt that their advisors were not interested in their progress through the program. Such a finding makes a lot of sense: although it is impossible for a graduate student to find a mentor who works *exactly* in the area he or she finds most interesting, it is essential that the student be mentored by someone who shares a commitment to the scholarly trajectory the student wishes to pursue. While Cheryl's work focused on an earlier historical period than either of our projects, she was tremendously interested in the contributions our projects could make to feminist historiography. Cheryl's commitment to the larger project of expanding the borders of rhetorical history was invaluable to us and her enthusiasm surely influenced the timely manner in which we both finished our dissertations.

Our ability to finish our dissertations in a timely manner depended, of course, on our starting them as early as possible. From the time she began working with us, Cheryl talked a lot about what Scott L. Miller, Brenda Jo Brueggemann, Bennis Blue, and Deneen M. Shepherd call the "future tense," gently pushing us to think about how seminar papers and conference presentations might fit into a dissertation project, even before the dissertation prospectus stage (397). When it came to writing our prospectuses, both of us had already identified and done extensive work on several of the proposed chapters of our dissertation projects. In these early stages, Cheryl also asked us about the kinds of scholarly work we wanted to do, the kind of scholars we wanted to be, and the kinds of classes we wanted to teach. Early on, both of us understood the dissertation process as one of the initial steps in defining ourselves not just as scholars but also as teachers because the classes that we choose to teach as junior professors often invigorate our scholarly interests.

Yet Cheryl's guidance affected more than the pace at which we completed our writing—it also affected the manner in which we situated our work in the field of rhetoric and composition. One of the central lessons Cheryl imparted to both of us was how to treat other scholars with respect, even if we disagree with a position those scholars have taken on a particular topic. The idea, she stressed, is to transform the tenor of scholarship from one that focuses on fault-finding to one that focuses on explaining the significance of another's project to one's own, thereby moving the scholarly conversation in a productive direction.

Cheryl's observation at the conclusion of *Rhetoric Retold* nicely sums up her perspective on scholarly positioning and scholarly mentoring: "We do not have to compete for bits of female rhetoric, nor do we have to scramble after a few pages of women's letters. Although neither Cicero nor Quintilian are offering up an esteemed female colleague for us to study, the opportunities for feminist work are endless" (178). This attitude of openness and shared scholarship rejects ideas of possessiveness over topics or research methodologies. Such a stance infused her advice on our research and writing, prompting us to see our work as that which derives from a spirit of contribution, involvement, and community rather than from the vantage point of an individual faltering alone into unknown territory.

In her introduction to this piece, Cheryl mentions that Corbett referred to her dissertation project as "instantly publishable." This comment reflects a respect for the contributions that graduate students can make to the field and, at the same time, positions the dissertation as more than simply an academic exercise—it becomes the first major publication of a scholarly career. As Julie Drew and Gary Olson argue in "(Re)Reenvisioning the Dissertation in English Studies," the dissertation should not be seen as an "academic exercise" through which graduate students "demonstrate[e] to their professors that they [have] a thorough grasp of research in the field" (59); but that, because of publishing pressures in the discipline, graduate students and their advisors must frame their dissertation as "the first serious scholarly monograph a scholar produces" (56). Echoing the respect Corbett had shown her work and recognizing the significance of the dissertation to our later careers, Cheryl regularly emphasized the "publishability" of the dissertation. When the subject of introductions and the conclusions came up, Cheryl suggested that we look not only to other dissertations as models but also to those books with which we were in conversation. Yet she also realized that the dissertation needed to get done, so her emphasis on publishability was always tempered with the knowledge that we could not be, and did not want to be, graduate students for years to come. Through Cheryl's advice, then, we framed our dissertations as serious scholarly endeavors that would certainly—if after a good deal of revision—become our first book manuscripts.

Working with Cheryl as our mentor was productive for us both: we finished our dissertations in a timely manner, and our dissertations were deemed "good" by others. Both our dissertations won the CCCC James Berlin Outstanding Dissertation Award. And we have both published extensively from those dissertations—Wendy's dissertation has been published as *Vote and Voice: Women's Organizations and Political Literacy, 1915-1930* (Southern Illinois, 2004), and Jess's manuscript, *On the Borders of Tradition: Female Teachers and Rhetorical Education, 1865-1911*, is currently under review at a university press.

THE FABRIC OF MENTORING—WENDY, JESS, CHERYL

The mentoring relationship involves professors acting as close, trusted, and experienced colleagues and guides. It is recognized that part of what is learned in graduate school is [. . .] socialization to the values, practices, and attitudes of a discipline and university, it transforms the student into a colleague.

—Michael Cusanovich and Martha Gilliland

In many ways, graduate students are like the first-year students that David Bartholomae writes about in "Inventing the University." While first-year writers have to learn the "peculiar ways" of "knowing selecting, evaluating, reporting, concluding, and arguing that define the discourse" of the university community, graduate students need to learn the same things about graduate study in general and about the academic field they plan to enter (623). One of the most effective ways that a mentor can help a graduate student "invent" the PhD program is to stockpile examples of the kinds of documents common to graduate study and faculty professional life: dissertation proposals, submission letters to journals, conference papers, grant applications, job application letters, job talks, book prospectuses, etc. All three of us recognized the value of seeing what these genres of advanced study look like, and whenever Jess or Wendy embarked on a new project, Cheryl provided models for them to work with. Of course, feedback and revision are central to the success of graduate students' forays into new academic genres, but this extended archive of mentoring documents was invaluable to Jess and Wendy and, most certainly will be to numerous graduate students in the future. The work of previous graduate students becomes, for future graduate students, threads in the mentoring fabric.

The mentoring fabric can also gain strength from resources outside of the individual mentor/mentee relationship. Cheryl, for instance, regularly enabled connections between new and senior graduate students, encouraging them to learn with and from each other. Now that Wendy and Jess have moved on to professorships, graduate students at Penn State continue to contact us (and we contact them) about the dissertation process, grant proposal writing, job opportunities, and conference panels we might collaborate on. Thanks to these connections, Wendy and Jess work within a mutually supportive group of professional friends and colleagues.

The greatest successes in mentoring, however, rely upon more than a graduate student and a faculty member within a particular department—mentoring is most powerful when it involves scholars at diverse institutions. Several of the opportunities provided to Wendy and Jess through their mentoring experiences with Cheryl enabled them to become part of an extensive and supportive network of scholars from across the country. The conference co-planning that Cheryl and Wendy collaborated on certainly enabled Wendy to develop long-lasting scholarly connections. One such network in which both Jess and Wendy participated, and one that all graduate students can participate, is the Coalition of Women Scholars in the History of Rhetoric and Composition. The Coalition sponsors a special evening session at the Conference on College Composition and Communication, the first part of which typically involves several featured speakers—both veteran scholars and current graduate students. During the second, and less formal, half of the session, graduate students meet with established scholars in small mentoring groups to discuss a variety of professional development concerns—finishing the dissertation, getting published, finding a job, getting grants, making tenure, and so on. But in addition to the opportunity for beginning academics to learn the ropes, they also have the opportunity to talk with the living, breathing scholars whose scholarship has sustained their dissertation work.

In addition to the Coalition meeting, CCCC also works to establish mentoring relationships in a number of other ways. Every year, the organization sponsors a Newcomers' Breakfast, a cost-free venue for newcomers to meet and talk with experienced CCCC members. This breakfast is an attempt to make first-time attendees feel "at home" within a large organization—and to make human contact with a person they've only read about. Other groups provide scholarly connections and administrative support, groups such as the Research Network Forum (in which new and established scholars discuss ongoing research projects and prospects for publishing that work once it is completed) and the Teaching and Mentoring Special Interest Group (a group that links experienced mentors with new mentors). Learning how to mentor is a central part of professional development for new scholars—efforts such as the Mentoring Special Interest Group (SIG) and this collection are important means by which to strengthen the mentoring fabric across the profession.

Reflecting on our experience and the opportunities available in the field, it seems that the sign of an effective and productive mentoring relationship is that it functions on multiple levels. Cheryl, Wendy, and Jess worked together to create and conduct courses, administer writing programs, hold conferences, direct and compose dissertations, and build working relationships inside and outside the university. Although establishing such a multifaceted mentoring relationship might be difficult in terms of time and availability, it seems important that we should work on the departmental, university, and disciplinary level to make these kinds of opportunities available for graduate students. As part of a long line of productive mentors and mentees, we hope that others are inventive in considering how they might construct mentoring relationships and the kinds of work that mentors and mentees engage.

Works Cited

Bartholomae, David. "Inventing the University." *Cross-Talk in Comp Theory.* 2nd edition. Ed. Victor Villanueva. Urbana, IL: NCTE, 2003. 620-25.

Brown, Stuart, Rebecca Jackson, and Theresa Enos. "The Arrival of Rhetoric in the Twenty-First Century: The 1999 Survey of Doctoral Programs in Rhetoric." *Rhetoric Review* 18.2 (2000): 233-43.

Cusanovich, Michael, and Martha Gilliland. "Mentoring: The Faculty-Graduate Student Relationship." *Council on Graduate School Communicator* 24 (1991): 1-2.

Drew, Julie, and Gary Olson. "(Re)envisioning the Dissertation." *College English* 61.1 (1998): 56-66.

Faghihi, F.Y. "A Study of Factors related to Dissertation Progress among Doctoral Candidates: Focus on Student Research Self-Efficacy as a Result of their Research Training and Experiences." Diss. U of Memphis 1998.

Glenn, Cheryl. *Rhetoric Retold: Regendering the Tradition from Antiquity Through the Renaissance.* Carbondale: Southern Illinois UP, 1997.

Heilbrun, Carolyn. *When Men Were the Only Models We Had: My Teachers Barzun, Fadiman, Trilling (Personal Tales).* Philadelphia: U of Pennsylvania P, 1991.

Miller, Scott L. Brenda Jo Brueggemann, Bennis Blue, and Deneen M. Shepherd. "Present Perfect and Future Imperfect: Results of a National Survey of Graduate Students in Rhetoric and Composition Programs." *College Composition and Communication* 48.3 (1997): 392-409.

Noddings, Nel. *Caring, a Feminine Approach to Ethics and Moral Education.* Berkeley: U of California P, 1984.

Ritchie, Joy, and Kate Ronald. "Riding Long Coattails, Subverting Tradition: The Tricky Business of Feminists Teaching Rhetorics." *Feminism and Composition Studies: In Other Words.* Ed. Susan C. Jarratt and Lynn Worsham. New York: Modern Language Association, 1998. 217-39.

Sharer, Wendy. *Vote and Voice: Women's Organizations and Political Literacy, 1915-1930.* Carbondale: Southern Illinois UP, 2004.

11 Mentoring across the Continents

Susan E. Thomas and George L. Pullman

George Pullman and Susan Thomas met at Georgia State University in Atlanta, where with very little conscious effort or self-reflection on either person's part they began to evolve a mentor-mentee relationship. George Pullman is still teaching at GSU and Susan is now Lecturer in English (equivalent to Associate Professor) at the University of Sydney, Australia, where she mentors her own PhD students in a similarly indirect and evolutionary way.

Susan: In December 2002, three weeks after defending my dissertation, I boarded a Sydney-bound plane for a new life in Australia. I had no guarantees of finding academic work (or any other type) in Sydney, but desperately needed a break after four years in a PhD program and was enticed by the idea of summertime in Australia. Fortunately, I was hired by the University of Sydney to start a rhetoric and composition program based on the American model. At first I was exhilarated at landing a tenure-track position at the largest university in the Southern Hemisphere, but the exuberance slowly turned to fear as I realized that none of my colleagues understood what "Rhetoric and Composition" meant, and most assumed it was some kind of remedial enterprise.

In a foreign academic environment where no one "spoke my language," I quickly realized that it wasn't necessarily what I'd studied in my PhD program but the mentoring relationship I'd established with George Pullman that would enable me to meet the challenges I now faced. In many respects, my professional life was mirroring that of my mentor, as I was recruited to start a rhetoric program. However, in my case, the environment was a bit trickier, as not everyone in a very traditional English Department was convinced that rhetoric and writing instruction fit the profile of what the Sydney English Department does.

Feeling isolated and frustrated and finding little moral support in my new department, I turned to the person I once called my supervisor, but whom I now call my mentor—George Pullman. Through my experiences as a new faculty member at the University of Sydney and through my prior experience as a PhD student at Georgia State University, I have come to realize not only the importance but also the vitality of the mentoring relationship.

When I met George Pullman, I was in turmoil of another kind, having begun graduate studies shortly after my first marriage had fallen apart. In a new city as well as a new stage of my personal life, I felt alone and fearful, knowing I would be tested as never before. The mounting self-doubt was initially debilitating, as I found myself unable to speak to most of the people I met in the English Department. I'd been advised to get in touch with George Pullman, so, nervously, I made my way to his office. Expecting a much older man, perhaps in a tweed jacket, I was surprised by the image I glimpsed through the open door: a young, smiling, seemingly accessible person with a photo of a pug dog and an Old English bulldog on his desk. In the minutes that followed, we spoke very little about rhetoric and composition or even graduate school, but of dogs and life in general. From that day, I began to develop the confidence I would need to get through the next four years—not because of anything specific I'd learned, but because I knew I had someone I could talk to. In the days and years that followed, that assurance would prove invaluable. George had an uncanny ability for getting the best work out of me, inspiring my best teaching, and perhaps most importantly, convincing me to be less doubtful and more accepting of my work and myself. I can't recall a single time when George advised me to "Do it this way," but amazingly, I always seemed to know which course to follow after seeking his advice. A true rhetor, George Pullman knew his pupil and was able to help me see new possibilities in my work and to accomplish things I'd never thought possible, even landing an academic position overseas—simply by believing in me and convincing me to believe in myself.

I'd never put much stock in the adage "It's not *what* you know, but *who* you know" until meeting George. A few months into my job at Sydney, a member of my selection committee confided in me that George's letter was the deciding factor in my appointment, as it revealed not only the kind of worker or scholar I was, but offered anecdotal evidence of the kind of colleague I was likely to be. Today, as I sit in my office in the Sydney English department, I realize that a genuine mentoring relationship offers the most valuable preparation for not only a career but also for the twists and turns of life and the associated challenges. Thanks to George's generous support and sound advice, I have been able to get the rhetoric program off the ground, develop four new courses, and convince my department to hire another person in my field. George has also helped me realize that my new colleagues were never "against" me, but just needed time to see what I—and rhetoric—were all about.

George's influence can be seen in all aspects of my teaching and my interactions with my own PhD students, especially when they are placed at ease by my open door, my interest in them as people and not just students, and certainly not least, the photos on my desk of my three Shih Tzu dogs.

George: My first mentor was my twelfth grade English teacher whose options for the final semester project, a reading of *Moby Dick*, included a Freudian interpretation of the novel. I couldn't help myself. And after reading *Interpretation of Dreams*, and coming up with a good deal of phallic nonsense (this was 1980) I went to Mr. Samuals three days before my presentation and expressed some doubt about what I was going to say. He handed me a copy of *The Ego and The Id* and *Civilization and its Discontents*, and said, "if you sleep between now and Friday you're a coward." And that was it: Nothing more than a challenge. Horrifically macho, I'll admit in retrospect. But it was perfect for me at the time. A teacher expressed confidence in me and that was all I needed. I don't remember what I said during the presentation; I don't imagine it made much sense. It never mattered.

Three years later, at the University of British Columbia, bored with literary studies I came across a course called The Rhetoric of Fiction. I didn't know what rhetoric was and I certainly had never heard of Nan Johnson, but the course title sounded exotic and at any rate it wasn't "literature". We read Wayne Booth. And I wanted to be like Nan when I grew up (I think I may actually have said that to her). She got me into Rensselaer Polytechnic's PhD program, and three years later James Zappen got me out, primarily by being intensely patient and endlessly encouraging.

None of these people took me on as a project. They never hooked me up with editors or otherwise held open any doors (although they did write important letters of recommendation). They never told me what to think or do. They led by example, by remote control. They liked what they did and they were able to effortlessly convey that enthusiasm.

Our relationship came full circle in September 2005 when George travelled to Sydney to be the plenary speaker at Susan's 'What Is the New Rhetoric?' conference, the first international conference on rhetoric in Australia. In the days and weeks preceding the conference, Susan looked to George for advice on how to present their discipline to a new audience. Ever the doubting Thomas, Susan was convinced she hadn't done enough to promote the conference—or perhaps she'd gone about it in the wrong way. Time would prove otherwise, however, as the conference attracted 80 delegates, spawned an infectious interest in rhetoric, and set into motion plans for a Rhetorical Society of Australia. Susan attributes much of this success to George, who fielded hundreds of e-mails, read and edited dozens of press releases and draft articles, and encouraged her that she could achieve her goals, even in a foreign environment. While in Sydney, George was interviewed on several radio programs, some with Susan, doing his best to help his former student and current colleague blaze a rhetorical trail in Australia. After the conference, we watched and listened with interest as conference-related newspaper articles appeared, radio shows aired, and favorable e-mails poured in. Our first professional venture as colleagues had been a huge success, and once again, George had inspired Susan's best work.

In introducing George at the conference's plenary session, Susan said, "Today I have the distinct privilege of introducing my colleague, mentor, and friend. Quintilian believed that to be a good orator, one first had to be a good man, and I can assure you that George Pullman is both."

We are currently working on a digital, cross-cultural project and wondering which country we'll invade next.

12 Chancing into Altruistic Mentoring

Doug Downs and Dayna Goldstein

Here's one story: Mentoring is all the rage. Faculty mentoring faculty, faculty mentoring grad students, grad students mentoring grad students, faculty mentoring undergraduates and schoolteachers. Programs for mentoring are springing up all over now, some of which actually *assign* mentors. Dayna, for example, as a PhD student has been assigned a faculty mentor and Doug as junior faculty has been assigned a tenure mentor. To us this feels analogous to requiring volunteerism, establishing by fiat what may be best left to ecology and time. Mentoring programs—particularly those that direct the relationship—if they do not preclude altruism, hardly seem borne on its breath. Assigned mentoring is to altruistic mentoring what security cameras are to honesty—relatively effective replacements, but not quite the same thing.

Here's a story that's not on the list above: graduate student establishes extracurricular relationship with undergraduate in an advanced writing course, a playful banter that turns to more writing courses that turn to serious questions that turn to special projects that, somewhere in there, had become mentoring in all but name. But why isn't it? You don't find *mentoring* in the typical TA Handbook of Undergraduate Relations. You don't find any other institutional expectation, support, or infrastructure for it either. Such mentoring, outside programmatic bounds, hardly could be anything *but* altruistic; there's simply no institutionally recognized percentage in doing it, and actually a significant risk of being censured for it. Our attempt at altruistic mentoring was essentially subversive, if not flatly illicit—in a research institution which quietly encouraged TAs to put studies first, research second, sleep third, teaching last, and pretty much left mentoring (even of other TAs, much less undergraduates) off the list entirely.

So we wonder: *is* there something subversive about altruistic mentoring in institutions of higher education? And if so, what hope is there of programming it? Here's the real story, short form: Dayna, a junior at the University of Utah, had the rare foresight to be looking for a mentor among her teachers—but had the misfortune to be doing so at a research institution where most students see as many TAs as they do faculty. Doug, a third-year PhD student, had just published a reflective essay on mentoring in *The Writing Instructor*, bemoaning students' lack of interest in being mentored, at least by TAs in required writing courses. Dayna appeared in Doug's advanced composition class as a bright and engaged student . . . and then began appearing at Doug's office hours and in his e-mail in-box, asking questions about his scholarship and interests. Doug thought nothing of it until Dayna asked whether it would be agreeable for her to take his rhetoric-based humanities writing class next semester. Doug found this puzzling (Dayna had already met the requirement that course fulfilled) but flattering enough to encourage her to do so. E-mails increased (particularly during the university's three-week hiatus for the 2002 Winter Olympics) and Dayna began requesting lists of reading, then sending Doug summaries of the books with complicated questions stemming from her readings. By the middle of the semester the two had agreed this might be . . . mentoring. By the end of the semester they had designed a summer project, an independent readings course led by Doug and assisted by Dayna in which five students designed an advanced popular nonfiction writing course. (The two went on to get the course adopted by the university and taught it the next summer.) Dayna went into a rhet/comp master's program, fulfilling Doug's goal of luring her into the field, and the mentorship continues as she begins her PhD.

And, so, here's a fourth story, the interpretive one, the one about us trying to understand why and how this worked. As O. L. Davis has said, most authentic mentorships are understood in hindsight. Now we recognize the mentoring as altruistic—based on an ethics of care, nurturing, concretely and emotionally involved, present (Lauer 234) and subversive in the domain of the research institution. We noticed that it was not just Dayna who sought attention from a faculty member; Doug sought attention from students, or a student, *as* a mentor.

Dayna and Doug both saw giving attention as a legitimate means of getting it. These are not necessarily wholly altruistic motivations—they are ethos-tempered—but they *are* altruistic effects. Nor was the attention dishonest: Dayna sincerely *was* interested in Doug's work and professional activities; Doug sincerely was interested in Dayna's intellectualism and well-being as a student. The mentorship, then, was rooted in genuine goodwill and other-interest as much as self-interest.

We noticed that the mentorship relied on a specific intermingling of personalities and worldviews; this particular relationship was rooted in particular characteristics and knowledges of the people involved. Dayna understood the importance of a mentor enough, and had the right degree of aggression and patience, to actively pursue a mentorship, to press, to make first moves. She had the ability for sincere flattery and an ease that made her non-threatening. Her academic interests and capabilities (such as reading, interpretation, and reasoning) were sufficiently developed to be intriguing and challenging to Doug. Both combine intensive inquisitiveness with easy-going personal manners. Doug also maintained an attitude of independence and impatience with rules-for-their-own-sake that made it possible to sustain a mentorship between actors not institutionally authorized to do so. As much as Dayna had a drive to see behind the stage to the structures holding it up, Doug had a drive to expose that structure and give fieldtrips to anyone interested. Perhaps the shortest way to talk about personality issues is to say that we clicked—we simply got along well. Dayna was willing to learn more and Doug was willing to guide her learning.

We are also both intensely reflective people, and that reflection drove the mentorship as well: after the first semester, active pondering of what was the nature of this relationship consumed a notable portion of our discussions, which were carried on mostly through e-mail and occasionally in office hours. It was a long time before Doug, particularly, was willing to actually call it mentoring, and his reticence connected back to altruism as well. There is risk in mentorship: the participants assume some level of responsibility for each other. Doug felt strongly his lack of institutional support, his newness to academe, the impermanence of a TA position, and his own scholarly inexperience. The fear of inadequacy, of doing more harm than good, made him want to call the mentorship something else—a lesser commitment. And as much as Dayna availed herself of Doug's influence, she was cautious to test it to make sure it was beneficial. There was a long process of getting comfortable in the roles, defining boundaries, establishing the relationship.

Dayna's reflection revealed her own altruism: always she wanted to know, "What are you getting out of this?" Aside from the pleasure of both the attention and the opportunity to joust with a student while guiding her, there truly were other tangible benefits that made the relationship two-way, with both members growing as people. While her understanding of given readings grew, Doug used her musing about them to help him study for PhD comprehensive exams. He took on projects, such as a directed readings course and creating an upper-division course, that were rarely undertaken by TAs. Perhaps the greatest gift Dayna gave Doug was a way to *teach* in a research university. Correspondingly, Dayna was gifted with a learning environment that was tailored to her and attenuated some of the institutional limitations of a large school. The freedom found in subversion allowed for a mutual shaping in a smaller institutional shadow.

Mentorships, if they are altruistic, are a love story of a sort society has a hard time recognizing, stripped as they are (or at least as ours is) of physical gestures and the accoutrements of romantic, familial, or other charitable relationships. (Though our process certainly had an aspect of "wooing.") That love, the desire for the best of the other, is essentially what we try to capture in this term "altruism." In our case, that relationship was one of tentativeness, mutual service to each other's best interests, and bidirectional appreciation of the other's gifts and insights. It's an example of how mentoring can work in a collaborative rather than an authoritative programmatic milieu—may actually subvert that authoritarianism. However altruistic mentoring is brought to life in institutional settings, we suspect it will require a subversive element.

Works Cited

Davis, O. L., Jr. "A View of Authentic Mentorship." *Journal of Curriculum and Supervision* 17.1 (2001): 1-4.

Lauer, Janice. "Graduate Students as Active Members of the Profession: Some Questions for Mentoring." *Publishing in Rhetoric and Composition.* Ed. Gary A. Olson and Todd W. Taylor. Albany, NY: SUNY P, 1997. 229-36.

13 Graduate Student Writing Groups as Peer Mentoring Communities

Lisa Cahill, Susan Miller-Cochran,
Veronica Pantoja, and Rochelle L. Rodrigo

In *Writing Permitted in Designated Areas Only*, Linda Brodkey describes a common image of the writer: "When I picture writing, I often see a solitary writer alone in a cold garret working into the small hours of the morning by the thin light of a candle" (59). Based on our collective experiences as members of a writing group that began in 2001 when we were all full-time graduate students, we have found that graduate student writing groups can be used to contest the myth that scholarly writing, or scholarly development, occurs best in isolation— or, in other words, primarily when the scholar labors alone. Instead, as a result of our experiences, we argue that scholarly development can occur when writers are able to invite others "into the garret" as they compose their scholarly documents and construct/develop their professional lives or when they decide to step out of the garret as writers.

Graduate study is a key time when students need support from their peers as well as safe, productive opportunities to test new ideas and writing styles. Graduate student writing groups often provide such a space because they enable the members to help one another evaluate and participate in the social construction of disciplinary knowledge. At the same time, when group members meet to discuss someone's writing, they have the opportunity to practice the spoken and written literacies that will gain them access to their discipline. They can also help each other negotiate knowledge construction and decide how to contribute to or challenge certain literate practices or acts. In other words, in graduate student writing groups, participants peer-mentor one another in their professional development as teachers, scholars, and members of their disciplinary communities. In this reflection, we share our writing group experiences as a way to illustrate the benefits of this kind of peer mentoring experience.

Graduate Student Socialization: Shelley's Story

I remember sitting in my first rhetoric and composition seminar after I had "converted" from being a literature graduate student. The faculty member teaching the class repeatedly talked about her writing group and how helpful it was for her, her writing, and her professional identity (and sanity). Being a little insecure about my new disciplinary status, I started to search out friends for help and then suggested that we might emulate our mentors by starting our own writing group as a way to mentor each other through the different stages of graduate study.

Participating in a writing group was one of the best things I could do in order to "catch up" with and discuss disciplinary knowledge. This is a process that I continue to participate in even after having completed all course work for my degree program because I continue to learn from my writing group. For example, I have never researched nor worked in a writing center; however, thanks to years in a group with two members who are very involved in writing centers, I now actually know a great deal more about theoretical and practical issues related to writing centers.

All of us were in different places in our graduate careers when we started our group; however, none of us can imagine progressing through our program without the support of one another. As a grassroots effort, starting this group represented our choice to complement the formal mentoring we received from professors with informal mentoring from our peers, thus marking our move from formal instruction on what it "means" to be in rhetoric and composition to actually "being" a rhetorician and/or compositionist. As a group that has met consistently for five years, our writing group membership has changed from solely being part of our lives as graduate students to being an important part of our professional identities and practices.

Benefits of Writing Group
Participation: Veronica's Story

Participating in a writing group has affected my development as a teacher, researcher, and scholar. As a writing instructor, I always assign structured peer review in my classes. However, participating in my writing group has heightened my awareness of what I ask my students to do. Sharing writing that is personal or that took a lot of struggle to produce is a difficult process, but the feedback can be invaluable. In class, I refer to my own experiences in writing group to let students know I understand their struggles and that I can also predict some successes.

In my efforts to help make peer review more effective for students, I assign time in my class so that students can actually talk with one another, share ideas about what works and what doesn't, and get clarification on their peers' comments, much as I do with my writing group. My goal is to help make students feel more accountable to each other and to themselves in the writing process; in this way, students can begin to see themselves as peer mentors instead of only peer reviewers. In writing group, I know what I can do with my writing and what I need help with. I can work with my strengths and my weaknesses, and I can also learn to ask specific questions about my own writing. Likewise, in my writing classes, I ask students to first reflect on their writing needs before peer review is conducted so that their reviewers can provide specific feedback.

As a member of my writing group, I have also developed skills to become a thoughtful researcher and scholar. Listening to my peers' concerns and incorporating their perspectives into my writing has helped me to construct more complete arguments for different audiences. As a result, my confidence about my writing has increased.

By working together, we have also provided one another with useful opportunities to present at conferences, collaborate on publications, and share resources. We have also become a community of support for one another and the support goes beyond writing. As our friendships have grown significantly, so has our commitment to one another's professional and personal successes.

Promoting and Developing Literacies: Lisa's Story

My participation in writing group has been an important part in the development of my disciplinary, professional, and social identities because of its influence on the development of my academic literacies. When we began our writing group five years ago, I was taking courses to work toward my graduate degree and I was teaching. As a teacher, I was learning methods to facilitate the social construction of knowledge in my first-year writing courses, while also searching for a relationship between the social construction of knowledge and my *own* scholarly writing. Although my course work taught me about genre and the importance of understanding that conventions and reader expectations vary from genre to genre, I still needed to apply those principles to the scholarly writing expected of me in my degree program and in the professional conference arena. My writing group membership became a way for me to achieve these goals.

Writing group meetings offered me opportunities to learn from my peers' experiences and to discuss, without being overly concerned about being evaluated by my peers, the features of genres like the conference proposal, literature review, and methodology chapter in a dissertation. Because each of us in the writing group were at different points in our graduate degree program when we first began meeting, we were able to coach one another through the different steps by sharing examples of our writing, discussing what we knew about different professors' expectations, and providing feedback about a conference proposal or a course paper *before* submitting the work for evaluation. In other words, the value of our writing group was proven early on because we saw that we could benefit from one member's experiences in the dissertation writing process while another member, who was still taking courses, could update us on recent research in different areas of rhetoric and composition. As a result, we realized that we did not have to know everything all of the time; we could look to one another for support.

The literate practices that we are expected to engage in on a daily basis—such as defending a dissertation, developing new course syllabi, writing institutional reports, assessing program development data, and negotiating workplace issues like salary, team building, as well as supervisory and teaching responsibilities—are some of the main motivations we share for continuing our writing group membership. Writing group meetings function as a safe and productive opportunity to ask questions and receive advice about writing styles, appropriate ways to approach classroom and workplace scenarios, career choices, and strategies for balancing work and life. As graduate students, we began our writing group participation because we were seeking ways to be mentored through our course work and through the requirements and expectations of our degree program. As we have moved through our degree programs and as we have developed as scholars and professionals, we have maintained our writing group membership—even as members move away—because we realize that the social support and mentoring contribute to our success and confidence.

Mentoring Roles: Susan's Story

As I conducted research for my dissertation and wrote the first draft of each of the chapters, my writing group mentored me by giving me helpful suggestions. They offered a "testing ground" where I could bring my data, conclusions, and interpretations, and they asked me the kinds of questions that my committee would eventually ask. Likewise, as I respond to the work of my colleagues in the writing group, I practice the social etiquette of providing constructive criticism to a colleague, and we discuss how to successfully negotiate the process of responding to readers' needs while maintaining the integrity of our own purposes as writers.

In our writing group, we continually learn to negotiate the intersecting and overlapping roles that we each have in the group. When we bring our work to the group, we come to be mentored, and when we read and comment on the work of our fellow writing group members, we mentor them. Our writing group roles help us to grow accustomed to the professional roles we play in our careers as faculty members, program coordinators, and active scholars in our discipline. As professionals working in postsecondary environments, we engage in similar kinds of negotiations as we mentor and are mentored through experiences such as the peer review process for journals and conferences, the tenure review process, the performance evaluation process, the selection of faculty awards, the mentoring of graduate students and colleagues, and the development of program assessment initiatives. In these professional and disciplinary spaces, we are often expected to mentor others while also knowing when we ourselves need to seek out a new mentor. In other words, we need to be able to move back and forth between these roles, and in a writing group we have the opportunity to learn how to listen to and use constructive criticism, to "practice" being mentors ourselves, and to negotiate similar types of roles as faculty members at our individual institutions.

Stepping out of the Garret

Through our participation and maintenance of our writing group, the importance of peer mentoring has taken center stage in our lives.

Based on our collective experiences, we ideally see peer mentoring being integrated as a structured part of graduate degree programs. One way to do that is to help students organize and develop their own writing groups. However, if structured peer mentoring opportunities are not part of a graduate degree program, students can still take steps to construct peer mentoring groups on their own. Without explicit discussions of expectations and without methods for navigating or negotiating particular literacies, graduate students may run the risk of remaining outside the power structures that serve to validate knowledge and that have the potential to effect change. Hence, peer mentoring through writing groups offer graduate students communities that support their socialization and empowerment.

Work Cited

Brodkey, Linda. *Writing Permitted in Designated Areas Only.* Minneapolis, MN: U of Minnesota P, 1996.

14 Mentoring Undergraduates in the Research Process: Perspectives from the Mentor and Mentees

Angela Eaton, Linda Rothman, Jessica Smith, Robin Woody, Catherine Warren, Jerry Moore, Betsy Strosser, and Randi Spinks

We would like to tell you about our mentoring project between seven undergraduate mentees and one assistant professor mentor, learning about research methods and conducting a research project together. The project resulted in this book chapter, two student conference presentations, one national conference presentation, and an article manuscript currently under review. It was an exceptionally rewarding experience for the mentor and mentees—many of whom said it was the most beneficial experience they had in their undergraduate career. In this chapter, we explain how we structured the project, what mentoring techniques were used, what we would change, and what the benefits were.

ORIGIN OF THE PROJECT

When I joined the faculty of Texas Tech University, I intended to conduct a research project with graduate students to help develop their research skills, in which proofreading methods were tested for efficacy. In faculty orientation, however, I learned about Tech's Vice President for Undergraduate Research and overall initiative of involving undergraduates in research, so I decided to tailor the project to undergraduates. In my classes, I announced that I would be giving an independent study course called *Introduction to Research Methods* in the spring, and that the ultimate goal of the class would be to produce a publication.

I explained the importance of research to graduate studies, indicated that a graduate school application would be stronger with the inclusion of a research methods class and perhaps a publication, and noted that I would be able to write an extremely strong letter of recommendation after the class. Overall, I stressed that it was an opportunity and not an obligation.

Seven students registered for the three-credit class. These students were bright, enthusiastic, and hardworking, but they were by no means carbon copies of each other. The mentees varied widely in their demographics, from 19 to 45 years old, six female students—Linda, Jess, Betsy, Cat, Robin, and Randi—and Jerry, our one male student. Six of the students were senior technical communication majors, and one student was a sophomore business major from a technical communication service course.

Mentoring Techniques

There were several techniques I used to mentor these students, but the most important technique—a concept that prompted every other—was to treat them as research partners instead of students. I referred to them in e-mails and on Web pages as my research partners. When I was with a mentee and another faculty member walked by, I made sure to introduce my mentee and stress that she or he was doing research with me.

Group Consensus on Every Decision

As part of treating the mentees as research partners, we made every—and I mean *every*—decision together, from agreeing on the first day about how many hours we would spend per week, to writing and editing this chapter you are reading now. At first, they were a little nervous that they got a say in every decision, but they quickly became confident and took themselves and the project more seriously. Betsy noted, "Dr. Eaton did encourage us to feel our way through the process without telling us the exact answers so that we could define our own learning experience. I was surprised that she let us decide some of the most important aspects of the study, but it helped us become more involved with the outcome instead of feeling like we were just told what to do."

Group consensus did take more time. It would have been easier and faster to design the study myself and assign them portions of it. However, learning how decisions are made in research is just as important as learning how to conduct the study itself; as an added benefit, they could explain the reasoning behind every feature of the study, because we had designed it together.

Flexible Deadlines

My students were busy people—all of them save one worked at least twenty hours per week and took two to five classes, and many had spouses and families. In the spirit of treating them as colleagues, no one was penalized for late work. I only occasionally needed to give them the gentle prodding scholars give each other. Linda remembers, "You told us we were not to apologize for anything in the project, especially as far as time frame, because we were all busy and were working on this project not just for a class, but beyond it as well. And it all worked out well, because it seemed we all were able to do a little more at times, and a little less at times, and it all got done with the group effort. It made for a comfortable working relationship, and none of us quit the project because we didn't have time." Cat, who was carrying a full load, noted, "If a few of us were not able to meet the required hours for one week, we could easily compensate for the next."

Jerry noted, "One element that aided the mentoring process was the fact that it was a group. Each group member took his or her responsibilities very seriously. No one wanted to be seen as the reason that goals and deadlines were not being met." Linda concurred, stating, "I enjoyed the relaxed approach and not putting us on too strict of a timeline. Self-discipline with completing our tasks and the overall project is another thing we will have to conquer to be successful in graduate school, and I think we learned that a bit in this project."

Personalizing Scholarship

One of the most important things I tried to do in the mentoring process was to show them that scholars are people. I let them know that I had also gotten tired of reading for a literature review, and that I had also wondered exactly when I had read enough literature. Reading studies for the lit review, they noticed that other scholars had made mistakes in their own work, and we discussed the difficulties in designing strong studies. I let them see that I didn't always know the answer, and that I often double-checked my initial inclinations using research texts. While I probably would have been more comfortable showing them a completely polished persona, I wanted them to know that imperfect people can be scholars (actually, only imperfect people are scholars), and they were scholars, too.

Socializing with Mentees

Part of the fun of a research partnership is socializing—meeting at a conference, having lunch together, having someone to share your excitement with about the project. I made an effort for us to social-ize together in a way that was appropriate for a faculty member and undergraduate students. We socialized at the conference we attended together, and we had dinner together before we did the data analysis. I also had a large end-of-year barbeque for the group where we met each other's partners and children, and they presented me with a wonderful plaque thanking me for the mentoring. Socializing helped cement the mentoring relationship; one mentee remarked, "I was surprised by how genuinely interested our mentor was in our futures, whether they lied in academia or industry. Her interest was a motivation to succeed."

How We Structured the Course

First, we created a contract describing the readings, assignments, and requirements for the course that was signed and filed. We agreed that the class would meet once per week for an hour and a half, and that they would work 5 hours outside of class per week. The five hour time limit kept frustration down—no matter how time-consuming each task was, they were able to have a stopping point each week. Cat noticed, "The class, itself, gave us time to not only work directly on our research, but also allowed us time for learning aspects beyond our main objective (i.e., how to organize a written study, the types of research available, etc.). I know this class was one of the main reasons why I did not feel so overwhelmed with the process; I was committed to a class rather than an outside obligation."

The 6.5 hours per week was slightly less than the average amount of time spent on a 3-credit class, but we all knew that by the time the research project was over they would have put in much more than an average amount of time for a class. I explained that we would try to finish the research project in one semester, and that if we weren't able to finish they weren't obligated to continue working over the summer. The project did go well into the summer and next fall, and all of the students continued to participate on a volunteer, no-credit basis.

The course was called *Introduction to Research Methods*. The grading scheme was simple. Eighty percent of the students' grades came from participation—reading the textbook, participating in class discussion, and conducting the project. Twenty percent was determined from two research response papers, explaining the strengths and weaknesses of two research projects described in journal articles. By the end of the semester, we eliminated the second response paper because the students had critiqued so many articles for the literature review that it wasn't necessary to show their mastery of course concepts with a second short response paper.

We used a course webpage to hold the course syllabus, the outline of our literature review that was updated with each new article summary, and our list of references so that students could determine if an article had already been requested from the library. We also used a Web chat board to discuss issues about the study between our weekly course meetings.

While working on the literature review, the mentees were also learning research methods. We talked about the purpose of a literature review, noting that we should learn from the results, but also get ideas from other scholars' methodologies. A few of the students initially had trouble summarizing the articles. Betsy noted, "The research experience was completely different from what I expected it to be. I've performed research in biology classes, but this research was something entirely new. Starting out the lit review, I did not really know what to pay attention to. I would skip over all the equations and numbers. Later, when we learned their importance, I began to include them into my reviews. I designed an outline for myself to follow while reviewing the studies; that way I would not forget to look for certain information."

Jess mentioned, "For the first portion of the semester, I felt a bit overwhelmed by the sheer size of the project, specifically the literature review, as we tackled that rather large task first. I think most of us shied away from voicing our struggles because we did not want to be the one who could not handle the task. Yet as the semester progressed, we began chatting more and more about the project, discussing both concerns and exciting developments." They quickly grasped the task and were soon producing graduate-quality work. I read all of the summaries and checked them against the original articles to ensure that they were accurate.

While designing the study, we also covered the human subjects review process. We discussed the importance of the process, its history, and when it occurs in the research process. The students read the forms from our Office of Research Services, looked at the original federal regulations, and discussed whether our proposed study would be exempt, expedited, or a full review. The students determined our work would be exempt and chose which exemption reasons we should apply under. I wrote the description and sent off the forms.

After the study was designed and we received human subjects (internal review board, or IRB) approval, we conducted a pilot study. For the first data collection, three students accompanied me to class to see the process. I collected the majority of the data because my students often worked or had class during data collection times.

Presenting the Preliminary and Final Results

West Texas A&M's 10th Annual Student Research Conference

A real turning point in the mentee relationships came when the students entered the West Texas A&M's 10th Annual Student Research Conference. The students wrote a proposal and were accepted. Only two presenters were allowed, so they decided to write the presentation as a group and two volunteered to make the presentation. In class, we discussed matters of professional development—the purpose of conferences, their format, how questions should be fielded, and how to respond when you don't know the answer.

The evening before the conference, the students met to finish their slides. We calculated the freshly collected pilot data, and I showed them how to do the data analysis. I did not help in designing the presentation because it was a student conference. After the data analysis, I realized that I had to leave and trust that they would finish. I knew they were very responsible students, and that they had certainly pulled all-nighters before, but I was worried. I left, knowing I had to trust them.

The next morning we met for a nice breakfast before carpooling. I noticed a difference in them immediately—they seemed a bit giddy, excited. They seemed more like a team than a class. We carpooled to the conference, had lunch together, watched other presentations and made ours. The students presented very well and were able to answer questions from the faculty judges with confidence. Later, we went to the awards ceremony. Randi, who worked full-time that day, drove two hours just to be at the awards ceremony with us.

Although their presentation had been accidentally misclassified into Fine Arts (mostly literature papers), their presentation was runner-up for "Best Paper." The conference also prompted the first publicity we received for the project, becoming an English Department announcement and an entry in the Arts and Sciences newsletter for being accepted and for placing. This presentation resulted in their first publication, in the proceedings of the conference.

Robin's Perspective, One of the Presenters. The conference at West Texas A&M was an experience that I would not have had, had I not been involved in this research project. Presenting at a conference is a rare opportunity for most students, undergraduates in particular. So often, undergraduate students are unable to attend conferences because of time and funds. If an undergraduate were to even attend a conference, it seems to be even rarer that he or she should present a study or paper.

When we heard about the Student Research Conference, we knew immediately we wanted to enter our research project. For most of us, we had never presented at a conference. Not only that, but we did not know really how to write a proposal for such a conference. So, we built the conference presentation into our course structure and worked on the proposal as a team. In all actuality, most of us didn't really know each other that well until we started this conference presentation. Until this part of the project, I think we were mostly just students in a classroom together. But when we started working on the conference and seeing the possibilities at hand, we really came together as a team.

We split the work so that all of us could be involved in the creation of our presentation. Though I was one of the two presenters, I know our presentation would not have been what it was without the help of the entire project team. Each of us went above and beyond to get the project done, even spending one late night working at school during the final push to get the presentation done before we headed to the conference the next morning.

The conference itself was one of the best opportunities for growth for me personally. Naturally I'm not a comfortable public speaker, but I volunteered to present at the conference for two reasons: 1) I knew it was going to be a good opportunity to get over my fear of public speaking; and 2) I knew my teammates would encourage me through the process. My teammates and my mentor helped me grasp the concepts applied in our research so that I could present them clearly and with confidence. Prior to the presentation, we went through several trial runs to get their feedback on the presentation. Everyone was honest and encouraging, and during the actual presentation, it was nice to look out at the audience and see my teammates and my mentor cheering me on.

So often we hear that teamwork is the foundation of any great project. I think in this project in particular, teamwork and mentoring were the key elements. Working closely in a small group on such an intense project made us a tightly knit group. We all fostered new friendships with colleagues that we might have otherwise just considered acquaintances. Not only that, but we were given the opportunity to work closely with a new faculty member whom we all respect.

Cat's Perspective, One of the Presenters. Presenting my first research study in front of a panel of judges was nerve-racking to some degree, but rather exciting as well. With my index cards full of information, not to mention the acquired knowledge of the study itself, I felt in control and confident throughout most of the presentation. Although Robin answered most of the questions put forward by the judges, I found myself thinking the same as she. One other factor that contributed to the optimism was the support we received from other student presenters and professional judges. Both the positive feedback and the conference as a whole allowed us to refresh our minds and easily resume our work.

Jerry's Perspective. The Student Research Conference represented a change in the way we (the students) saw ourselves. Until the conference came along, our project had the feel of many other projects. Once the group started working on our actual presentation it began to feel more real. We were already a group of students; this presentation turned us into a team in many respects.

We met the night before the presentation with Dr. Eaton to design our presentation. Our mentor was present for the first few hours to help firm up our data. She did eventually leave. That left our group to finish the presentation design on its own. It was from this point forward that we felt like a team instead of just a group.

We stayed until rather late into the night. One of the presenters ordered pizza, and we kept on working and brainstorming. I remember it as being a good night. It was a kind of good that comes from satisfaction as opposed to coming from pure fun. We tried to plan for every possibility, and by the end of the night, felt like we were ready.

Jessica's Student Conference Presentation

After the first student conference, Jessica proposed a presentation to an Honors national conference. Here is her account.

I gave a presentation of the preliminary data at the 2004 National Collegiate Honors Council Conference in New Orleans. The conference is a gathering of all member Honors Colleges and Programs from across the country. I created and presented a poster at the student poster presentation session, which took place in a room where approximately forty other students were presenting posters of their research. Conference attendees filled the room during the two-hour session, perusing posters and talking to the students when they had specific questions regarding a project. I had also presented a poster at the conference the year before, but that experience did not prepare me for the tremendous interest in the poster presenting our preliminary data.

I talked to students, faculty, and deans about the outcomes of the research and received multiple business cards and requests from many visitors for the final outcomes of our research. The majority of individuals I spoke with were professors who were disturbed but not entirely surprised by our findings. Student leaders, particularly fellow English students, were excited to discuss reasons for the findings, and nearly every person I talked to wanted to know what the next step in our research would be. Students recommended that we test older students, perhaps comparing senior English majors to senior engineering majors. A few professors recommended we test professors because they were disturbed by their colleagues' disregard for grammar in both writing their own documents and grading their students' papers.

Of the forty posters in my session, mine drew the most attention and conversation. After all the other students had packed up and left, I was still talking to professors and students who wanted to learn more about the project, ask what I thought were the reasons for our results, and recommend possible next steps for our research. By the time the last person left the room, I had talked thirty minutes past the end of the session. It was awesome.

Association for the Teachers of Technical Writing (ATTW) National Conference

In addition to the student conferences at which we presented preliminary data, we submitted the final results of our research project to the 2005 Association of Teachers of Technical Writing (ATTW) annual conference in San Francisco and were asked to do a poster presentation. I had received a late opportunity to be out of the country during the conference, so we determined that Linda would present it for us. I wrote the poster, and to practice her presentation, we presented the information to a graduate online research methods class at TTU, so that she could become familiar with the types of questions people might ask.

Linda's Account of the National Conference. This was my first experience participating in such a presentation and my first experience in attending a conference in the field. This was an amazing experience for many reasons.

First, I was there as a representative of Texas Tech University and of the Technical Communication program at TTU. Undergraduate research is a new direction for many universities, including Texas Tech. Since ATTW is the largest gathering of technical writing professors in the country, our undergraduate presentation at ATTW met this goal beautifully. Two 30-minute presentations were scheduled, but, because of the interest in our project, both presentations lasted over an hour. In fact, as I was taking down the poster after the second presentation, a conference attendee said, "Are you the one from Texas Tech? I wanted to talk to you." Needless to say, I promptly put the poster back up and spent another 20 minutes or so talking to her. I spoke with people from all over the country, including many who wanted to know what our follow-up study would be, where the study would be published, and how they could get more information to implement undergraduate research programs in their institutions.

Next, being at the conference as an undergraduate allowed me to get a "sneak peek" at what to expect when I return as a graduate or even as a professional in the field. I felt that I had some built-in leeway for error because I was an undergraduate, but most people assumed I was a graduate student and were shocked when they found out that I was not. They were impressed that undergraduates had undertaken such a huge project (777 subjects) on a topic that was an important part of their careers on a daily basis.

Lastly and most unexpectedly, I was very pleasantly surprised by the amount of interest in both our study and the undergraduate research process in general. Our initial hypothesis was not supported by the results, which was a little disconcerting. However, what I found at the ATTW conference was that although most people were also surprised by the results, they were most interested in what suggestions we could make based on those results. One professor lamented, "I teach English teachers. Now what do we do?"

This undergraduate research project allowed me to represent Texas Tech to academic professionals from all over the country, to practice my skills of presentation, and to bring home "kudos" for my research partners and to affirm that we were indeed doing something that many people were interested in and from which they could benefit.

AFTER THE CONFERENCES

By the end of all the conferences, we had collected the remainder of our data. The mentees then coded our papers for six variables, a massive undertaking. Each paper of the 777 participants needed to be coded twice so we could calculate inter-coder reliability. To make the task easier, we constructed a key that had all of the errors in the paper identified. Students took home packets of papers and entered the error counts into a cover sheet, and I entered all of the counts into our statistical analysis program. At that point, our semester ended. Some of the students moved away after graduation, but we kept in touch via e-mail and the Web board.

For the data analysis, those students who were still living in Lubbock met with me one evening to discuss it and our conclusions. Then each group member volunteered for writing a section of the final article or to proofread it. Finally, we edited our work via e-mail.

What We Would Do Differently

The mentoring experience was overwhelmingly positive, but there are a few things I will do differently with the next group. For example, I will explain the literature review differently, explaining exactly what needs to be summarized in an article; being used to graduate students, I assumed they would know which information was most pertinent.

The largest problem was that I simply underestimated the amount of time it took to conduct the study. While my previous research projects had taken a year and a half to two years, I expected that one shared with seven others ought to take a fraction of that time; it did not. Overall, the amount of time spent on this project was rather average for a quantitative research project, but my students, who were used to semester-long projects, did become a bit frustrated with its length. It took a year to conduct the study and submit it initially.

For one student, it was her only complaint about the process, and another noted, "The not-so-good aspect was the great amount of time that was dedicated to this study as well as any other study that people have and will do." However, it did give them an accurate picture of scholarly work. This fall, when I introduced the next mentoring class, I mentioned that it was at least a full year commitment, but that only one semester of it received course credit.

Mentoring Benefits

Initially, I wanted to do this project primarily because of the benefits to the students. However, I enjoyed benefits also. I enjoyed working with seven enthusiastic, hardworking students, teaching a topic I think is vitally important. Being a new faculty member, I appreciated developing relationships with the students quickly, making me feel more connected to my new institution. But most importantly, rather than mentoring taking away from my research time, a dilemma often faced by female faculty, mentoring allowed me to work closely with students while advancing my own research agenda. Our work together counted toward an eventual course release, and the national conference presentation, this chapter, and the research article will add to my CV, as will the follow-up study we have begun.

I have taught this same subject to graduate students and undergraduates, and I think there are very specific benefits about beginning mentoring and research methods training early, showing them what to do before they become intimidated by the process. And administratively, our work together gave my research agenda publicity within the school.

In addition to my personal benefits, the mentees noticed benefits including being exposed to a new kind of learning, building relationships, and making graduate school easier.

A New Kind of Learning

For these students, this research was an entirely new kind of learning. It wasn't until the first conference that I realized that they had only seen the most static part of academia—the theories and studies that make it into textbooks, which students are then asked to understand, memorize, and apply, and the course projects that rarely are seen outside of the classroom. By participating in the conference, these students were able to take part in the side of the academy most undergraduate students never experience—the part outside the classroom, the knowledge production, the life of the scholar. When faculty members asked them serious questions about their work at all of their conferences, they converted into experts—for once, no one *anywhere* knew more about the topic than they did. It's a powerful moment that usually doesn't come until late in graduate work, and they had that feeling while still being undergraduates.

Robin. From an undergraduate perspective, the mentoring process is more valuable than any other aspect of my undergraduate career. Undergraduates rarely get the opportunity to be mentored by their faculty members, let alone be taught the fundamentals of empirical research. The best part of this mentoring relationship was the opportunity to work closely with a professor whom I admire and has taught me a great deal about not only research, but also professional development.

Cat. The benefits that I got from the mentoring were not only the sense of pride and knowledge I received, but also the newfound credentials I have because of it. The great aspects about mentoring under Dr. Eaton were the ability to learn additional information about myself and my fellow research partners (the skill of meeting and talking with new people was further improved upon), the ability to learn research terminology and apply that to actual scenarios, the opportunity of constructing a presentation and presenting it to a panel of judges, and the sense of pride I felt after knowing I contributed to society through a study that will hopefully be read by many who are eager to use the information to help other people.

Jerry. The entire process was an awesome experience for me. I felt then and still feel now that the research we were doing was important. I learned so much about research and the IRB process. In fact, anytime I read or hear about someone having a new study out proving this or that, I think to myself, "I sure would like to get a look at their study design." My mentor gave me a solid foundation in research. I can even hear about research studies every once in a while and can tell right away that they are total crap.

BUILDING RELATIONSHIPS

Jess. The best example I can provide of our developing relationships is our group development of the slide show that we prepared for the conference at West Texas A&M. The meeting began at 5pm and lasted approximately four hours. As the time passed, I personally became more and more animated and comfortable with my fellow mentees. We ordered pizza, sat on the table, laughed, and struggled to collectively write and agree on approximately fifteen slides. From that night on, I have felt much more at ease with my research partners on a personal level. Last spring, a year after the research semester, a few of us even began meeting for a monthly game night (and just to give you an idea of our relationship with our mentoring professor, she sometimes joins us for game nights).

Cat. Not only was the mentorship beneficial in regards to the study, it also contributed to a stronger relationship between me and the other researchers. The mentorship allowed seven acquaintances to grow as friends through each others' encouragement and aid. For example, our first meeting seemed to be rather formal since most of us did not know exactly what we were getting into. As time went on, however, laughter was something that was always present—that and the occasional pizza.

And as for our mentor, Dr. Eaton, she is now not only a wonderful professor but also a friend. In this one-year duration, Dr. Eaton has clearly addressed her expectations of us in a tactful but nurturing way, representing what I believe to be a great leader. Dr. Eaton is, by far, the greatest professor I have ever had, and it is through this mentorship that I have the utmost respect for her.

Randi. I told everyone that asked me about the research class (family, friends, classmates, etc.) what an awesome opportunity it was. I was so excited to have a professor actually take the time to mentor me and teach me the importance of research. Throughout the whole process I feel like we bonded as a group and formed some really important relationships. Now if we have a question or are confused about anything related to this in the future we have a group of people willing to contemplate and/or answer our questions. Not only that but we also have developed lasting friendships with each other and our mentor.

Jerry. I know I developed some special relationships. To start out with I only knew two of the eight people in our mentoring group really at all. I had been in other classes with Robin and Betsy and worked with them on past projects. We had a very interesting dynamic as a group. We spanned in age from 19 to 44 (I think). By gender, we were seven females and one male (that being me). We learned many things about each other. We were constantly talking either in class or on e-mail. I have never been impressed with any group that I have been a part of as much as I was impressed with our mentoring group. At times I was a little intimidated by how bright everyone else in that group was. They were awesome.

Dr. Eaton quickly became the favorite professor of my academic career. She made everyone of us a better student. Take it from me, she was not a soft touch as a professor and could be as tough as she needed to be. However, she was fair and let all of us know that she cared not only about the research but about each of us as people.

In fact, there were two instances I remember well that showed how deeply she cared about her students. The first instance was when we went to the student conference in Canyon, Texas. Even though she could not be a part of the presentation, she went with us to the conference. Not only that, but she gave a couple of us a ride to the conference in her personal vehicle and offered to help out financially if any of us just could not come up with some money for the trip. The second instance occurred after the semester was over and any obligation she had to us or we had to her had passed. We were all invited to a cookout at her home. A good time was had by all. It was at this event that our group presented Dr. Eaton with a plaque to let her know how much we appreciated all she had done for us as students and mentees.

Dr. Eaton. I was a bit surprised at how wonderfully all of our relationships had developed. As an instructor, it's something you hope for but can't control. I have kept in touch with all of the students, meeting for coffee to discuss graduate school options, receiving chatty e-mail about new jobs in new cities, being invited to game night at Robin's new post-graduation house, and watching Randi's young son grow through the pictures she sends. I was surprised at how quickly the project made TTU feel like home.

GRADUATE SCHOOL IS EASIER

A large benefit of research mentoring is that it simply makes graduate school less intimidating to the students. Having completed a research project and submitted it for publication prior to the first graduate class really gives these undergraduates an advantage. Betsy, Robin, and Jess used the experience in their graduate school applications, explaining their abilities and describing their own research agendas; they were accepted. Betsy pointed out, "I believe since we were all undergraduates, we were quite eager to learn since we knew we were gaining ground on our graduate career by participating in an opportunity that normally does not come around until graduate school." When asked about this project, the chair of my department, Dr. Sam Dragga, remarked, "This effort gives students a splendid opportunity to develop and practice their research abilities but it also offers extraordinary insight on the life of the scholar. The students develop a clear sense of how their instructor manages a research project, develops presentations and publications from that research, and integrates that research in the teaching of classes. If students are considering a life in the academic profession, this experience offers a vital and practical orientation."

Jerry. There was another big advantage to the mentoring program; the entire idea of post-graduate work did not seem as that big of an obstacle. Our mentoring group attended the student-led conference in Canyon, Texas to present some of our preliminary findings. This conference was competitive and our group was up against students working on post graduate degrees while all of us were still undergrads. While I did not hear every group present, I heard a few of them. I can honestly say that our presentation and research was so much better than most of what I heard.

Jess. The prime benefit for me was the learning experience; Dr. Eaton moved especially slowly in explaining concepts (because we were undergrads), and that helped to build quite a strong foundational understanding of research methods. Just learning the research process as an undergrad was benefit enough, but my opportunity to prepare a presentation for two different conferences was an intangible benefit both for me personally and for my application to graduate school.

Linda. I believe this experience has been invaluable. I am so grateful for the opportunity to learn the research process and to have opportunities for publishing (eventually up to three or four articles started by this project) and presenting. Those are both opportunities I never thought I would have had as an undergraduate. I now feel that in graduate school I can focus on content and not so much on process. I also believe I will have a much better chance of attending graduate school because of this research. What an excellent CV item: published/presenting as an undergrad! And to go back even further, I had only toyed with the idea of graduate school -- this helped push me over the edge.

Robin. A personal benefit of mentoring was the chance to develop, implement, and complete a research project of such a large scale. Research at the undergraduate level is rare, but is so valuable to the participants. My experience has prepared me for graduate school in that when I start work on my own research agenda, I am aware of the steps to take and the time that is necessary to complete a project. This skill set will be valuable when I start work on my own research agenda in graduate school.

Dr. Eaton. My favorite anecdote from the mentoring experience came from Robin, a senior in the group about to apply to the Master's program at Tech, an anecdote which exemplifies the benefit of undergraduate mentoring in research. She rushed into my office between classes to drop off a packet of papers she had coded, and asked breathlessly,

"Dr. Eaton! I have to run but I have a quick question."
"Shoot, Robin, what is it?"

"How different is the kind of research we're doing from a Master's thesis? On my application, I'm trying to decide between a thesis in the Master's or not."

"It isn't."

"What?"

"If you do a Master's thesis, it will only be you instead of eight of us, and you'll be doing it under the supervision of a committee instead of in a group. But other than that, it's exactly the same."

"Wow," she paused. "That's going to be easy. Gotta go!"

I've never before heard any student refer to a Master's thesis as "easy."

Advice to Prospective Mentors

In this section, we provide advice to prospective mentors and mentees.

Jess. Carefully select the students you want to mentor. Taking volunteers tended to work in our case so only those students actually interested participated. I would be wary of offering incentives because you may end up with students who have no interest in the program/research. Also, emphasize personal responsibility and the importance of being able to work and meet deadlines independently, as we did for our five hours of work per week.

Linda. I would want the mentors to know how much they are appreciated. I would also want to tell them not to expect graduate work, because we are not graduates, but with the right guidance, we can get close. And when we are graduate students, we should be able to do graduate level work because of their mentoring.

Cat. For many who are interested in improving their mentoring ability or even starting out, I believe that mentorship is a great learning experience and should therefore be encouraged. Not only did I learn about the research that was derived from the study that I worked on under the mentorship of Dr. Eaton, but I also learned the essentials of research such as writing an abstract, a literature review, and what to look for as far as inconsistencies are concerned.

Randi. When I look back at my undergraduate career at TTU, having a mentor was the most important experience that I had. I think that by taking one person or a small group of people and mentoring them you are planting a seed that will continue to grow long after the formal mentoring process is over. Take the extra time to explain and go over details. A lot of the time when your mentees claim they understand, they really wish you would go over it one more time so that they can really confirm to themselves that they get it. Dr. Eaton always took the time to make sure that all of us were following and understanding what she was saying.

Robin. Overall, mentoring was one of the most valuable experiences of my undergraduate career. I have encouraged others to find a mentor and complete a project with that mentor, and I think each undergraduate should make it a goal to complete a project under the guidance of a mentor.

Dr. Eaton. I think that every student needs to be somebody's favorite, to have a connection, knowing that person will delight in their accomplishments, and support them with recommendation letters and encouragement. I think that every scholar has that person in our background, someone who stood before us in the classroom, then beside us as a mentor, and now stands behind us as a friend. Mentoring is a mutually beneficial way to become that person for your students. As one of my mentees wrote, "I have my very first mentor!!!! At 40, that's quite a feat!"

Work Cited

Crosland, Harold R. *An Investigation of Proofreaders' Illusions*. Eugene, OR: U of Oregon P, 1924.

15 Webs of Mentoring in Graduate School

Jennifer Clary-Lemon and Duane Roen

When we invoke the metaphor of a web, we evoke several images: the spider's web, with a discrete center, radial lines of silk running from it, woven spirals and threads. In this web spiders nurture their young, and it is here that they hunt and kill their prey. It is shelter, lifeline, and sticky silk. We might also imagine a web in more contemporary terms, in thinking of the World Wide Web, where information allows us access, connection and interconnection, networks, and extensions of ourselves in virtual form. Or we might see the Web's potential for isolation, alienation, and separation.

In these multiple ways, we see the web as a fitting metaphor for both mentoring as a scholarly practice, and graduate school as the locus of that practice. The mentoring done in graduate school is an extension outward, both from individual mentors and mentees in informal mentoring situations, as well as extensions of our institutions as they develop and maintain formal mentoring programs (see Canton and James, Hood and Boyce, and Herr). Strong mentoring in graduate school often offers "shelter" for incoming, junior scholars by helping them cope with the identity crisis that often comes with pursuing a degree in higher education. The idea that one "can't go home again," as well as the potential for social alienation from home cultures, may be eased somewhat by having mentors that not only function along professional lines, guiding a mentee through research and teaching expectations, but also those who function along personal lines—those who are explicit about the sometimes "uninviting territory" (Okawa 507) of academe, especially to female junior scholars or junior scholars of color. Mentoring in its ideal form provides a network of colleagues, a connection between and among generations, disciplines, institutions, and interests—a "validation process" of "real acceptance into that social collegial network which assists with promotion, advancement, and recognition" (McCormick 189). Yet it is not without its own pitfalls and stickiness; traditional mentor roles have been critiqued as androcentric, promoting competition, elitism, and exclusion (i.e., "socializing protégés into the 'rules of the game'" [191] in which such rules are potentially detrimental or discriminatory). A scarcity of successful, senior-level mentors of color and female mentors are oft-cited problems that formal and informal mentoring face (Hansman, McCormick).

It may be a myth to assume that this territory will ever be more inviting, especially with the overwhelming number of scholars who see themselves as not fitting into the academy. Yet such territory may be mapped as a space that connects us, mapped through our stories and experience. We also need to clarify what we mean when we talk about mentoring. Mentoring relationships in academic settings often involve senior scholars working with junior scholars. For example, such relationships might involve tenured faculty mentoring tenure-track faculty and graduate students, faculty at any rank working with graduate or undergraduate students, or advanced graduate students working with recently admitted graduate students. If we consider mentoring to mean that more experienced people "show the ropes" to less experienced people, then academic rank should not always be the factor defining the roles of mentor and mentee. In some knowledge domains a graduate student can easily be more experienced or knowledgeable than a full professor—for example, in the use of digital technologies for teaching. Also, the nominal mentee is not the sole learner in the relationship. That is, if the mentor is the kind of reflective practitioner that Donald Schön describes, then the mentor is learning by monitoring and evaluating his or her mentoring activities and their effects on the mentee.

It is perhaps a lack of these kinds of critical definitions, as well as the lack of an impetus to construct them, that leads to the invisibility of mentoring, especially within built-in institutional reward structures. The invisibility of mentoring, then, is a place where we need to begin. For us, a way to increase the visibility of mentoring activities is to see mentoring as a scholarly activity, rather than service to the profession, or "grooming" partnerships between protégés and experts in a field. To see mentoring as scholarly—contributing to new knowledge, research, and teaching—gives mentoring the place and value in our disciplines and institutions that it deserves, as goes far in getting mentoring on the ballot of activities that reward scholars for their time and effort.

Graduate school, for many of us, is the center of our web—it is where our journey began, where we began to map our territory. We may see radial lines of connection between graduates and undergraduates, faculty and graduates, graduates and graduates. We may also see power lines radiating out from that center, lines that denote differences in class, race, gender, sexual orientation, and disability. Yet we also see mentoring as part of a new, broader agenda of universities to value connectedness and to move beyond an evaluation of the professoriate that is relegated to teaching, research, and service. In this piece we also hope to move beyond this given agenda to assert that mentoring is, as Gail Y. Okawa suggests in "Diving for Pearls," "more than an academic exercise" (507). In describing our own experiences as both mentors and mentees, we hope to contribute meaningfully to a growing body of work about mentoring in recent scholarship. We see our stories of mentoring not only as a framework for others and as a testament to and support for successful mentoring models, but also as a way of honoring those activists—those mentors—who are co-tellers of the stories we share here.

"MORE THAN AN ACADEMIC EXERCISE": STORIES OF PERSONAL AND PROFESSIONAL MENTORING

Jen's Stories. In July 2005 I was in Urbana, Illinois, for the second-round review of CCCCs convention proposals. As the only graduate student there, working as an assistant to the 2006 program chair, Duku Anokye, I found myself at an upscale restaurant on the Saturday evening of the review, surrounded by names that I had heretofore only read about. As I looked around the table at Cheryl Glenn, Paul Puccio, Gwendolyn Pough, Jaime Mejía, Sharon Mitchler, Deborah Holdstein, Fred Thomas, Risa Gorelick, Jacqui Biddle, and Eileen Maley, I wondered how in the world it was that I came to be there, in this surreal experience, at this surreal table. Then I looked to the two people whom I knew at the table, Duane Roen and Duku Anokye, and thought it even stranger. I was conversing, with these book writers, these scholars, these teachers, as though it were the most natural activity in the world. That is to say, by virtue of having a seat at that table, I felt like a real colleague (instead of the impostor I thought for sure they'd recognize me as). I began to think of mentoring in a new way—not necessarily in the one-to-one, protégé-expert relationship but as a "serendipitous byproduct" (Healy 10) of being in the right place at the right time. Such mentoring was performed by a multitude of experienced scholars who simply demonstrated a willingness to relate their experiences to my own, to offer helpful advice, and to appear as people rather than as glossy magazine covers.

The literature has defined mentoring in many ways: as sponsorship (Zeldich), as master teacher, as guide (Daloz), as "Opener of Doors" and "Developer of Talents" (Schein), as guru (Levinson), as supportive boss (Phillips-Jones). More recently, mentoring has been recognized as more complex than any one of those labels. Indeed, I think it's more complex than even the concept of mentoring to which we refer here as an activity that is both reciprocal and transformational—that is, often on the mentee end of graduate education. Mentoring may not always be reciprocal; sometimes it may even be serendipitous. Perhaps, like the Supreme Court's definition of obscenity, we don't know quite what mentoring is, but we recognize it when we see it. Regardless of the many forms that mentoring may take, then, perhaps we can at least agree that mentoring is important, not just as a move to induct a new generation of scholars into the academy but also as an act of transformation in and of itself—a transformation of how we see teaching, of how we see service, of how we see our profession. It may even change who get gets to speak, who gets to be heard, and who gets a seat at the table.

Before I can talk about how I ended up in Urbana, having a seat at a very real table, I have to admit first that I never knew I wanted to do this—pursue a PhD, teach, write, all of it—for a living. I took a few courses in my masters program, not really knowing what I was doing, aimlessly trekking through course papers (and receiving, as I recall, not very high grades on them), thinking of a life in publishing or, well, I wasn't quite sure. The difference between that woman and the one that I am today, to be sure, is the result of the people who have encouraged me along the way. I realized—and perhaps all graduate students realize this at one time or another—that the difference between having great mentors in graduate school and not having them is, as one of my undergraduate students recently put it, the difference in seeing graduate school "as a one-hour flight to California rather than a seven-hour drive." So these brief stories are the stories of my one-hour flight, rather than seven-hour drive, through graduate school.

After a few courses in composition theory during my master's degree coursework, I began to realize what I was in for. I had taken an autobiography course with Peter Vandenberg the semester before when he approached me in the hall one afternoon. He explained that he was an editor of a journal, and that his assistant had just bailed out on him at the last minute, leaving him in the lurch as an exhibitor for a conference. He wanted to know if I was available as a fill-in that weekend to go to Minnesota. Because I had nothing better to do, I went to my first CCCC meeting as an exhibitor. I knew nothing about the culture of the conference, or even its purpose.

On the drive back to Chicago, Pete and I chatted about our lives, our plans, and our families. During the last leg of the trip, he asked me if I would like to apply to be his assistant for *Composition Studies*. I suppose I could say the rest has been history, but it has been so much more story than that. Pete gave me my first insight into the field; he explained the editorial review process; he explained schools of thought in rhetoric and composition with words that I could understand long before I read Hairston's "Winds of Change" or Kent's *Post-Process Theory*; he gave hard but fair feedback on course papers; he put up with my incessant questions; he introduced me to "names" in the field at subsequent conferences; he talked about PhD programs with me; he helped me figure out what a "statement of purpose" was when applying to do PhD work. Once I successfully navigated the process and moved away, Pete would invite me to collaborate on publications, inquire about my progress towards the degree, and try to coordinate conference presentations with me so we'd have a chance to catch up. Perhaps most importantly, Pete treated me like an equal and a friend, allowing me to see details of his life, sending me and my husband postcards from places he would travel to, asking me to keep an eye out for certain garage sale "treasures" for his eBay passion.

If it weren't for Pete, I would have been convinced that I did not possess the right "stuff" for PhD work, certainly not the right stuff to be a teacher, and undoubtedly stuff so atomically small as to not even remotely resemble the stuff of a publishing scholar. I completed my master's degree work at a commuter campus offering a terminal degree. I was most often invisible both the times I was on campus and the times I was off. Having someone cheerlead for me gave me the courage to quiet, to some extent, the voices crying "fraud!" in my head; it gave me support to move beyond the terminal. It also made space for me to seek out similar experiences with others when I went on to my PhD work. Effective mentoring pays forward and leads us to seek out, not only other great mentors (and mentees), but also a recreation of great mentoring to others. That is, "this kind of modeling involves learning *who* to be" (Zeldich 26), but not just learning how to be a teacher or scholar. Good mentoring teaches us, in graduate school, how to mentor others. It teaches us to recognize unfair and unethical behavior, how to celebrate our own successes, how to champion others' success.

Because of a powerful mentoring experience with Pete, I was able to seek similar experiences once I enrolled to do PhD work in rhetoric and composition. Believing, perhaps for the first time, that I had a "right" to be there, I got involved with my graduate student community, becoming president of the graduate student association in our department. As a result, I met Duane Roen, the faculty sponsor of the organization. Duane is a notorious mentor in our department and at our institution more widely—co-authoring articles with students, giving presentations not only through the department but through the graduate college on topics such as effective conference presentations and constructing vitas. Working alongside Duane in some of these workshops, I was able to trade some of my outsider status for insider status. When Duane asked me to enter into collaborative projects with him, I felt that I had the right stuff. And when my name was listed first on this piece, I didn't feel like an impostor. I felt instead as if my plane has finally touched down.

Mentoring has catalyzed a chain reaction for me, encouraging me to be the type of graduate student who opens the door of opportunity knocking rather than looking through the peephole and engaging the deadbolt. I have begun to see mentoring in most places I look; when I first applied to be Duku Anokye's assistant for the 2006 CCCC program, I was delighted to be offered the position. At this point you may be thinking, "She doesn't need any more mentoring. She's had more than her fair share and she's already first author on this piece." And you may be right—I've benefited from great career advice, and I hold my stuff in higher esteem than I used to. Still, I was fortunate enough to enter into the serendipitous experience of finding yet another person (and this time a woman!) willing to take the time to sit down with me and share her experiences of academe, let me ask questions about balancing work and family life, and not think less of myself. Further, she has proudly introduced me at every meeting as her assistant, and seated me—literally—at the table.

From metaphors of planes, tables, and webs, I have grown to see mentoring as an integral part of graduate education. I know, also, that my experience is neither unique nor universal. I approach my mentoring experiences cautiously; as a white woman, I know that gaining access to these experiences has been made easier for me by virtue of the color of my skin. I wonder, though I can't yet articulate, about the fact that I have had two white, male mentors and one female mentor of color. I know also that although we may want to see mentoring as valued in the universities of the millennium—a form of teaching, research, and service—that that change is slow in coming. Out of these realities, I've begun a fledgling peer mentoring program in our department that both challenges graduate students to be great colleagues, models, and friends, as well as encourages new graduate students to ask the right (and wrong) questions in a non judgmental atmosphere. Peer mentoring is not nearly the same as some of the great one-to-one relationships we have with long-standing experts in our field, but it holds in it a kernel of *who* it is we want to be and what it is we want to see of the academy: a diverse, supportive environment. It also paints a clear picture of what models we strive to get away from—colonial practices, the isolation and invisibility of the ivory tower, the theory of personal genius, and the reproduction of existing power structures and elite institutions.

Duane's Stories. Just as Geneva Smitherman and Victor Villanueva worked with mentors who helped them believe that they could succeed in academia (Okawa), I too have benefited from such mentors who helped me overcome persistent doubts in my abilities—even before I entered graduate school: Joyce King, my eighth-grade English teacher, who fostered my love for reading and writing; Clair Stein, my eleventh- and twelfth-grade English teacher, who challenged me to think more critically; Nicholas Karolides, who modeled scholarly, inspired teaching in my undergraduate and master's English education programs; Gene Piché and Michael Graves, who in my doctoral program, invited me to join them in research and publication; Les

Whipp, who involved me in the Nebraska Writing Project; Charles Cooper and Yetta Goodman, who vigorously supported my bid for tenure in 1988. Because of these and other mentors, I developed a steadfast commitment to mentoring early in my career, and I have tried to remain faithful to that pledge. Although the institutional rewards for mentoring are not always readily apparent, the intrinsic rewards are—as the popular credit-card commercial says—*priceless*.

Throughout my career as a university faculty member, I have collaborated with other scholars—usually junior scholars and most often graduate students—in much of my published research. I have done so because my graduate school experience with senior scholars such as Gene Piché and Michael Graves helped me believe that I could do publishable work. In listening to graduate students over the last several decades, I have frequently heard them talk about the benefits of collaborating with someone who has been there before. I also need to confess, though, that I have benefited immensely from these collaborations. Working with younger scholars such as Jennifer has helped me to see fresh approaches to problems. I also freely confess that I enjoy interacting with others to complete tasks—something that I learned as child growing up on a dairy farm in Wisconsin, where we worked together to milk cows, plant and harvest crops, and repair buildings and machinery.

Throughout my years as a university faculty member, I have conducted hundreds of workshops for small and large groups of graduate students in English as well as students in most other fields on campus. These sessions have focused on such topics as constructing vitas, writing letters of application, preparing for job interviews, constructing teaching portfolios, building courses, writing for publication, assessing learning, developing effective writing assignments, promoting learning and thinking through writing, and preventing plagiarism. On the one hand, I thoroughly enjoy these conversations, and I love to see the learning that results from them. I also see such learning in the materials that graduate students send me weeks and months later—CVs, syllabi, writing assignments, comments on teaching evaluations, and the like. I don't know if it's a weakness or a strength or a delusion, but I love to feel that I'm making a difference in graduate students' lives. On the other hand, I sometimes wonder why my workshops are necessary. When graduate students tell me that no one else has ever discussed these topics with them,

I wonder why. Shouldn't these topics be integral to graduate education? Shouldn't all faculty routinely discuss these topics with graduate students?

I have often taught seminars for first-year teaching assistants/as-
sociates in writing programs. These experiences have been both rewarding and immensely challenging. The rewards come from seeing
relatively inexperienced teachers develop confidence and expertise
in the classroom; the challenges come from trying to meet the needs
and to appeal to the interests of graduate students in a diverse range
of fields—rhetoric and composition, literature, fiction and poetry
writing, English education, linguistics, and teaching English as a
second language.

At my institution people make jokes about my frequent Saturday-
morning meetings with graduate students at Starbucks. Although I
admit that these meetings do give me an excuse to enjoy my favorite
beverage, what I like most about these meetings is that the setting
is so conducive to leisurely conversations about mutual interests—
research, teaching, and even non-academic topics. During these
conversations, I appreciate the observation that Gail Okawa makes
about the time that mentors and mentees spend together: "I've noted
that mentees see time taken as a gift given, an end in itself, while the
mentors instead see it as a vehicle, a means to an end" (527). At some
point in the Saturday-morning conversation at Starbucks, the graduate student will inevitably offer an apology for taking my weekend
time, and I am always struck by this gesture. My view is that I'm
having a good time drinking coffee, talking about topics that interest me a great deal, and hanging out with some very interesting
people. What could be better than that?

MENTORING AS SCHOLARLY ACTIVITY

If institutions expect faculty to engage in a particular activity, there
must be clear rewards for that activity. Those rewards can come in the
form of tenure, promotion, salary increases, and awards. Because the
academy so highly values scholarly activity, faculty routinely earn tangible rewards for activities labeled as "scholarly." Therefore, one practical means of rewarding faculty for mentoring is to consider mentoring
as scholarly activity. To do that, we can turn to the work of Ernest
Boyer, who, when he published *Scholarship Reconsidered: Priorities of
the Professorate* in 1990, offered a powerful argument for revising the

definition of "scholarship" to include four kinds of work: discovery, application or engagement, integration, and teaching and learning.

The scholarship of *discovery* is roughly equivalent to traditional concepts of research. Gail Okawa's qualitative study of relationships between mentors and protégés reveals how mentoring can function as "activist practice" (508). Okawa's study, "grounded in methods of narrative inquiry" (510), offers first-hand accounts of the mentoring that Geneva Smitherman and Victor Villanueva have experienced—both as protégés and as mentors. Smitherman's and Villanueva's testimonies, as well as those of their protégés, demonstrate the productive power of effective mentoring in shaping young scholars' careers. Such accounts also make us wonder how many careers have languished in the absence of mentoring. Studies such as Okawa's can serve as calls for further research on mentoring, which can have many purposes—for example, making mentoring more visible.

The scholarship of *application/engagement* is concerned with the question, "How can knowledge be responsibly applied to consequential problems?" (Boyer 21). With regard to mentoring, the question becomes something like this: "Given what we know about mentoring, how can we apply that knowledge to the mentoring opportunities at hand?" By responding to this kind of question, we can help to equip faculty with a range of tools for effective mentoring.

The scholarship of *integration* is concerned with "making connections across the disciplines, placing the specialties in larger context, illuminating data in a revealing way, often educating nonspecialists, too" (Boyer 18). The scholarship of integration leads us to consider the ways in which mentoring can be interdisciplinary. Many possibilities emerge: teams of faculty and graduate students teaching in interdisciplinary learning communities, cross-college professional-development workshops sponsored by the institution's graduate college, courses that attract graduate students from multiple departments or even colleges, interdisciplinary research teams consisting of faculty and graduate students.

Likewise, the scholarship of *teaching and learning* aims to make teaching publicly available to other scholars, as well as the object of other scholars' scrutiny and critique. We might do this by direct instruction about mentoring ("effective teaching"), by familiarizing ourselves with best practices about mentoring ("scholarly teaching"), and by writing about teaching faculty how to mentor ("the scholarship of teaching and learning") (Boyer 49).

In the 1990s as faculty and administrators began discussing Boyer's ideas, as well as those of other innovators such as Shulman, a common question emerged: "What are the criteria for evaluating the four kinds of scholarship?" In 1997 Charles Glassick, Mary Huber, and Gene Maeroff addressed that important question when they published *Scholarship Assessed*. After conducting extensive research on the ways that faculty get evaluated in the United States, Glassick, Huber, and Maeroff concluded that there are seven important criteria for evaluating any kind of scholarship. That is, effective scholarship is marked by (1) clear goals, (2) adequate preparation, (3) appropriate methods, (4) significant results, (5) effective presentation, and (6) reflective critique. If we combine Boyer's four categories of scholarship with Glassick, Huber, and Maeroff's six criteria for evaluating scholarship, we derive a table that can be used to pose some additional heuristic questions about mentoring. By responding to these questions, we can more clearly see the diverse purposes of mentoring, the need to conduct research on mentoring, the ways that we can enhance the quality of mentoring, and the means for evaluating and rewarding mentoring.

In Table 1, we combine Boyer's four categories of scholarship and Glassick, Huber, and Maeroff's six criteria for evaluating scholarship to pose questions that can help mentors design, deliver, and evaluate mentoring.

Just as these six criteria have been used widely in higher education to evaluate the traditional areas of research, teaching, service, and administrative work, they can also be adapted—as we have demonstrated here—to evaluate mentoring. If we analyze and evaluate mentoring in systematic ways, we can reveal its value to the department, college, and institution. Once our institutions understand its value, then we realize how important it is that we offer rewards to faculty who mentor— especially those who excel at mentoring.

Conclusion

To evaluate mentoring as scholarly activity, we need to make mentoring visible in multiple ways—by sharing our stories, both to one another within our disciplines, and also to our departments and institutions. We also must be aware of the ethical considerations and conflicts within mentoring. Although there are many ways to define ethics, one

Table 1. Combining *Scholarship Reconsidered* and *Scholarship Assessed* to Evaluate
Mentoring

		Four Categories of Academic Scholarship Boyer 1990			
		Discovery	Application	Integration	Teaching
Six Criteria for Assessing Scholarship Glassick, Huber, Maeroff, 1997	*Clear Goals*	What are the goals of our research on mentoring?	How can we apply knowledge about mentoring to serve students' professional and personal needs?	How can we work with colleagues and graduate students in other fields to foster mentoring?	What are our goals in mentoring? How might we communicate those goals to mentees?
	Adequate Preparation	How can we prepare ourselves to conduct meaningful research on mentoring?	How can we prepare ourselves to mentor effectively?	What can we learn from other fields to enhance the quality of mentoring?	How can we effectively instruct members of the profession in the practices of effective mentoring?
	Appropriate Methods	What research methods will most effectively answer our questions about mentoring?	What mentoring methods will be most effective in this particular situation?	What mentoring methods in science will work in rhetoric and composition?	What mentoring methods can we apply to teaching? What teaching methods can we apply to mentoring?
	Significant Results	What difference will this research make in mentoring?	What difference will this mentoring make in the professional and personal life of this person?	What difference will mentoring make in interdisciplinary partnerships?	What difference does mentoring make on teaching?
	Effective Presentation	How can we most effectively share our research on mentoring?	How can we make mentoring visible within our departments?	How can we make mentoring visible within our colleges and institutions?	How can we make mentoring visible in our classrooms?
	Reflective Critique	What has our research revealed about the nature of mentoring?	How can we mentor more effectively in the future?	How well have we used the mentoring practices of other fields?	How can we teach others to mentor more effectively in the future?

useful approach is to treat ethics as a reflection of values. We can begin to define mentoring ethics with some direct questions—ones that are easy to ask but more challenging to answer: What do members of our profession value? How can members of our profession exemplify those values in mentoring? So, for example, if we value full-time, permanent faculty positions, then our mentoring should help graduate students secure such positions. If, like Emily Toth, we want "women to have power in academia NOW" (xi), then we should, as Toth does, describe strategies for becoming empowered. If we value scholarly teaching and the scholarship of teaching and learning, then our mentoring should help graduate students to succeed in their teaching. In short, our performance as mentors is unethical if we fail to identify and exemplify our field's values. Further, as Donald Schön warns, when we fail to live by our professional values, we invite and deserve "expressions of disapproval and dissatisfaction" (7).

Of course, deciding what to value in mentoring is just one of the conflicts that we encounter as we strive to mentor (and be mentored) effectively. We must recognize that many times what mentors value may not be what mentees value, and vice versa; we must contend with the principle that values are changing, and that mentoring itself is critiqued for sanctioning elitist behavior. While we may not be able to "solve" conflicts of values outright, we can stress the idea that effective mentoring is flexible and negotiated, personal *and* professional. We must evaluate and assess how our mentoring is (or is not) meeting our mentees' needs. We must diversify mentoring experiences, encouraging cross-gender, cross-discipline, cross-race, cross-sexuality, cross-ability mentoring. We must reward mentoring activities as we would any other scholarly activity, providing faculty reassigned time (especially for those faculty of color and women who are our key mentors in diversifying the future academy, but who often are overloaded with committee work), mentoring credit towards tenure and promotion, and giving public recognition for mentoring activities. We must extend the definition and goals of mentoring—by joining coalitions and committees that address mentoring; by beginning and continuing conversations about how, where, and why mentoring is done (in collections like these, in community forums, in special-interest groups such as the 2004 CCCC SIG "Opening the Gates of Academe through Mentoring: How to Help Students and Colleagues Enter and Succeed" or 2006 session "Generating Mentors in Composition: Beyond the Great Chain of Being"); by not seeing mentoring as a generic process subsuming mentees "into an assumed heterogeneous academic culture" (Okawa 529); by being aware of our own subjectivity—as insiders and outsiders—throughout the mentoring process.

This same kind of flexibility is needed to address other pitfalls and rough spots of mentoring—for example, acknowledging how gender and race dynamics may affect mentoring relationships. We must continue to dialogue honestly about the sticky parts of the web—about stereotypes that sometimes cling to the roles of mentor/mentee in opposite-sex mentor partnerships (such as mother-son/daughter, "father-daughter," or "chivalrous knight-helpless maiden" (Hansman 66); about the "cultural, rhetorical, and linguistic sacrifices [. . .] that some scholars must make to gain entry and achieve full participation as they make their way in academe" (Okawa 508). We must recognize that mentoring is a varied, webbed practice with diverse ends, and work against the isolation and invisibility that many of us feel as we enter graduate school.

WORKS CITED

Boyer, Ernest. *Scholarship Reconsidered: Priorities of the Professoriate*. Princeton, NJ: Carnegie Foundation for the Advancement of Teaching, 1990.

Canton, Marcia E., and David P. James. "Models in Mentoring through Faculty Development." Frierson 77-92.

Daloz, Laurent A. "Mentors: Teachers Who Make A Difference." *Change* 15.6 (1983): 24-27.

Frierson, Jr., Henry T., ed. *Diversity in Higher Education: Mentoring and Diversity in Higher Education*. Greenwich: JAI Press, 1997.

Glassick, Charles, Mary Huber, and Gene Maeroff. *Scholarship Assessed: Evaluation of the Professoriate*. San Francisco: Jossey-Bass, 1997.

Hairston, Maxine. "The Winds of Change: Thomas Kuhn and the Revolution in the Teaching of Writing." *College Composition and Communication* 33 (February 1982): 76-89.

Hansman, Catherine. "Mentoring and Women's Career Development." *Women's Career Development Across the Lifespan: Insight and Strategies for Women, Organizations, and Adult Educators*. Ed. Laura L. Bierema. San Francisco: Jossey-Bass, 1998. 63-71.

Herr, Kay U. "Mentoring Faculty at the Departmental Level." *Mentoring Revisited: Making an Impact on Individuals and Institutions*. Ed. Marie A. Wunsch. San Francisco: Jossey-Bass, 1994. 81-91.

Hood, Stafford L., and Jennifer Boyce. "Refining and Expanding the Role of Professional Associations to Increase the Pool of Faculty Researchers of Color." Frierson 141-60.

Kent, Thomas, ed. *Post-Process Theory: Beyond the Writing-Process Paradigm*. Carbondale: Southern Illinois UP, 1999.

Levinson, Daniel J. *The Seasons of a Man's Life*. New York: Knopf, 1978.

McCormick, Theresa. "An Analysis of Five Pitfalls of Traditional Mentoring for People on the Margins of Higher Education." Frierson 187-202.

Okawa, Gail Y. "Diving for Pearls: Mentoring as Cultural and Activist Practice among Academics of Color." *College Composition and Communication* 53.3 (February 2002): 507-32.

Phillips-Jones, Linda. *Mentors and Protégés*. New York: Arbor House, 1982.

Schein, Edgar H. *Career Dynamics: Matching Individual and Organizational Needs*. Reading: Addison-Wesley, 1978.

Schön, Donald A. *Educating the Reflective Practitioner: Toward a New Design for Teaching and Learning in the Professions*. San Francisco: Jossey-Bass, 1991.

Shulman, Lee. "From Minsk to Pinsk: Why a Scholarship of Teaching and Learning." *The Journal of Scholarship of Teaching and Learning (JoSoTL)*. 1.1 (2000): 48-53. 22 August 2003 <http://www.iusb.edu/~josotl/Vol-1No1/shulman.pdf>.

Toth, Emily. *Ms. Mentor's Impeccable Advice for Women in Academia*. Philadelphia: Pennsylvania UP, 1997.

Zeldich Jr. Morris. "Mentor Roles in Graduate Studies." Frierson 23-40.

16 Mentor or Magician: Reciprocities, Existing Ideologies, and Reflections of a Discipline

Barbara Cole and Arabella Lyon

Within the mentoring literature, mentors are most often described in the frame of youthful Telemachus' wise and overseeing friend, Mentor, who is repeatedly described as a capable senior giving to a callow youth.[1] Although some attention is devoted to the tensions between mentors and their juniors,[2] few acknowledge what the mentor receives from the relationship beyond a feeling of generosity or "doing good" in the world. This frame of mentoring proves too simple as it is insufficiently self-reflexive. After all, the original Mentor who was to maintain Odysseus's household and educate his son failed, and Penelope's suitors were running the estate when the father returned. One's reasons for mentoring, its outcomes, and the nature of the relationship are far from simple.[3]

In this essay, we examine our acts of mentoring graduate and undergraduate students within the composition curriculum. We are most concerned with graduate students learning to teach and their relationships to mentors who inevitably have more complex motivation than simply giving, but we are also concerned with undergraduates learning to write. While we may blur the definitions of teaching and mentoring occasionally, we examine a specific set of obstacles to forming mentoring relationships within an English composition practicum. Beginning graduate students who resist composition pedagogies have complex motivations for their refusals, but such resistance can be a source of growth for mentors and new teachers alike. We believe that the conflict in the teaching of English teaching assistants (TAs) can be applied to other disciplines.

At the crux of any discussion of preparing graduate students for teaching writing is the question of ideological indoctrination. Much of the literature on TA training suggests that this indoctrination occurs during graduate student education and professionalization. In "Resisting The Faith: Conversion, Resistance, and The Training of Teachers," Nancy Welsh discusses the dangers of "convergent theory of teacher instruction" (387). Building on Wendy Bishop's work on the need for congruence between a teacher's preexisting attitudes toward composition and the changes she is asked to make in her pedagogical approaches, Welsh demonstrates that still, in certain seminars, students are forced to speak the discourse of specific composition schools; their practices are curtailed by faculty who circumscribe methods of composition instruction. Marcy Taylor and Jennifer Holberg, in a historical study of TA training discourses, analyze the disciplining and figuring of the teaching assistant. Drawing on Ken Macrorie's ten case studies of graduate experiences ("Tales of Sadism and Neglect"), Taylor and Holberg similarly focus on the process of defining and training graduate teachers as a source of tension. The education of graduate students, then, is seen as a process of indoctrination rather than one of mentoring. So, too, the TA practicum is sometimes viewed as a scene of violence and/or conversion as opposed to a site of mentoring.

Instead of focusing on what happens during the teaching seminar, we instead suggest that problematic ideologies and disciplinary tensions are well-established before the graduate student begins preparation for teaching. Like Bishop, we are interested in the context of teacher education, but we define the context more broadly than attitudes toward composition. The tensions, refusals, and frustrations of the TA classroom are not necessarily created by the pedagogy of the teaching practicum, but rather arise from broader disciplinary and intellectual beliefs that affect the faculty member as well as the students. The four ideological tensions that we identify as most prevalent arise symptomatically as "problems" of English study as new graduate teachers are forced to negotiate the disciplinary terrain without the experience of the discipline. In remaining unspoken and unidentified, these ideologies reverberate as pedagogical deflections throughout the graduate students' teaching and professional life. Consequently, such ideologies become both the causes and effects of disciplinary attitudes toward teaching at large.

Incorporating Althusser's distinction that ideology inscribes the imagined representations of the real, we interpret TA behaviors as indicative of already-established indoctrination into ideologies at both institutional and disciplinary levels. In a perverse manner, the tensions that trouble beginning teachers are symptoms both of their successful identification with certain aspects of the discipline as well as their struggle with other repressed aspects of the discipline.

Beginning teachers, we find, arrive in their graduate program already having accepted, in varying degrees, the following four binaries:

1. romantic notions of creativity and genius over models of pedagogy and process;
2. the necessity of perfect competence over the incompetence that is part of learning;
3. the reification of literature against fear and loathing of the student text; and,
4. the valuing of theoretical enterprise over praxis.

The first two ideological tensions are connected in that they reflect the teaching assistant's identity through her conceptions of the *writerly self* and *teacherly self.* Hard as it is to develop a professional sensibility, these two tensions are complicated by the inherent political challenges of representing the *writerly* and *teacherly* selves within a discipline and the academy. The second two tensions are subsets of the larger doctrine privileging research over teaching, and, because they are so broadly imagined and so supported by an institutional base, are the more recalcitrant to address. All four ideologies are fostered by the values of departments of literature which remains the dominant field in language departments, such as English. Of course, there are other ideologies at work in departments and the academy, and English departments outside of Research I or II status tend toward a more complex understanding of the relationship between the discipline and undergraduate education. Most graduate students, however, have only limited access to these alternative worldviews. Hence, these four ideologies are chosen as representative for their continual influence in the teaching practicum as evidenced in TA writing, articles on composition theory, and class discussion.

These four ideological tensions also haunt the lives of many faculty. As graduate students have less experience to draw upon and because faculty often project their anxieties on to those they mentor, TAs are thereby subjected to the ideological tensions that faculty may evade, deny, and repress due to their privilege within the institution. Simply put, faculty have more choices in what they teach and how they teach it. They can assess student products and avoid process assignments, stay within fields of acquired competence, and spend days discussing literature and never mention student texts (or vice versa). This model of the *ideal* teaching situation is readily accepted by undergraduates who literally partake in it for years and are subject to disciplining for failing to participate fully in the reigning ideology. Well-schooled in the hegemonic discourse, the brightest of undergraduates then carry forward this disciplinary apparatus to their own graduate experience.

Moreover, a graduate student's ability to reflect on or negotiate these ideological tensions is further limited by the ambivalent definition of her role. If one is a teaching assistant, is one a teacher, a figure of knowledge or authority, or is one an assistant, an aide to someone whose agency is privileged? As Taylor and Holberg have noted, graduate students are named as "academic other," passed over on the schedule as staff, faculty, or instructor (610-12). It is because of this ambivalent definition of role that beginning teachers need mentoring in ways that allow them to define their place within the discipline. Given their marginal space, how then do graduate students address these four tensions? Do these tensions ultimately hinder or help a graduate student learn to teach and come to success in academic life? If the tensions are addressed, can our teaching (not training) of graduate teachers become mentoring in the rich sense of nurturing their own potentials rather than instilling our values as rhetoricians?

Romantic Notions of Authorship: the Writerly Self versus the Grammarian

The closest tension to the identity of the graduate student herself is her writerly self. From time to time, all writers feel discomfort with the notion of the self as a writer. New graduate students, especially if they are teaching writing for the first time, experience more discomfort. Not only does the role of writer lack clear criteria for success, but the transition to graduate school tests the previously competent undergraduate self. Furthermore, since for many graduates most of their previous writing was assigned essays with clear deadlines and little more than a grade for evaluation, they have had little opportunity to reflect on existing writing strategies or to develop more complex ones. This relative lack of experience with the writing process is made more problematic by their success as writers. The undergraduates who become graduate students have not struggled with cohesion, syntax, or punctuation. As teachers readily acknowledge, their historic success creates cognitive distance from their struggling undergraduates students. Though rarely voiced, when it is we hear graduate students questioning: how do I teach writing process when I am not even sure what my own process is? How do I teach writing process when I simply sit down and do one draft?

Consequently, if her own writing process is opaque, the graduate student has either to build a rich model of writing, accept the romantic model of writing, or teach what is most transparent about writing: the rules of grammar. Without adequate mentoring and modeling, the complexity of approaching, questioning, or, perhaps most threatening, theorizing one's own writing process may result in an acceptance of a romanticized view of writing (which in another seminar would be harshly critiqued) or the pedagogical deflection of focusing on grammar. If process is ineffable and a romantic approach fails to work in the classroom, grammar is documented nicely in the handbook, and no consideration of process (neither the instructor's nor the student's) is required. The notion of standards or rules in this realm is defined and much safer for the new TA who yearns for a regimented curriculum in which she feels her mastery of the material. Furthermore, even freshmen, who fail to accomplish *romantic genius*, can be evaluated. "Everyone should be able to master the grammar of their own language," claims the multilingual graduate student.

A mentor here must make explicit the writing process of the discipline as required in professional outside reviews. As well, she should be able to demonstrate her own approaches, limits, and strategies within the writing process. This act of reflexivity may not change the mentor's practices, but it refocuses her attention upon her own writing as well as all writing to the benefit of both the teacher and the graduate student. The act of making public models of writing makes more complex each choice made within the generation of a text. It forces reflexivity upon the mentor.

Public Confession: The Competence / Incompetence Bind of the Developing Teacher

If, in the freshman classroom, graduate students are asked to make public their model of writing, in the graduate teaching practicum seminar, they are asked to reflect upon their classroom practices; too often, this translates into reflecting on their competence and incompetence as teachers. Well-aware of departmental and institutional valuing of competence, most graduate students fear both the implications and professional ramifications of publicly admitting to not knowing what to do or how to do it. Such fears are hardly unsubstantiated. While the fear of losing one's teaching assistantship usually isn't valid, there are always cases. Though the purpose of a teaching seminar is to foster good teaching, create confidence, nurture the development of articulate theories of pedagogy and only incidentally to prevent any loss of funding, it is unrealistic to expect graduate students to feel so safe. Yet they are asked to reflect upon their practice and indeed must do so in the process of developing their teaching.

Graduate teachers have a variety of defenses against this risk. Silence and retreat, confession, and bragging are the most common. Silence is perhaps the hardest defense to intervene in, but mentors should not make King Lear's mistake and assume that silence is negation. Silence does not mean a graduate teacher is unengaged; simply, she is protecting the imaginary of her competence. The occasional graduate teachers will openly divulge the "dirty secrets" of the classroom, rapt with guilt, shame, defiance, mock bravado, or, even worse, seeming unawareness that the secret shared might be judged unfavorably. We find this posturing makes it difficult to assess practice because what facilitates understanding are not confessions, but careful description, analysis, and offerings of alternative strategies. Other graduate teachers, however, overcompensate by offering public confessions of brilliant teaching moments laden with Hollywood images of what classrooms should look like. Such teachers publicly cast themselves in scenes reminiscent of *To Sir with Love* or *Dead Poet's Society* and silence their incompetency phobias (though they may simultaneously increase those of others). While one is loath to deny moments of brilliant teaching, this defense reduces the possibilities for developing self-reflective teachers, and further limits the disciplinary understanding of what constitutes teaching. Ideally, the mentor repeatedly models description, analysis, and strategy formation, offering real examples from her classrooms for critique. The mentor who demonstrates her own strategies and offers them up for evaluation can move graduate teachers beyond defensiveness and into intellectual engagement with their practice of pedagogy. In this reflexivity, graduate student teachers become open to engaged mentoring, and the mentor's own teaching is subject to public analysis and development.

THE GLORY OF LITERATURE VERSUS FEAR OF STUDENT TEXTS

Our third binary arises from a familiar privileging of poetics over rhetoric and cultural studies.[4] Most first-semester graduate students, though new at teaching, are already fully indoctrinated in the English department's ideology of *belles lettres*. When the new graduate teacher faces difficult student texts, she feels uncertain and may react with what might be understood as a fight or flight response to such a text. Aware that she cannot "fight" the text and her student, the common response then falls under the "flight" category. The graduate student flees student writing by simply deflecting attention elsewhere. This flight from student writing consequently diverts freshman and curricular attention towards literature. Some graduate teachers become convinced that, if only they were armed with the perfect syllabus, text, or lesson plan, they could look out at a class full of eager students engaging classroom discussions and turning in papers of intellectual substance and aesthetic lyricism. The lament is repeated with minimal deviation: "If only I could teach what I work on." The desire to teach literature or theory to freshmen is part of an earlier elite, recalcitrant ideology. While many graduate teachers forsake fiction and are willing to read the right cultural studies texts in the composition classroom, many of these resist embracing student texts and workshop models, preferring to structure syllabi around readings. While most can provide a careful critique of canon, the move to privileging student texts remains a tension even within composition studies as evidenced by the huge market for readers.[5]

Unlike discussions of writing processes and classroom strategies, teaching how to read student texts is less about the identity of the mentor and student. Perhaps here is a moment within the TA practicum when the practicum leaders do not have transparent return on their endeavor as the skilled reading of student texts receives little disciplinary reward. The social positioning, however, is useful because, in broadening the definition of reading within the discipline, the mentor serves her own research and disciplinary purposes. More than simply expanding into new historicism, rhetoric, or cultural studies, recognizing the complexity of developing writers also recognizes the intellectual work of teaching writing.

SEEKING PRAXIS OVER THEORY

While the discipline values theory over practice and literati often are disdainful of composition because of its inadequate theorizing, paradoxically new graduate teachers often complain of inadequate discussion of praxis and too much emphasis on theory in the practicum. After all, the dominant discipline has taught them that the teaching of writing is a transparent and easy undertaking. Furthermore, the application of theory evades many graduate teachers (Leverenz and Goodburn 22). The first-time teacher's response here, again, is akin to the response of the first-year writing student. Just as freshmen protest that the teacher is simply refusing to show them how to write by withholding the secrets of the trade, so, too, new graduate teachers lament: "You know how to teach this; why don't you just show me how?" Just as freshmen protest that the teacher is leaving too large a cognitive gap between the assignment and the paper, the new graduate teacher laments, "This is too time consuming an approach to teaching me how to teach."

Here we identify the latent ideology of the institution as professional training establishment, one in which easy answers are given. While those of us in the humanities would argue for the merit of discussion, process, and dialectic, within this paradoxical tension, the teaching graduate student is cast into the service frame of the university and responds with the voice of the service university. Like students of nursing or accounting, they ask for precise knowledge within a defined pattern of praxis. While they are skilled in the methods of the humanities, the tensions in the new, corporate university lead some away from humanistic practices. Adequate mentoring and practicum teaching require direct address to the political context of teaching writing and public recognition of the intellectual and financial sacrifices assistantships demand of students. Acknowledging the complicity of all faculty in the exploitive system is an important step in building a meaningful mentoring relationship, but the difficulty of acknowledging one's own place in the system exceed the command of many faculty.

Faced with these four tensions between the belief system of a teaching practicum and that of the literary seminar, between the enterprise of teaching and that of institution, how should we proceed in the teaching practicum? Faced with the tensions between giving and receiving within a mentoring relationship, how can mentors lead learning? What theoretical understanding might improve the classroom practices of the seminar and the composition class? What would make the ideological dynamics in the discipline productive rather than destructive to teaching?

What might real mentoring look like? The following story, from Cole's first semester of teaching, seeks to remind us of the enigmatic, magical aspects of learning, and to acknowledge that all players in this drama—mentors, new teachers, and first-year undergraduates alike—manifest some desire for easy answers within the classroom.

One afternoon, Cole recalls, a student appeared at my office hours, asking if we could "just talk." For ten minutes, we reviewed his most recent revision, before his comments drifted to freshman frustrations. What appeared at first to be typical complaints of dorm life, however, became more urgent, almost a monologic meditation on everything from the American education system to capitalism. "I never questioned any of this before" he confided as he proceeded to talk about his parents' decision to leave their lives in communist China in the hope of giving their son better opportunities in the land of the American Dream. "I feel like I have to make money to make them proud," he lamented, "and now I see that there is something wrong in that goal."

And so the scene plays out: the teacher is cast as pedagogue or priest, compelled to absolve the American-ness of student's ideas, to free him of his guilt. "So what's the answer?" he asks. It is, of course, an impossible question, rendered even more impossible by the sincerity in his eyes, his hopeful expectation for a concrete solution. This desire, this hope, this moment, might be the most difficult part of teaching or mentoring. We problematize, we question, we complicate, we push. Even more, we ask—no, we require—that our students problematize, question, complicate, and push. And then, after all of this questioning, we are left to say: there is no answer.

Understandably frustrated by the seeming evasion of this response, the student gets up to leave only to turn back at the door. "Can I do some magic for you?" he asks, a grin replacing the despair which gripped him moments ago. Without waiting for a response, he whips a deck of cards from his pocket and launches into a series of tricks which, surprisingly, prove mesmerizing. Shuffling the deck like a veteran card shark, he performs his tricks with the panache of a true magician, complete with hand flourishes, dramatic flair, and a performer's sense of timing and repetition. "Did you see it?" he asks each time he makes a card disappear. The pace is frenzied despite my cliché outbursts demanding, "How did you do that?" Unphased, he proceeds with his trickery, smiling sheepishly in the face of my frustration. "Remember this," he commands each time he holds up a card. "Queen of Hearts." "Remember this: Ace of Spades." Though I am embarrassed by my girlish fascination, I remain too distracted with gleeful astonishment to assume my more teacherly stance. Momentarily abandoning my professional decorum, I am more concerned with understanding how this is happening. I truly want to know how he does it. But, each time I urge him to reveal his process, he plays humble, shrugs his shoulders, and squelches his proud grin by launching into a different trick before I can stop marveling at the last. "I wanted to show you something I was good at," he finally explains, "because English is something I've never been good at." Nodding, I implore him to do the same trick over and over again but slower—as if by analyzing it or seeing it one more time, I might be able to understand. "No, really," I insist, "I want to know." But he just flashes a knowing smile, reversing the tables: "Remember? It's like you said. There's no answer."

This anecdote offers particular insights into the mentoring relationship, reminding us that, as teachers, we are all faced with the difficult realization that "there are no answers." But, so too, it is useful to remember, we are all still very much students, insisting "I want to know." Remember this: each new teacher wants to know how we do it and no amount of reading theory seems to translate immediately into flawless praxis. In the teaching of graduate students, conversion to our personal visions of English is a fantasy, and the integration of beliefs is a comfortable goal, but both are non-productive, failing to create the hybridity, the recognitions and fissures which produce the new. This tale is a crucial reminder that the desire of new teachers to know easily and quickly is no different than the first-year student's desire for formulaic answers and basic how-to solutions to the complex question of how to write, and it is little different from the experienced mentor's desire for easy transitions for new teachers. The process of becoming is a process of struggle and trailblazing. Finally remember:

at the anecdote's end, the student's offering to the relationship is extra-disciplinary, outside the institutionally-defined relationship. Cole's gains—and she has gains in both understanding and satisfaction—come from actions that are not embedded in ideological and institutional structures.

The goal of a teaching seminar must not be conversion to the reigning ideologies of composition (as Welsh already warned us); it is too cheap a trick. Neither graduate students nor faculty benefit by conversion or adherence to static beliefs in various forms of composition theory. This is not to say that professors of rhetoric and composition do not have knowledge, but that the evolution of knowledge requires an open forum, tricks performed slowly enough that they can be apprehended as method, not trick. Difficult as it is, it is more productive to ask beginning graduate students to embrace the multiple identities expected of them in the discipline, to speak in multiple tongues, and ultimately to achieve the rich identity as scholar and teacher. While this offers a richer sense of what English means, it is not an approach without problems for—if this is done without full disclosure and discussion—it diminishes the graduate students' agency within their education. Furthermore, without full disclosure of the fissures, we limit the potential for a full, conscious engagement with the heterogeneity that is "English" and so diminish the possibility of disciplinary change.

Appropriate interventions in these ideological tensions require foregrounding the tensions themselves, unsettling the complacency and common assumptions of both sides, opening possibilities of experiment and transition, and in doing so, creating multiple models of classrooms. That is, in fostering ideological critique, we conceive the new disciple of English as a pre-political subject ready and able to enter the antagonistic process of becoming politically aware of the tensions within the discipline, both between literature and composition and within composition studies. In seeking a more dynamic and complex subjectivity, we would offer the new teacher (and ourselves) a model based on Homi Bhabha's "enunciatory subject," the speaker who creates and is created. In turning to postcolonial theory, we do not wish to collapse the distinctions between nationalism and disciplinarity, but we do want a materialist and historical model of subjectivity and identity, one responsive to the problems of power, hierarchy, and ideology. In discussing hybridity in identity formation, Bhabha writes:

> In the enunciatory subject—which is a subject in per-
> formance and process, the notion of what is to be
> authorized, what is to be deauthorized, what will be
> signified, what similarity or similitude will be articu-
> lated—these things are continually happening in the
> very process of discourse-making or meaning-making.
> They are not subjects which are already given to the
> process of enunciation. The most important thing
> about the process of enunciation as a kind of border-
> line concept is that the borders between objects or sub-
> jects or practices are being constituted. (qtd. in Olson
> 19)

The practicum should be open to the hybridity of the discipline and,
furthermore, understand speaking as constituting the practices of the
discipline, speaking as authorizing and deauthorizing disciplinary
ideologies as well as disciplinary subjectivity. Ideally seminar speakers—faculty and graduate students—can find generative borders and
fissures within composition and literature. Hybridity—so easily said,
so obviously part of the postmodern English department—offers an
alternative means of intervening in the ideological tension, but one
that offers more risks to the subjects and the practices of teaching than
conversion.

Early on, graduate students need to see and grapple with the institutional ideologies. Through such a process, they become disciplined
in productive rather than restrictive ways. As Homi Bhabha teaches
us, "any change in a statement's conditions of use and reinvestment,
any alteration in its field of experience or verification, or indeed any
difference in the problems to be solved, can lead to the emergence
of a new statement: the difference of the same" (22). If we wish for a
practicum in writing to generate a real knowledge and commitment to
the politics of education, if we want to mentor in ways that allow our
students to develop beyond us, if we want to benefit from mentoring,
we must engage the "dissensus, alterity, and otherness" implicit in
training across disciplinary apparatuses (23). If mentoring new graduate students creates a space where one is neither compositionist nor
literati, then our political possibilities are opened. Our conflicting interests, discourses, and even our identities are visible for examination,
critique, and transformation and evade ritualized reproductions. After
all, pedagogy, like writing and magic, is an evolving process that re-

quires openness to improvisation, welcomes the possibility of surprise, and offers unique enunciatory potential.

Mentors cannot simply, with a wave of their hands, pull accomplished teachers out of the proverbial magic hat; nor can they claim to be unaffected by whatever magical moments arise within the mentoring relationship. The trick, in the end, is not that the TA comes to understand that there are no simple answers to the question of how to teach. Rather, the real trick emerges in the act of reciprocity: the mentor comes to understand that she has been mentoring herself all along as much as the teacher-in-training. The mentor has not forced her assistant into a box only to then disappear, but they both—mentor and TA alike—have, quite magically, reappeared in new and wonderful ways.

NOTES

1. See Faye Crosby's "The Developing Literature on Developmental Relationships" for 18 definitions based on a senior interested in the progress of a junior colleague (12-13).

2. For example, Mara Holt and Albert Rouzie are unusually forthcoming about tensions within a healthy mentoring relationship. W. Brad Johnson and Charles R. Ridley even advocate "idealization" in mentoring, but they include a chapter "When Things Go Wrong" (109-124).

3. Andy Roberts has a lively discussion about this misreading of Mentor.

4. Rhetoric and poetics: the tensions and hopes documented in Winifred Horner's *Composition and Literature* (1983) have changed little.

5. What is perhaps agreed upon in composition studies is that the high text is used not as a model, but as a lesson in reading as an academic and an engaged author (Elbow 380, Salvatori 661).

WORKS CITED

Althusser, Louis. "Ideology and Ideological State Apparatuses." *Lenin and Philosophy*. London: NLB, 1971. 121-73.

Bhabha, Homi. *The Location of Culture*. London: Routledge, 1994.

Bishop, Wendy. *Something Old, Something New: College Writing Teachers and Classroom Change*. Carbondale: Southern Illinois UP, 1990.

Crosby, Faye J. "The Developing Literature on Developmental Relationships." *Mentoring Dilemmas: Developmental Relationships within Multicultural Organizations*. Ed. Audrey J. Murrell, Faye J. Crosby, and Robin J. Ely. Mahwah, NJ: Erlbaum, 1999. 3-20.

Elbow, Peter. *Everyone Can Write: Essays toward a Hopeful Theory of Writing and Teaching Writing*. New York: Oxford UP, 2000.

Holt, Mara, and Albert Rouzie. "Collaboration and Conflict in a Faculty Mentoring Relationship." *Dialogue: A Journal for Writing Specialists* 8 (2003): 75-95.

Horner, Winifred, ed. *Composition and Literature: Bridging the Gap*. Chicago: U of Chicago P, 1983.

Johnson, W. Brad, and Charles R. Ridley. *The Elements of Mentoring*. New York: Palgrave, 2004.

Leverenz, Carrie Shively, and Amy Goodburn. "Professionalizing TA Training: Commitment to Teaching or Rhetorical Response to Market Crisis?" *Writing Program Administration* 22 (1998): 9-33.

Olson, Gary A., and Lynn Worsham. *Race, Rhetoric, and the Postcolonial*. Albany: SUNY P, 1999.

Roberts, Andy. "Homer's Mentor: Duties Fulfilled and Miscontrued?" 1999. 22 June 2008 <http://home.att.net/~nickols/homers_mentor.htm>.

Salvatori, Mariolina. "Reading and Writing a Text: Correlations between Reading and Writing Patterns." *College English* 45 (1983): 657-66.

Taylor, Marcy, and Jennifer L. Holberg. "'Tales of Neglect and Sadism': Disciplinarity and the Figuring of the Graduate Student in Composition." *College Composition and Communication* 50 (1999): 607-25.

Welsh, Nancy. "Resisting the Faith: Conversion, Resistance, and The Training of Teachers." *College English* 55 (1993): 387-401.

17 Transformative Mentoring: Thinking Critically about the Transition from Graduate Student to Faculty through a Graduate-Level Teaching Experience Program

Amy C. Kimme Hea and Susan N. Smith

The first step in transitioning from graduate teaching associate to graduate faculty happens with the signing of a contract, but meeting the challenge of teaching, rather than taking, graduate classes is a slower process, one that requires reflection and continual negotiation. In their 1997 graduate student survey, Scott L. Miller, Brenda Jo Brueggemann, Bennis Blue, and Deneen M. Shepherd reported the bad news that graduate student informants felt under-prepared for their future lives as faculty (397). As graduate programs continue to thrive and others develop, the range and type of graduate courses also grows. From teaching MA and PhD students to building graduate-level teaching practica for students and adjuncts, many newly conferred PhDs will be responsible for organizing courses beyond the undergraduate courses where they gained most of their teaching experience. Graduate teaching requires the selection and introduction of theories and practices, the establishment of relationships with students who are in process of becoming future fellow faculty, and even attention to different forms of writing than most of us teach in our undergraduate courses. These requirements are not only key to the development of a graduate-level course, but they also represent many pressing issues, including knowledge creation, reflective practice, authority, power, and literacy. In other words, introducing graduate students to the demands of graduate-level teaching is not simply a matter of providing a simulation of their future teaching position but rather a means of challenging our own institutional practices and structures.

To get at such issues of graduate-level teaching and to provide another mentoring opportunity in the University of Arizona Rhetoric, Composition, and the Teaching of English (RCTE) Program, Dr. Amy Kimme Hea, a then second-semester graduate faculty member, developed a graduate-level student teaching apprentice pilot program. Working together to pursue the development of graduate-level teaching, Kimme Hea and Sue Smith, an ABD graduate student in RCTE, co-taught a graduate-level spatial and visual rhetorics course, English 696e. Drawing on our mentoring relationship, we discuss some of the problematics raised by our pilot—particularly issues of power and authority. We argue that although—or even because of—such issues, we believe mentoring graduate students to design and teach graduate-level courses is important to their professional development and to our own fields' shared commitment to strive for reflective praxis. Knowing that our local context at the University of Arizona (UA) shaped our pilot program, we examine our own institutional mentoring situation. To do so, we draw on James Porter, Patricia Sullivan, Stuart Blythe, Jeffrey Grabill, and Libby Miles' (610-642) concept of institutional critique to analyze the apprenticeship proposal, the graduate course materials, some classroom moments of the apprenticeship, and the reflective documents directly related to our mentoring. In our examination, we investigate the "zones of ambiguity, or spaces that house change, difference, or a clash of values or meanings" related to our own mentoring experiences (Porter et al. 624). Through this analysis, we hope to create a broader and deeper understanding of the larger role of mentoring, especially in relationship to advanced teaching opportunities. Our discussion concludes with key points about our own insights into the transition from graduate student to graduate faculty.[1]

Mentoring

The UA's writing program has well-established, formal mentoring opportunities. All new and returning graduate teaching assistantships (GATs) are assigned to preceptorship groups led by teaching advisors (TEADs) in the writing program. Throughout their first year, graduate students attend weekly preceptorship meetings that offer ongoing pedagogical support to develop critical, reflective teaching practices. After this first year of preceptorship, experienced GATs report to a TEAD and receive annual TEAD reports based upon classroom observations, but they are not required to attend weekly meetings, just one pre-semester orientation session each semester. These positions provide experienced GATs a chance to work with placement, enrollment, curricula, pedagogy, technology, and teacher development programs, in addition to special projects. A few GATs work as junior WPAs, and they participate, more or less fully, in teacher development, policy making, and other WPA duties (Barr-Ebest 215; Gunner 315-330; McNabb 40-87; Micciche 432-458; Weiser 45-49). In her study of graduate student WPAs, Catherine Latterell squarely situates her mission as "productively defin[ing] graduate student WPAs' roles and responsibilities (and rethink[ing] our own) through postmodern ethics of action that casts authority as dynamic yet responsive" (33). Citing the flexibility of power, authority, and knowledge-making in a postmodern ethics of action, Latterell urges members of our field to see that graduate student-faculty collaborations and reflective practices lend themselves to the development of critical, ethical writing programs. Latterell astutely asserts that junior WPA work should lead to a critical questioning of our writing program practices. In fact, our own graduate student teaching apprenticeship was both an attempt to extend, and perhaps even challenge, the mentoring options in our graduate program and a means to investigate sites of power, authority, and knowledge that are embedded in our graduate-level teaching practices.

INSTITUTIONAL CRITIQUE

One aspect of the transition from graduate student to faculty member is negotiating new institutional pressures and demands. In our view, institutions are physical locations and the practices that exist within those sites. From the brick and mortar buildings to offices and classrooms, these physical spaces affect our academic lives and figure our relationships to institutional practices such as teaching, tenure, and promotion, among others. Even though institutions are both material and figural, they are not fixed or stable. Because institutions are represented through discursive and material practices, we academics have opportunities to change institutions through our practices. Porter et al. aptly discuss the complex roles institutions play in our lives noting that "institutions are certainly powerful, they are not monoliths; they are rhetorically constructed human designs (whose power is reinforced by buildings, laws, traditions, and knowledge-making practices) and so are changeable" (611). Mentoring, as we have noted, is arguably an "institution" in our own field and many others, but despite its widely accepted status as a professional practice, mentoring is not stable, fixed, and unchanging. We acknowledge that although certain mentoring practices—aid with publication, teacher development, and administrative training—are widespread across our graduate programs, the theories grounding these practices are not universal. We believe, then, that to understand better the implications of mentoring as an institution, we must examine mentoring practices in their local context. Taking mentoring as an institution in the sense that Porter, et al. suggest, we want to locate the opportunities for agency and change that are located between the official "map" of mentoring and our lived experiences as mentor and mentee. To do so, we will interrogate the gaps of the discursive and material spaces of our graduate student apprentice pilot as it was constructed through a range of documents and moments. As Jeffrey T. Grabill, James E. Porter, Stuart Blythe, and Libby Miles state in their return to institutional critique, "documents can be revised, and because their wording can influence subsequent decisions, change may be possible." (225). To begin analyzing options for change, we want to examine some of the central texts of our pilot and their relationship to the ways we experienced the apprenticeship. The documents we consider include the apprenticeship proposal, the course materials, and our reflective reports. We also draw upon classroom moments that highlight different aspects of our mentoring. These sites of inquiry reveal both the tension of integrating a new aspect of mentoring in our local culture and the zones of ambiguity—spaces where values clash—in the discursive formations of our mentoring relationship. Before we turn to the documents and their connection to our lived experiences in the apprenticeship, we provide information about our own local mentoring context in UA's Writing and RCTE programs as well as insight into our relationship prior to participating in the apprenticeship pilot together.

Local Context

The RCTE Program also offers a range of formal mentoring activities in addition to undergraduate teaching and WPA activities. Peer and faculty mentors are assigned for all new GATs in the program, and weekly colloquia are used to discuss program and professional issues. In addition, the RCTE Program Handbook (2005-2006) defines chairing exams and working on dissertations as mentoring students in our program. Finally, all RCTE students share a written annual review with the RCTE Director. RCTE faculty and graduate students alike see these mentoring activities as a way to foster community. However, the range of local mentoring opportunities caters to the "first-year experience." In our local context of mentoring, our graduate student teaching apprenticeship was unique: It was an effort to engage an advanced RCTE graduate student in a formal mentoring opportunity.

We had an informal mentoring relationship that grew out of our roles as graduate student and faculty in a previous graduate course. As we read in that course, a mutual respect developed. When the apprenticeship pilot was approved, we thought our collaboration would be ideal because of the focus of the course, spatial and visual rhetorics, and our already well-established working relationship. We reasoned that the apprenticeship would offer Sue an opportunity to discuss visual rhetoric readings—her research area—with an interested group of colleagues, provide Amy a chance to discuss course development with an invested colleague, and give other members of the course an opportunity to share in course discussion with a professor and an advanced student. The even broader benefits of the apprenticeship would be its ability to challenge our local construction of mentoring and our understanding of graduate-level teaching.

Proposal

Despite Amy's status as a new graduate faculty member at UA, she had experience teaching graduate courses—English 502I: Computers and Composition Mentoring and English 502M: Professional Writing Mentoring—as a graduate student administrator in Purdue University's composition and professional writing programs. These teaching situations were part of Purdue University's ongoing teacher mentoring. Once responsible for teaching these computer composition and professional writing mentoring practica, Amy understood the value of preparing and teaching graduate courses. In his essay on Purdue's writing program, Irwin Weiser acknowledges the potential complications of having graduate students teach other graduate students, but he also argues that "mentoring is professional development, of a kind not available through class work, and as such, I believe it has an important role to play in the preparation of soon-to-be-faculty" (47). Having experienced the benefits of such a program, Amy was committed to integrating some aspect of her own formative experiences teaching graduate courses in her new position as a graduate faculty member. The development of an apprenticeship pilot seemed one such option.

To begin providing the type of reflective graduate teaching experience that she had valued, Amy created the apprenticeship proposal with Sue's input. This proposal was presented to and approved as a pilot program by the RCTE program faculty and two RCTE graduate student representatives at a monthly meeting. The document outlines "1) the goals and structure of the graduate-level student teaching apprenticeship and 2) measures to balance the graduate student apprenticeship and his or her dissertation progress" (Apprenticeship Proposal). Knowing that UA graduate students rarely earned the right to teach even 400-level courses, we attempted to situate this mentoring opportunity within the boundaries of the UA's culture, stressing certain safeguards in terms of graduate student workload and class member rights. Weighing too heavily on effectively managing the graduate student position, our proposal objectifies graduate students and usurps their power to negotiate their own workload requirements and their relationship with other graduate students. In effect, this document reifies certain top-down models of mentoring that we had hoped to disrupt.

This language of protection also is found in descriptions of the graduate student apprentice and the graduate students taking the course. For example, in a note, the proposal states, "At no time will the graduate student grade or evaluate his or her fellow graduate student colleagues enrolled in the course" (Apprenticeship Proposal). Despite one of the goals of the apprenticeship being to provide a critical view on graduate-level teaching, we see that the proposal attempts to attend to program constraints rather than advocate for critical inquiry. The document, in effect, was written to anticipate concerns from faculty and graduate students in terms of workload, and it tried to speak to the worst-case scenario, preventing the most obvious cases of abuse of power from faculty or student. Through the language of protection, however, our proposal mistakenly identifies power as a "possession" of the faculty member to be "borrowed" by the graduate student apprentice. Rather than identifying the complexities of negotiating power

and authority within our own local context and positing a more complicated view of the classroom and our roles within it, our proposal
reaffirms the hierarchical relationships of mentor-mentee and faculty-
student that we were trying to bring into question.

Following the Modern Language Association's (MLA) "Advice
to Graduate Programs," which states that graduate programs should
"provide adequate training, including course work, workshops, or *apprenticeship* programs" (55, emphasis added), the proposal defined our
pilot as an *apprenticeship*. Later in the final vote on adopting the apprenticeship as part of our mentoring line-up, our English Graduate
Student Union (EGU) representatives on the RCTE faculty committee conferred with their constituency about the proposal's adoption.
The EGU is made up of graduate students from all the department
programs, and it represents students' interests in most of our departmental committees, including our program committees. In its final
deliberations on the apprenticeship, the EGU supported the effort to
provide graduate students with this type of experience. They agreed to
vote for the measure in the RCTE committee. This group, however,
argued for a change in the language of the apprenticeship, calling for
our mentoring to be titled, "Graduate-Level Student Teaching Experience" (GLSTE) (personal conversation, Thomas J. Kinney, September
30, 2003). Because of the underlying metaphor of indentured servi-
tude in apprenticeship, projecting long hours in service at no pay, and
perhaps the unvoiced metaphor of the master, graduate students right-
ly requested this name change. We agree that this shift in language is
positive, and it more closely reflects the need to see power relations
as constructed through discursive spaces, such as the proposal. We
also note, however, that this name change to "graduate-level student
teaching experience" has its own complication of leaving no specific
"name" for the graduate student role. The naming raises important
issues of the type of teaching and mentoring relationships which we
are comfortable with, ones that typically do not take into account the
collaborative goals of this mentoring option. From this point on in our
work, we will refer to the apprenticeship as GLSTE, demonstrating
our commitment to the shared goals of collaborative teaching.

COURSE DOCUMENTS

Another discursive location where issues of power and authority are
revealed in the GLSTE is in the course materials themselves. Working

to construct this new course to accommodate issues of spatial and visuals rhetorics, we collected a wide range of articles and books from
many disciplinary areas, totaling more than 200 potential spatial and
visual articles, books, and other resources. As part of the experience,
faculty and graduate student participants share in the creation of the
course with the faculty member providing insight into her decision-
making about policies, projects, course readings, and other aspects of
graduate-level teaching. The graduate student and faculty member are
asked to negotiate course days where the graduate student will teach
the course, preparing course readings and activities and defining other
aspects of the daily plan (Apprenticeship Proposal). In preparation
for our first negotiation meeting, Amy had created a possible line up
of course readings, projects, and policies. We discussed that plan, re-
vamping certain aspects of the projects, and we identified the days
when Sue would teach the course. That allowed us to place readings
into those particular course days to serve Sue's interests. Our other
planning meetings also reflected the respect we share for one another,
and we talked about course learning objectives, certain theories, writing projects, the sequence of projects, their evaluation, the range of
readings, the schedule, and other resources.

Our own behind-the-scenes collaborations, however, are not
well represented in the course materials (See http://www.u.arizona.
edu/~kimmehea/svrhet/svrhet.htm for the course website). That is,
while we grappled with the material and discussed the seemingly in-
finite possibilities of texts and projects, the course policies page reifies the power hierarchy and division of faculty and graduate student.
From the policies page:

> We are pilot testing a new component of the RCTE
> program in our course, the graduate student appren-
> ticeship. This opportunity is being developed to offer
> advanced graduate students the chance to learn how
> to plan and teach graduate-level courses. Sue Smith is
> our graduate student apprentice. Based upon her own
> research interest in visual rhetoric, Sue will offer her
> expertise to our class. (Kimme Hea, "Course")

Much like the proposal's efforts to *protect* the graduate student participant and those graduate students taking the course, this part of
the policy statement serves to diminish the collaborative, reflective

teaching practices that we had already engaged in when planning the course. We did include an extensive bibliography of resources that we did not directly integrate into the course readings, but this page of resources could have been better defined as the result of our collaborative efforts, providing a meta-discussion on the development of the class and our choices. Even though the GLSTE was designed to offer a new type of teaching opportunity to an advanced graduate student, it was not intended to place the student or the faculty member in a rigid, hierarchical relationship as this part of the syllabus seems to denote.

By the time the semester began, we had many hours invested in the course. Some institutional practices of the local program were unknown to us at the time and unanticipated in the proposal or course materials. This new course did not easily fit into the RCTE course requirement schema. Most entering RCTE students come with MA degrees in hand, and their MA coursework often fills the elective slots in RCTE requirements. The entering student can expect to take courses for about two years to complete all the required courses. Our course was an oddity: a topic new to the field and an elective in programmatic terms, and so its potential constituency was limited from the beginning. We were lucky, however, that the minimum number of students enrolled, but we had other constraints in terms of timing. The course met on Mondays, and due to both UA's spring semester which always begins mid-week and the Martin Luther King Holiday, we did not meet as a class until the third week of the semester. Our course was unusually placed in terms of our credit structures, time, and location—a basement room with no windows, no conference table, a low ceiling, and minimal technology (one old-fashioned overhead projector). Our ideal of beginning collaboratively with students was tainted by these institutional and material spaces.

Despite our efforts to create a space in the class for collaborative engagement, we noted in the first weeks a resistance to our co-teaching positions. We had reviewed the syllabus, which had been provided weeks in advance of our first class meeting, and we discussed in some detail the GLSTE and our rationales for piloting it. We asked for student input and suggestions related to our pilot. Students knew that Sue would be attending class, reading the material, and leading the discussion during two sessions. The resistance manifested itself in students asserting an allegiance to one or the other of us, varying over the semester. This *choosing* became evident in the material space of the classroom. Until midway in the semester, we sat next to one another during class. When students spoke, it seemed they were addressing both of us. On Sue's second teaching day, however, she elected to sit across the room from Amy. One student physically turned to face Amy, leaving Sue to talk to the student's back for most of the session. Despite the fact that Sue had framed the course day and was leading the discussion, this student defined Amy as the teacher for that day. Another student brought in off-topic material, demanding discussion, but only on Sue's teaching days. While we attempted to handle the situations with some grace, these episodes underline the power of students to resist shared models of authority and the complications of our GLSTE for other members of the course, who enrolled without involvement or investment in the process. Classroom management is generally no problem for Sue, then a 9-year veteran of college teaching, but she became acutely aware that any unpleasantness reflected not only on her, but on Amy. Any negativity might play out in Amy's course evaluations, once again underlining the ambiguous nature of power in the classroom. Even though we had hoped our efforts to negotiate the complexities of the classroom and instantiate a shared model of expertise and authority would encourage student involvement in the topic and format of the course, we learned that students had a challenging task to situate themselves in relationship to two teachers, and some did so more easily than others.

We understand this resistance as part of the complicated definition of graduate faculty. Many graduate students feel they have a great deal more at stake in their course work beyond the material being covered in the classes. Graduate students are aware that they will continue to work with faculty as they take more courses, prepare for exams, establish committees for their major projects, apply for teaching and administrative opportunities in the program, and go on the job market. Graduate students may look for small ways of resisting having to negotiate with two teachers, much less one. More surprisingly, however, we found this resistance to be absent from the course evaluations, which highly ranked the class material and teaching. In our reflections on the course, we discussed the moments of classroom tension and their absence in the course evaluations as a point of reference for the pressures that come in negotiating the graduate course, issues of expertise, exercise of power, and constructions of authority.

REFLECTIONS

The third discursive site is our post-experience reflections. As part of the GLSTE proposal, we each were assigned to write a reflective memo to the Director of the RCTE program. Our memos discuss, in much more positive terms, the relationship of mutual teaching we developed through the pilot program. In fact, the discursive space of our reflections more accurately demonstrates the value we found in the pilot program.

In her memo, Amy asserts that "Articulating my rationales for readings and categories of the course planning was incredibly valuable to my formulation of project objectives and lesson plans for the course" and later that "This sort of productive discussion continued throughout the semester [. . .]. Sue and I discussed the class dynamics and reading selections, brainstorming ways of approaching certain types of questions and thinking about possible revisions to the reading line-up if she or I decide to teach a similar course in the future" (personal correspondence, Amy C. Kimme Hea, May 13, 2003). These statements demonstrate Amy's commitment to a collaborative relationship between the faculty mentor and graduate student mentee. We also see in this memo the respect we shared as we came into this project, and the respect we developed through a more critical view on graduate faculty as both mentor and teacher. In the close of her memo, Amy suggests that members of the RCTE program should expect

> the graduate-level student teacher to take on quite a bit of responsibility negotiating the material for the course and the unique relationship of being "in-between"— not quite a student like the other graduate students and not quite a professor like the course instructor [. . .]. I believe the apprenticeship provided an effective means to reflect critically upon graduate-level teaching and to introduce a graduate student to concerns that are not typical of undergraduate teaching—that is, preparing students to be your future colleagues. (personal correspondence, Amy C. Kimme Hea, May 13, 2003)

Sue's reflection also discussed the benefits of the GLSTE to her scholarship, particularly the opportunity to read in her area of specialization with an interested group. Usually dissertating students are

isolated from all but their dissertation director, considering any connections and discoveries in the future dissertation and not in a classroom of graduate student peers. In other graduate teaching contexts
such as guest speaking invitations or other single-session presentations,
advanced graduate students may have some sense of the teacher role
in a graduate course. These opportunities, although valuable, are not
geared to exploring the rationales behind the construction of an entire
course or negotiations that happen in a classroom between faculty and
graduate students. Sue's position is discussed in some detail in her reflection as she states that

> Normally, as a student begins a dissertation, course-
> work is complete, effectively cutting off future inter-
> actions with others with similar interests. I not only
> participated in a personally relevant course, but I saw
> the topic as formulated by Amy, through new eyes.
> This binocular vision of visual rhetoric is very instruc-
> tive. I also carefully read four or five articles or a book
> each week, a particularly useful activity for my schol-
> arship. This exposure led me to a better understanding
> of the shift in discussion of visual rhetoric over the last
> ten years, as people incorporate material from growing
> interdisciplinary input. (personal correspondence, Sue
> Smith, May 12, 2003)

Sue points to the need to continue mentoring opportunities for advanced graduate students, noting that too often, advanced graduate
students, post-coursework, are readying for and writing the dissertation—solitary scholarly acts. The GLSTE allowed Sue to see her
dissertation topic as evinced in class discussions, to locate the areas
of consensus and dissonance in the broad and varied theoretical landscape as she was beginning to write about the topic and to reflect on
notions of power and authority throughout the program, confirming
that she prefers undergraduate teaching.

   Our reflections complete, the GLSTE was adopted, by unanimous
vote, as a mentoring option in the RCTE program. In this piece we
have presented some of the complications of taking on such a mentoring
experience, and we have investigated some of the discursive constructions of the mentoring that reveal the ways we failed to instantiate
some of our shared collaborative goals and visions of the mentoring.

Institutions do change. Practices such as advanced mentoring opportunities for graduate students are now seen as part of the RCTE program and its commitment to reflective teaching.

CONCLUSION

As we review these documents and our classroom experiences, we are
aware of the clash between our own values of reflective teaching and
the narrower discursive space of protectionist language and material
spaces of our class assignment, location, and interactions. We also better understand the complications of challenging traditional mentoring
and teaching practices. The occasional clashes were balanced by moments of group insight and camaraderie, but issues of authority and
power in a graduate-level course continuously reappeared in our classroom. We believe these issues appear in every class, but our ability to
talk about what went on probably heightened our awareness of them.

As rhetoric and composition programs continue to pursue ways of
building mentoring opportunities, they should remain mindful that
a range of advanced-level, especially graduate-level, teaching experiences can inform our understanding of reflective praxis. Here, we
want to suggest that any such opportunities should consider a set of
factors, including but not limited to, the program's local culture of
mentoring, broader discussions within the program about the transition from graduate student to future faculty member, and open forums
on negotiating issues of power and authority as teachers and scholars
in the field. We also feel strongly that taking on a graduate-level teaching opportunity should acknowledge, but not play into, the possible
pedagogical "dangers"—dissonant views between mentor and mentee,
workload issues, and privacy guidelines. Without a tolerance for, or
even encouragement to take risks, this type of mentoring opportunity
may only reify hierarchical power structures and negate for the faculty member and graduate student any real opportunities to challenge
our understanding of teaching and learning. Finally, whether graduate
students become graduate faculty is not the issue, at least not for us.
Mentoring is not merely about mimicking future workplace contexts,
but it is about providing a range of intellectual and pedagogical experiences that raise new complications in regard to ethical, critical, and
invested practices to both parties as scholars and teachers. Faculty and
graduate students are both served by the opportunity to negotiate the

classroom with another teacher and scholar, challenging the boundaries of existing institutional constructs.

NOTE

1. As a matter of procedure, we refer to each of us by first name when acting individually, by the first person plural when acting together.

WORKS CITED

Ebest, Sally Barr. "Mentoring: Past, Present, and Future." *Preparing College Teachers of Writing: Histories, Theories, Programs, and Practices.* Ed. Betty Pytlik and Sarah Liggett. New York: Oxford UP, 2002. 211-21.

Grabill, Jeffrey T., James E. Porter, Stuart C. Blythe, and Libby Miles. "Institutional Critique Revisited." *Works and Days* (2003): 219-37. 14 August 2005 <http://www.english.iup.edu/publications/works&days/>.

Gunner, Jeanne. "Professional Advancement of the WPA: Rhetoric and Politics in Tenure and Promotion." *The Allyn and Bacon Sourcebook for Writing Program Administrators.* Ed. Irene Ward and William J. Carpenter. NY: Longman, 2002. 315-30.

Kimme Hea, Amy C. Apprenticeship Proposal to Rhetoric, Composition, & Teaching of English Faculty. October 2001.

—. "Spatial and Visual Rhetorics Course Website." 2003. 8 August 2005. <http://www.u.arizona.edu/~kimmehea/svrhet/svrhet.htm>

Latterell, Catherine. "Training the Workforce: Overview of GTA Education Curricula." *The Allyn and Bacon Sourcebook for Writing Program Administrators.* Ed. Irene Ward and William J. Carpenter. NY: Longman, 2002. 139-55.

McNabb, Richard. "Future Perfect: Administrative Work and the Professionalization of Graduate Students." *Rhetoric Review* 21.1 (2002): 40-87.

Micciche, Laura R. "More Than a Feeling: Disappointment and WPA Work." *College English* 64.4 (2002): 432-58.

Miller, Scott L., Brenda Jo Brueggemann, Bennis Blue, and Deneen M. Shepherd. "Present Perfect and Future Imperfect: Results of a National Survey of Graduate Students in Rhetoric and Composition Programs." *College Composition and Communication* 48.3 (1997): 397-409.

MLA Committee on Academic Freedom and Professional Rights and Responsibilities. "MLA Advice to Universities and Graduate Programs on Graduate Student Rights and Responsibilities." 1998. 22 June 2008 < http://www.mla.org/grad_student_rights>.

Porter, James E., Patricia Sullivan, Stuart Blythe, Stuart, Jeffre T. Grabill, and Libby Miles. "Institutional Critique: A Rhetorical Methodology for Change." *College Composition and Communication* 51.4 (2000): 610-42.

RCTE Program Handbook. (2005-2006). 8 August 2005 <http://www.u.arizona.edu/%7Ercte/handbook.htm>.

Weiser, Irwin. "When Teaching Assistants Teach Teaching Assistants to Teach: A Historical View of a Teacher Preparation Program." *Preparing College Teachers of Writing: Histories, Theories, Programs, and Practices.* Ed. Betty Pytlik and Sarah Liggett. NY: Oxford University Press, 2002. 40-49.

18 A Mentoring Pedagogy

C. Renée Love

I used to think that mentoring consisted of finding "the one great teacher," someone who would become a lifelong tutor, adviser, and friend, and, of course, such mentoring relationships exist, but other approaches to mentoring exist as well. For instance, we may have been mentored by a colleague or someone else in our academic or professional community. Much like the thoughtful rhetorician who must constantly adapt to meet the needs of different audiences and contexts, our mentoring relationships may also shift or evolve over time, transformations influenced by changes in our academic positions, career stages, and personal needs. In addition to outlining three approaches to mentoring—*traditional mentoring, collegial mentoring, and network mentoring*[1]—I argue that teachers may include a *mentoring pedagogy* in their classes, a method that encourages students to explore the benefits of mentoring relationships. I conclude by suggesting how teachers may promote mentoring not only by acting as mentors but by helping our students find mentors who may enrich their lives. To this end, I use assignments that allow students to research and write about professionals in their respective fields, an epistemic approach to writing that also creates opportunities for continuing the tradition of mentoring. Through specific pedagogical practices, we can apply rhetorical strategies to mentoring, teaching our students diverse approaches to mentoring while also widening the audiences and contexts for mentoring.

TRADITIONAL MENTORING

As Mitch Albom suggests in *Tuesdays with Morrie*, mentors often appear in the form of inspiring teachers, and I, too, have certainly benefited from the wisdom of teachers who have shared their experiences and knowledge with me. The mentoring relationship Albom describes in the book depicts an excellent example of a traditional mentoring relationship. Albom and Schwartz become friends through a Sociology class that Albom takes at Brandeis University; Schwartz, the Sociology professor, becomes one of Albom's favorite teachers. After graduation, the two lose touch, but during the last months of Schwartz's life, Albom and Schwartz rekindle their friendship. Through weekly visits they fondly call "Tuesday classes," Schwartz passes on some of "life's greatest lesson[s]" to Mitch Albom, his favorite student. Such mentoring relationships may help us reach the next stage in our academic, career, or personal success, but we may also learn from other kinds of teachers.

COLLEGIAL MENTORING

In the context of academics, many of us are familiar with the practice of mentoring graduate students, whether we have benefited from such mentoring or have served as a mentor, helping graduate students develop teaching and scholarship methods, skills that also promote professional development. We may also find mentoring relationships through organized mentoring programs designed to help new faculty members; such organized partnerships help newcomers adjust to new academic settings. However, rather than relying exclusively on just one colleague for assistance, we could likely benefit from several sources of guidance. Mary McKinney, a psychologist and career coach for academicians, reminds us that "guidance will come from many sources in a variety of forms. One member of [the] department will explain the history of the political divisions" while "another may be willing to read [one's] manuscripts." Whether in the form of one colleague or half a dozen, finding reliable advice that will help us meet the challenges of our new roles and contexts will certainly strengthen our chances for success.

NETWORK MENTORING

We may also gain insights on our work practices through conversations with colleagues and other professionals. I call this form of mentoring "network mentoring," a description influenced by Tim Sanders's *Love Is the Killer APP*. Sanders, the Chief Solutions Officer at Yahoo!, attributes his success to factors from being a prolific reader to sharing knowledge with colleagues. Sanders argues that "the more you read, the more you know, and the more knowledge you have to pass along" (42). By passing along knowledge and gaining the respect of colleagues, we build ethos within our communities, which, in turn, creates meaningful networks; the people in these networks will, likewise, share their knowledge with us, creating a culture of connection and inspiration, an environment that fosters creativity. Furthermore, I find that by sharing knowledge with others, and learning from others, we create epistemic networks, webs of positive influence, feedback, and information that produce new knowledge.

Network mentoring does not require a major time investment, for we can often gain valuable feedback through a conversation, an e-mail, or phone call. As professors, writers, and scholars, one of our primary responsibilities may be to pass on the knowledge we have gained, and our students do not have to be the only benefactors of this knowledge. Seek out the people in your professional community, and talk with them about their work. Learn some of their strategies for teaching, writing, presenting, or whatever interests you, and share your knowledge in return.

MENTORING PEDAGOGIES

Perhaps becoming a teacher is the homage we pay to our teachers and mentors. By including assignments that allow students to explore mentoring practices, as well as conceptions of success and inspiration, students can learn strategies for how to enhance their own academic and professional success. I define such approaches as "mentoring pedagogies" because the practice extends beyond the mentoring of individual students, although such one-on-one mentoring may also occur. A mentoring pedagogy refers to a philosophy of teaching that introduces students to both conceptions of mentoring as well as strategies for identifying mentors who would best meet students' needs; through reading, research, writing, and discussion activities, students can learn how to find the "right" mentoring relationships, based on students' respective disciplines and goals. The resulting essays may even become the first steps in students' journeys to finding mentors, whether they find these "teachers" within the academic community or beyond. Mentoring pedagogies also promote epistemic writing opportunities. Because students research and write about the professionals who genuinely interest them—that is audience-specific professionals—our students can learn from professionals in their respective fields.

To begin such mentoring conversations, I assign a book or film that emphasizes a mentoring relationship or an inspiring or successful individual; texts that focus on the transmission of knowledge or the passing on of a legacy also often work well for this pedagogical approach. After textual analyses, reading, researching, and discussion activities, students write essays on topics like the following ones.

Assignment Ideas

While I use these assignments in my writing classes, which include Composition, Business Writing, and Writing in the Disciplines courses, the assignments could easily be adapted across the disciplines to meet the needs of students in diverse fields. Students develop essays in stages, and cultivate a philosophy of writing as a process, but for the sake of brevity, I did not include either the various stages of the writing process or the due dates. I have used these writing prompts in my classes, suggesting topics influenced by the mentoring pedagogy I describe:

Composition Approach

- Can you recall an inspiring experience or an inspiring person? Why are these situations or people inspiring? What characteristics define inspiring people? In *Tuesdays With Morrie*, Mitch Albom describes his relationship with Morrie Schwartz, a teacher who continued to inspire Albom even years after their class together.
- Using the book *Tuesdays With Morrie*, as well as additional examples, examine the idea of "the inspiring." Why did Schwartz inspire Albom? Does Schwartz inspire readers, too? Discuss the topic of the inspiring in terms of *Tuesdays With Morrie* and other inspiring figures. Through an exploration of inspiring people or situations, construct an argument that demonstrates your view of the inspiring. In the conclusion of the essay, you might reflect on the value of the inspirational. In other words, do we need inspiration to thrive? Why do we need inspiring people or situations? Can we learn anything about our own lives from inspiring people? Can such people become mentors

for us? Can we enhance our opportunities for success by considering the path taken by people like Schwartz, Albom, and others who inspire us?

An Approach for Professional Communication Courses

- Explore your discipline outside the textbook and classroom by learning from professionals in your field. In this project, learn more about your area of study through two forms of inquiry: an interview with a professor in your field and research on a distinguished figure in your discipline: a scholar, writer, scientist, artist, or other well respected professional. Try to learn as much as possible about the discipline you have chosen, as well as career opportunities that exist for you. What can you learn from these professionals? Do they suggest any strategies for maximizing success in your chosen major? Could such professional inquiries constitute a form of mentoring? Does this project prompt you to think about the value of having a mentor? Present your interview and research findings in the form of a short research paper. Next, write a letter or e-mail to a professional in your field, ideally the professional you researched for the assignment. In the letter, demonstrate your familiarity with the individual's work, and then make a discipline-specific inquiry or request for advice on a relevant subject.

- In this project, using at least two forms of inquiry, write an essay that demonstrates success strategies for professionals in your field. Use Tim Sanders's *Love is the Killer APP* as the first source. What could respected colleagues, managers, teachers, or professionals teach us about the path to career success? Identify and research a respected figure in your field, and research this individual's career, work, and philosophy. What can you learn about your discipline and opportunities for success through an examination of this person's career, writing, teaching, or work practices? You may even have your own insights about career success, and you may use these insights in the essay, too, but include research to support your argument.

A Literary Approach

- In a class that uses literary works, students might consider a text such as Toni Morrison's *Song of Solomon*. After discussion of the text, students could explore in writing the value of transmitting knowledge and resources. Have they ever benefited from such help? Have they ever shared their knowledge with someone else? What does the text, *Song of Solomon*, suggest about the continuation of such legacies? Morrison seems to clearly advocate a philosophy of sharing and networking in passages like this one:

> We live here. On this planet, in this nation, in this county right here. No where else! We got a home in this rock, don't you see! Nobody starving in my home; nobody crying in my home, and if I got a home you got one too! Grab it. Grab this land! Take it, hold it, my brothers, make it, my brothers, shake it, squeeze it, turn it, twist it beat it, kick it, whip it, stomp it, dig it, plow it, seed it, reap it, rent it, buy it, sell it, own it, build it, multiply it, and pass it on – can you hear me? Pass it on! (235)

These assignments could be adapted to meet the needs of students across the disciplines, and I strongly recommend the inclusion of mentoring pedagogies across the curriculum; such assignments would provide opportunities to expand mentoring traditions, allowing a wider audience of students to learn from successful professionals, to benefit from mentoring, or to become mentors themselves.

CONCLUSION

As Jonathan Fields reflects in *Chop Wood, Carry Water*, "there are many ways of being a teacher and of being a student" (Fields et al. 30). As I think of my own mentors and life's lessons, I know that I have occupied both roles in many different forms. I realize that I have never had one great teacher or mentor; instead, I have been lucky to benefit from the guidance and insights of a number of mentors, professors, and colleagues, and, at times, even strangers who passed along something of themselves to me perhaps purely for the sake of continuing the legacy of knowledge. Whether we have benefited from traditional, collegial, or network mentoring relationships, as teachers we can encourage students to consider the value of mentoring relationships by providing assignment opportunities in which they might identify mentors, role models, or successful professionals in their respective fields. Including a mentoring philosophy enriches not only one's pedagogical methodologies and course assignments, but, perhaps most important, it enhances our students' success beyond the classroom. Much like a thoughtful rhetorician must consider the audience and context of discourse; similarly, mentoring relationships may also involve rhetorical considerations of audience and context. Our mentoring relationships may change depending upon the ever-changing contexts of our lives, changes that also create possibilities for developing new relationships or chances to renew old ones. Our mentors might change depending upon our needs and roles, and we, too, are part of the change, finding ourselves, at times, in the role of the "mentee" and, at other times, in the role of the mentor, who passes on the knowledge that has itself been passed to us.

NOTE

1. Special thanks to Mary Lynn Polk and Branimer Rieger for helping me formulate the title of this section.

WORKS CITED

Albom, Mitch. *Tuesdays with Morrie: An Old Man, A Young Man, and Life's Greatest Lesson*. New York: Broadway Books, 1997.

Bumiller, Elisabeth. "If They Gave Nobels for Networking." *The New York Times* 5 June 2005. Sec. 4: 1-4.

Capriccioso, Rob. "Aiding First-Generation Students." *Inside Higher Ed*. 26 January 27 January 2006 <www.insidehighered.com/news/2006/01/26/freshmen.>.

Fields, Rick, Peggy Taylor, Rex Weyler, and Rick Ingrasci. *Chop Wood, Carry Water*. New York: Putnam, 1984.

McKinney, Mary. "Collegiality: The Tenure Track's Pandora's Box." *Inside Higher Ed*. 23 June 2005. 13 July 2005 <www.insidehighered.com/careers/2005/06/23/mckinney>.

Morrison, Tony. *Song of Solomon*. New York: Knopf, 1977.

Sanders, Tim. *Love Is the Killer APP: How to Win Business and Influence Friends*. New York: Three Rivers Press, 2002.

19 Textual Mentors: Twenty-Five Years with *The Writing Teacher's Sourcebook*

Nancy A. Myers

When I was twelve, I received Louisa May Alcott's *Little Women* for Christmas. It was the first hardback book that was truly mine—not the family's, not the library's, and not the school's. By the time I was back in my sixth-grade classroom the first week of January, I had absorbed all 546 pages on the March family. I cried for Beth, laughed at Amy, struggled over Meg, and rebelled with Jo. I was proud of having read it so quickly and of being able to keep it in my room, prominently displayed, because it was mine and only mine. Before I was 40, I had read *Little Women* more than twenty-five times. It became a regular and anticipated December event. Each reading offered me something new because the reading was always contextualized by my immediate circumstances. Not one of the March girls, but all of them have mentored me through the years. I learned patterns for living and acting, strategies for coping, and ways of thinking and reacting. Reading was and continues to be personal.

Little Women was my first introduction to textual mentoring; Amy, Beth, Jo, and Meg mentored by illustrating, guiding, and providing on a personal level. Just as importantly, an aspect of that early mentoring was my pride of possession, and that pride is characteristic of professional mentoring too. As graduate students and as junior faculty, we take pride saying, "So-and-so is my mentor," but in our heads we are saying, "I'm hers," meaning "She's chosen me because I've earned that right." Possession works both ways. Text has that dynamic process of possessing a reader and writer while simultaneously being possessed by them (Bakhtin, "The Problem" 126-27). Particularly in disciplines with pedagogical traditions, a text can provide that personal and professional access that is often viewed as the role of a human mentor.

Another twenty-five year relationship with text has also mentored me—*The Writing Teacher's Sourcebook* (hereafter, *Sourcebook*). My continually different and unique association with this text's four editions has instructed me in the power of text's ability to mentor. It has reinforced how even the professional is personal and how possession means more than pride of ownership. Between 1981 and 2006, the *Sourcebook*, an anthology of articles on the teaching of writing, has circulated nationally in four quite different editions in the discipline of rhetoric and composition. For the publication of the first two, I was a member of the intended teacher-audience; for the last two, I was teacher-editor. Across my history in the discipline, only the editions and I are the constants: the institutions, the people, and my responsibilities and needs were different in each context. Throughout all of those incarnations and differing relationships, the *Sourcebook* mentored me: illustrating, guiding, and providing various professional identities.

As the teacher-audience for the first two editions, my readings of and class-based experiments with stated and implicated strategies helped me develop from the novice teacher studying a text trying to understand teaching strategies and student composing processes to the seasoned educator actively using the text to revise and rethink already established and successful pedagogy. This mentoring began in 1981 when I was a new graduate teaching-assistant simultaneously teaching composition while enrolled in a graduate seminar, which included the *Sourcebook* as required reading. In the preface of that first edition, Gary Tate and Edward P. J. Corbett acknowledge this relatively new institutional support of teaching writing: "The growing demand in the schools for courses in writing has been accompanied by a realization of the need for professional training in the teaching of writing" (Tate and Corbett vii). While these graduate courses are common today, and while many of the faculty who teach them—mostly writing program administrators—are trained in rhetoric and composition, at that time this was not the case. Often Directors of Composition were English literature faculty, who had no training in teaching and pedagogy and little background in rhetoric and composition. They often trained themselves on the job, just as this director did. What this director did effectively for this seminar was her choice of books, including the newly published *Sourcebook*. Although this director did not mentor me, she introduced me, an inexperienced teaching assistant, to texts that did.

While other texts were beneficial later on, it was the *Sourcebook* that I gravitated toward first. The articles were short, theoretically and conceptually accessible, directly applicable to my class planning, and pedagogically useful. This edition mentored me, first, by providing me with a practical, yet theoretical, understanding of teaching writing. Second, it introduced me to a discipline and its habits—its multiple research methodologies and its multidimensional topics, interests, and concerns, including writing genres, rhetorical aims and means, composing processes, student writing, the relationship of teaching to assessment and pedagogical philosophy, and ways of reading and analyzing text whether student essays or essays in an anthology. I found my subject matter and my profession: teaching writing.

When the second edition of the *Sourcebook* appeared in 1988, I eagerly ordered it. I was in my second year as a fulltime lecturer, teaching multiple writing courses at various undergraduate levels. Moreover, because I had participated in a National Writing Project (NWP) Institute during my graduate work, I was appointed as the University Director of an NWP Site, for which I was responsible for designing and implementing systematic inservice on the teaching of writing for K-12 teachers. I was conducting workshops on all aspects of teaching writing. Again this new edition of the *Sourcebook* was timely for my needs and situation. With no human mentor to aid me, I came to this edition as the starting point for any topic. Seventy percent of the articles were new and the "Additional Readings" now became the focus of my research for the next workshop. The theory-practice connection that I recognized in the first edition was reaffirmed in the second, and since NWP promotes theory-practice relationships as a foundation for teaching, this edition was a credible and helpful place to begin my research on any aspect of teaching writing. First, this edition with articles chosen by editors knowledgeable of the discipline mentored me through its reliability and authority, just as a junior instructor would ask for research suggestions from a senior instructor. Second, the edition spurred me to examine and extend my own teaching and learning across these various writing courses.

The first two editions mentored me where my interests and energies were focused—in the teaching of writing and with other teachers discussing the writing classroom. As one of the teacher-editors for the

last two editions, my work with the re-conceptualizing of the anthology as a viable text within a discipline provided me with the knowledge
of the trends and directions in the discipline, of the audiences across
the various institutions, and of professional collaboration and publishing. While I was supported by established and helpful co-editors in the
compilation of these two editions, the anthology as a text of texts and
as what M. M. Bakhtin refers to as a "domain of culture," provided the
mentoring of my professional development and growth, my scholarly
identity (*Toward* 2).

In 1992 I returned to graduate school, this time at Texas Christian
University (TCU), to work on my doctorate in English with a specialization in rhetoric and composition. Being a seasoned teacher and administrator, I was excited about returning to formal education to learn
more about the discipline, its practices, and its expectations. Gary Tate
approached me that first fall—actually he called me into his office—
and asked me if I would like to serve as the graduate-student assistant
in the compilation of the third edition of the *Sourcebook* for a small
stipend. He did not know how much those first two editions meant
to me, nor did I know what it meant to be "the graduate student assistant," but I was willing to learn. Originally, my job was a combination of research assistant and photocopier of specified journal articles.
However, I soon asked about the reading and selection process then
asked to be involved in that so I could better understand how Tate and
Corbett made their decisions.

Where the first two editions had been based on providing a "wide
range" of articles on "the concerns of composition teachers" (Tate and
Corbett vii), the third edition focused on "pedagogical articles" (Tate
et al. v). Tate, Corbett, and I together read six years of two of the
leading journals in our discipline, and we equally divided the list of
other disciplinary journals among the three of us. We also discussed
and debated over which of the essays to keep from the second edition.
As the preface to the 1994 edition states, we expanded our definition
of "pedagogical" to include history or theory articles that "suggested
either explicitly or implicitly, some fruitful practice or approach that
writing teachers could adopt in their classrooms" (v). It was within this
process of reading widely and debating specifically for articles in the
third edition that provided the mentoring, not just through Tate and
Corbett but through my new understanding of the characteristics of a
sterling article and of the burgeoning awareness of our critical develop-

ment both in content of the discipline and in the rhetoric of the articles. Thus, the textual mentoring became on one level an entrée to the discipline's "domain of culture" and on another level my individual insight into what comprises a sterling and relevant pedagogical article. I argued for a section on teaching writing with computers, and I maintained that Richard Fulkerson's "Four Philosophies of Composition" should return for its relevance. Because of this critical engagement with texts and with Tate and Corbett, I was added as the third editor for this edition and have continued since with that broader definition of pedagogical articles to embrace histories and theories that offer an association with application.

As a new assistant professor during the compilation of the fourth edition, I was an equal professional partner. When Tony English at Oxford University Press contacted Tate, Corbett, and me about a fourth edition, I was in my first year as an assistant professor. While all three of us wanted to see a new edition, I was eager to initiate the calendar for compiling the manuscript: for the research, discussions, and decisions over articles with enough time built in for me to actually assemble it. As the lead contact with Oxford, I had direct dealings with the publishing community for the fourth edition. Besides the experiences of textual mentoring that I had with the third edition, I grew yet again through the responsibilities of making the final list of returning and new articles that we collaboratively agreed on and of redesigning the organizational categories. Even as this edition possessed me, I possessed it: choosing, arranging, and shaping. I wrote in the preface that "[t]he constant mark across the four editions reflects a desire to offer new teachers a starting point, which deals with the immediacy of Monday's class yet simultaneously moves beyond it theoretically and practically" (Corbett et al. vii). With this statement, I not only referred to my own history with the *Sourcebook*, but I also began the mentoring process with other teachers through text. As my textual mentor, all four editions have provided a personal starting point for me in the profession. With the fourth edition, I hope that the *Sourcebook* invites others beginning work in the discipline to see that professional texts, as illustrators, guides, and providers, can mentor individual pedagogies.

My experiences with these four editions illustrate how texts can mentor. Each edition provided a different type of reading access to the discipline. I have all four editions prominently displayed in my library—a personal and professional place. Last year, I was asked by a friend and colleague what I had learned from my extensive and intense reading over the years with the *Sourcebook*. "Humility," I immediately replied. And also immediately, I thought of Jo March's declaration upon seeing the expansiveness of the Laurence library: "What richness!" (Alcott 59). That is how I always think of the published articles, collections, and books in academe. We are truly rich in our texts and in our communities. Both mentor us. They help us see new directions and strategies for dealing with our profession, ourselves, and our students. Best of all, both are still personal while being professional.

Works Cited

Alcott, Louisa May. *Little Women*. Illustrated Junior Library. New York: Grosset and Dunlap, 1947.

Bakhtin, M. M. "The Problem of the Text in Linguistics, Philology, and the Human Sciences: An Experiment in Philosophical Analysis." *Speech Genres and Other Late Essays*. Trans. Vern W. McGee. Ed. Caryl Emerson and Michael Holquist. Austin: U of Texas P, 1986. 103-31.

—. *Toward a Philosophy of the Act*. Trans. Vadim Liapunov. Ed. Michael Holquist and Vadim Liapunov. Austin: U of Texas P, 1993.

Corbett, Edward P. J., Nancy Myers, and Gary Tate, eds. *The Writing Teacher's Sourcebook*. 4th ed. New York: Oxford UP, 2000.

Tate, Gary, and Edward P. J. Corbett, eds. *The Writing Teacher's Sourcebook*. New York: Oxford UP, 1981. 1988.

Tate, Gary, Edward P. J. Corbett, and Nancy Myers, eds. *The Writing Teacher's Sourcebook*. 3rd ed. New York: Oxford UP, 1994.

20 A New Paradigm for WPA Mentoring? The Case of New York University's Expository Writing Program

Alfred E. Guy, Jr. and Rita Malenczyk

During a January, 2005, thread entitled "WPA Genealogy" on WPA-L, the writing program administrators' listserv, we were intrigued and moved by the tributes many WPAs paid to their mentors, traditionally defined as more senior colleagues or professors. Martha Townsend paid tribute to Susan Miller, David Schwalm and others; Doug Hesse and Bradley Peters acknowledged the influences of Richard Lloyd-Jones, Richard Gebhardt, and Louise B. Kelly; Joan Mullin named Muriel Harris. Other WPAs joined in, echoed ("What he/she said!") and acknowledged, too, the influences of friendships made through introductions at conferences and other professional gatherings.

However, turning to one another—and to our friend and colleague Lauren Fitzgerald of Yeshiva University—off-list, we spoke privately about the curious fact that no one who attended New York University wrote to participate in the discussion (see Guy). We were surprised by the absence of NYU from the conversation because among the three of us, we were able to name twenty-nine graduate students who taught in the expository writing program (EWP) there in the 80s and 90s who went on to become WPAs after graduate school. This number includes not only the two of us (and Lauren) but also WPAs who are perhaps better-known, such as Joseph Harris of Duke and Joseph Janangelo of Loyola University-Chicago, at this writing Vice President of the Council of Writing Program Administrators.

It may be that only a few former NYU-grad-students-turned-WPAs are on the WPA-L listserv. However, many NYU graduates may also think of the mentoring they received as different from the kind of mentoring that was discussed on the list. In "Graduate Students as Active Members of the Profession: Some Questions of Mentoring," Janice Lauer critiques the traditionally hierarchical understanding of mentoring as potentially introducing a problematic power dynamic in faculty relationships, a concern that highlights our sense that graduate students are not normally seen as mentors for each other. However, though there were several faculty members and administrators at NYU who mentored teachers directly—notably the late Geoffrey Summerfield, associate EWP director and Barbara Danish, director of the Writing Center—one of the strengths of EWP was how well it was set up so that advanced graduate students could assume what may have been the most crucial mentoring roles in the program. In this essay we describe the history and structure of NYU's expository writing program from our dual perspectives as past mentors and mentorees, discuss the nature of EWP's strengths, and speculate on the implications of those strengths for other programs and for how mentoring is defined. Although more experienced mentors can help guide novices to professional stature, taking a mentorship role can also be an invaluable experience in itself. Peers have something to offer that teachers cannot, and acting as mentors offers learning opportunities that let advanced novices develop much more rapidly into experts.

269 Mercer Street, Greenwich Village, is a relatively dark and, to the non-native-New Yorker's eye, narrow eight-story building tucked away in the middle of a not-so-busy block on the otherwise hectic New York University campus. However, the second floor—where the EWP was located from the mid- 1980's through 2005—belies first impressions. It is a large space, and open; the TA cubicles that crowd the floor are short enough to let in the light from the ceiling. The directors' offices, conference rooms, copying closet, and writing center tutors' carrels occupy the walls encircling the TA space. Occasionally, in true New York fashion, a mouse darts out of one of them and interrupts a conference. At the very center, in a space among the cubicles, sits a long table known in our time as, appropriately enough, "the center table." It was there that TAs would arrive after class to dump their books and papers and sit—to get to know their colleagues, graduate students whose disciplines ranged from american studies to English to

history to performance studies to comparative literature; to eat lunch; to (yes, we admit it) complain about students, a little too publicly, for which they would be occasionally and appropriately chastised by the directors; to get informal reviews of the films playing at the Angelika Film Center down the street, of the better and cheaper places to eat in the not-then-totally-gentrified East Village, of the sidewalk merchant on Broadway near Houston where somebody got that excellent Bolivian wool sweater.

However, the center table served a pedagogical purpose as well as a social one, and in fact it is difficult to separate the two. By the time we arrived in the late 80s, the originating reasons for the center table were no longer apparent, but the general structure of the Expository Writing Program—less hierarchical than some programs—managed, deliberately or not, to mirror it, though that structure did evolve over time and had to struggle to maintain itself in the process. The program was first organized in the 1970s. NYU has four primary undergraduate colleges, and the College of Arts and Science—then known as Washington Square and University College—was selected to manage all of the liberal arts requirements for students in the Stern School of Business, Tisch School of the Arts, and what is now the Steinhart School of Education. The English Department supervised the EWP, and the first EWP director, Paula Johnson, was a composition specialist.[1] Two of her early colleagues there were Cy Knoblauch and Lil Brannon, and the three of them also collaborated with Gordon Pradl from the Department of Teaching and Learning in the School of Education. Together, the four of them shaped a program based upon process models of teaching writing that also emphasized collaborative ways of administering the program. Neither of these approaches was popular throughout the rest of the university, and the EWP curriculum, in particular, was constantly under attack by faculty members who argued for more rigor, more texts, and more standardization. Johnson, Knoblauch, and Brannon eventually left due to this acrimony, and the English Department began to appoint non-composition faculty to direct the program.[2]

The two of us joined EWP late in this history (Rita Malenczyk in 1987, Alfred Guy a year later), after a middle period during which the English department instituted a draconian curriculum designed to protect the program from criticism: a graded paper due in every class, with readings, assignments, and lesson plans all centralized. But we recap these beginnings because several colleagues who predated us in the program cite the embattled dynamic as instrumental in shaping the collaborative culture that we came to value. Certainly there were parallels between the collaboration among the graduate students and the unity in strife that the program directors felt while withstanding a series of proposals to scrap the program in the 1980s. While we were TAs at EWP, the authors sometimes joked that the graduate students were left to run the program while the faculty directors were busy fighting for its existence. In retrospect, however, we recognize a higher degree of design. Some of the progressive elements that brought the program's curriculum under scrutiny were also visible in how the TAs were guided to mentor each other as teachers.

By 1987, when we first started teaching at EWP, this TA mentoring role was reflected in what were known as staff development groups (or SDGs). These were groups of teachers who organized themselves to explore a particular aspect of teaching and learning—for instance, feminist pedagogy or the influence of critical theory on teaching. Except for a one-day orientation, the SDGs were the only formalized mentoring structure, and tended to be multi-generational. They met on average every other week. First-year teachers had one additional requirement—that they participate in a bi-weekly discussion group led by a faculty member from the School of Education, who would also visit new teachers' classes.

Education department mentors did not teach the required freshman writing course, however, and in 1990 the EWP directors decided to honor TA expertise even more fully. They created eight TA positions that were to be half-teaching and half-supervisory. Called Mentors, these eight TAs combined the roles of the SDGs and the Education department mentors, leading a bi-weekly discussion group and visiting the classes of instructors in their group. In the first year, mentor groups were required of first-year teachers and optional for the rest. That changed the next year, when everyone was required to participate. Groups held approximately five meetings a semester. Mentors also visited the classes of everyone in the group, focusing on seeing the new teachers in the fall. Experience was distributed among the groups so that they had the same percentage of new, second-, and third-year teachers, and there was some further management as well—balancing gender ratios, spreading the strongest second- and third-year teachers around. In the first few years, topics for mentor group meetings were set by the Mentor and often grew out of an immediate-issues survey of the other members. Later, the program began to set the agenda for at least a few meetings each year. The most important role of Mentors, however, was to serve as contact people for new instructors. Most people met with their Mentor individually three or more times in their first semester of teaching, on both a scheduled and a drop-by basis, and usually had multiple phone conversations as well. Mentors reviewed syllabi, both for compliance with program guidelines and to troubleshoot issues such as badly spaced due dates or too much reading assigned in any given week. And, as one might expect, Mentors also saw the most visible signs of distress common to new and sometimes frustrated teachers: they learned, fairly quickly, to keep a box of kleenex on hand at all times.

There were other graduate-student authority roles as well, at least one of which preceded the mentoring system. During our tenure at EWP, there were five directors—the Director, Associate Director, Writing Center Director, Director of Staff Development, and Director for International Writing Courses.[3] Teaching in the program were roughly 100 instructors and graduate students from different disciplines. Each was hired based on an interview with the directors and professorial recommendations; a very few, fellowship recipients in the English Department, were guaranteed employment as a condition of their fellowship. TAs could teach for a maximum of three years.

Each year, however, two TAs whose performance was deemed exceptional were offered a fourth year, and these were called (appropriately enough) fourth-year instructors.[4] During Rita's first year and continuing until 1993, these two instructors held what were essentially graduate-student WPA internships. They were responsible for scheduling instructors into classes, revising the instructors' handbook each year and helping interview potential new TAs. They would also organize occasional late-afternoon wine-and-cheese discussions entitled "Food for Thought," held at the center table and centered (no pun intended) on a variety of pedagogical subjects. These instructors had the opportunity to innovate, as Alberta Grossman—fourth-year instructor during Rita's first year—did by developing the "Food for Thought" series. By the time Rita was appointed to the position three years later, the fourth-year instructors also attended regular directors' meetings. The position provided an introduction to all sorts of practical WPA personnel problems, such as scheduling, and to the "people skills" required to confront such problems: for example, instructors with seniority had priority for their preferred schedules, which more junior instructors would try to circumvent simply by telling the fourth-year person that they weren't available at particular times. Though their tactics sometimes required some strong-arming or bluff-calling by the directors, the fourth-year instructor learned the finer political points of keeping a variety of faculty members happy by working out compromises. During directors' meetings, one also learned the arts of negotiating with colleagues whose views are different from one's own but with whom one still has to work: again, a useful ability for any academic administrator to have. And, as might be expected, fourth-year instructors also functioned as intermediaries between the other instructors and the directors if, for example, an instructor had a problem he or she was tentative about taking to the directors: in this their roles and the roles of the mentors overlapped.

A story from Alfie's experience as a beginning instructor at EWP illustrates how the various authority roles available to graduate students influenced their colleagues' development as teachers. Alfie started teaching at EWP in 1988, his second year in graduate school. EWP director Jeffrey Spear interviewed him for the position. Once he was hired, fourth-year instructors Bonnie Borenstein and Kathryn Schwertman met with him to give him the handbook, find out his schedule requests, and answer questions. All seemed to be going smoothly until fall of 1988, when NYU's clerical staff went out on strike the week before classes started. Many graduate student teachers chose not to cross the picket line. With the blessing of the directors, a group of these organized alternate EWP orientations. Those who wanted to honor the strike met at a central location, and the veteran teachers divided them up into smaller groups. Alfie went with Rita Malenczyk and Rebecca Fraser—the two experienced teachers—and two other new teachers to the Waverly Street Coffee Shop, where they set about discussing evaluation of student writing.

In some notes written later, Alfie describes his experience during this meeting:

> The radical moment for me in this meeting came when we did sample grading. [Rita and Rebecca] gave us three texts and asked us to come up with grades. One had surface errors—I gave this one a C. Rita asked me to talk about my thinking. I remember feel-

ing flustered and saying things about it being disorganized. Rather than press, Rita talked about the paper's strengths relative to the others in a non-judgmental way. Her measured admiration for the student's originality was compelling and persuasive. I might have made this shift anyway—most good teachers eventually do—but the charged circumstances and Rita's level-headedness were epiphanic.

Alfie's story about Rebecca Fraser is similar, but from a different day:

> We shared a cubicle, and one day we were talking about the value of conferencing. I said something suggesting that writing was recorded speech, and she said that she thought there were kinds of thinking available in writing that weren't accessible in speech. I spent months thinking about that, and it really affected my teaching. Rebecca is also the reason I started using small groups, because I believed that if she did it, it must be good. I probably figured out why it was good about two years later.

In her well-known essay "Talking in the Middle: Why Writers Need Writing Tutors," Muriel Harris discusses the value—in fact, the indispensability—of tutors to writers' learning, asserting that tutors, who inhabit "a world somewhere between student and teacher," enable student writers to take greater risks and grow as writers "in ways that teachers cannot" (28). The "middle position" of the tutor, a more experienced writer who has no responsibility for formal evaluation or grades, allows students to explore their fears, processes, and weaknesses as writers more honestly and openly. Similarly, the position of the mentors at NYU—more experienced teachers, but without control over the TAs' future in the program—allowed, at least in Alfie's case, for more open, self-critical, and ultimately productive reflection on his teaching.

Opportunities for TA influence at EWP were not limited to one-on-one teaching. In May of 1989, Alfie and Lauren Fitzgerald, also a TA, were invited to participate in a committee charged to redesign the program's curriculum—still centrally adopted, but by this point allowing more choice of paper topics and reading assignments (if still from a common reader). There was a third TA on the committee, as well as two of the program directors. In an initial meeting, the committee decided on three broad principles: (1) To encourage more substantial revision by reducing the number of required essays, then six; (2) To suggest thematic units for the selections in the anthology (what is now *The Writer's Presence*, then called *The Winchester Reader*); (3) To illustrate varieties of informal writing that might precede each of the major essay assignments. A follow=up meeting was set for the next week.

After the meeting, Alfie and Lauren spoke privately about their concern that summer vacations would keep the work from being completed in time for the fall. They decided to meet twice during the intervening week, at which time they presented a plan to the committee. This plan assigned each selection in the reader (which they'd divided up and read) to one of three thematic units, offered four broadly conceived paper topics, and described 3 different possible pre-draft assignments for each of the units.[5] The curriculum was adopted unchanged. We tell this story not to underline Alfie's and Lauren's precocity, but to emphasize that EWP invited TAs to think big and then allowed their plans—when appropriate—to become the program.

After the end of our TA years at NYU, the structure of the Expository Writing Program changed and ultimately became less collaborative. Following a stint as a Mentor, Alfie became Associate Director of the program in 1991, and was able to observe these changes firsthand. Due largely to a 1991 program review that praised EWP and suggested giving it a higher profile on campus, the embattled dynamic that had (in part) fostered the authority-sharing ethos of the program gradually faded. A full-time director, Pat C. Hoy II, was hired as a full Professor in the English Department, with greater independence and authority than previous directors had held. At about the same time, NYU began to re-invent itself as a more elite institution, accepting students with higher SAT scores and stronger high-school records who were thought not to need freshman comp; as a result, fewer sections of first-year writing were offered, and teaching positions were eliminated or changed. The fourth-year instructor positions were replaced by more Mentors; more positions for experienced TAs who had used up their allotted teaching time, but were still ABD, were added, with the higher rank of "Instructor" and "Lecturer" and no responsibility for attending mentor groups. Eventually, the number of regular TAs teaching fell to about 40 percent of classes, with the rest covered by Instructors and Lecturers.

These changes have resulted in TAs having a smaller role in the administration and training of the program. But it's also arguable that their input is not as necessary as it once was, either. Since Pat Hoy's arrival, all five directors have taught one of the required freshman courses every year—something that hadn't happened since the program's inception. This teaching gave the directors a more genuine stake in the curriculum. As Hoy added more than 100 pages of day-to-day instructions to the Instructor Handbook by 2000, eliminating both the need and the room for TA-to-TA mentoring and development, the average EWP teaching evaluation also rose by more than 15 percent, largely due to the clearer and sounder pedagogy possible when a full-time professional compositionist has the chance to shape a program's curriculum.

It is difficult to see these changes as being for the worse, especially given the dysfunctional relationship between literature and composition that helped produce the program structure we have described. Occasionally, the EWP as we recall it reminds us of some of the programs described in L'Eplattenier and Mastrangelo's *Historical Studies of Writing Program Administration*, in which resourceful and plucky souls manage to accomplish something called "writing program direction" against what we would consider long odds. Those programs, however, were situated in the early 20th century, not in the 1980s. One could argue, perhaps, that a school with the profile of New York University should have paid more attention to what was going on in its writing program, that someone upstairs should have asked if graduate students should really have been doing all that stuff. And, of course, not all the TAs had the positive experiences we had. Because of the power-sharing dynamic of the program, the directors were reluctant to openly articulate a single pedagogy for the writing classes, with the result that TAs who did not accept the implicit program philosophy tended to spend a lot of time muttering about "hidden agendas" when their syllabi or teaching approaches were criticized.[6] Some, if not all, of these mutterings may have been justified.

Furthermore, mixed-authority models sometimes risk exploitation, as low-level employees are charged with responsibility without being granted the agency of managers. In our view, however, writing programs are a natural site for teaching authority through sharing it, and a little mess is a small price to pay for a vastly enriched environment in which to try on professional roles. For us, the experience we gained by working at EWP has been invaluable for thinking about how to best administer writing programs. In a post to the WPA listserv in January 2005, Pat Belanoff—who was a TA at NYU during the Paula Johnson years—says that under Johnson (who began the peer-mentoring approach at NYU) she began to learn "that collaborative decisions are almost always the best." Later, working at SUNY-Stony Brook with Peter Elbow, she built upon Johnson's approach: "[B]y sharing decision making with everyone in the program I simply made better decisions."

In commenting on Pat's post in an e-mail exchange with Alfie, Rita concurs:

> I would have to say that I learned that too—it's one of the reasons, I think, why I can't really conceive of making decisions in any other way. At ECSU [Eastern Connecticut State University], where I've been WPA for over ten years now (and it was my first full-time job out of grad school, and has been my only WPA job), this works because my department values consensus and faculty governance, so thinking about NYU and my experiences there help me realize why I've stayed at ECSU so long even though it hasn't always been easy. Faculty here are suspicious of decisions handed down from above, and my NYU experience has helped me fit in well here because I don't do that. And these aren't just administrative decisions, either: they're matters of curriculum. We have a writing program in which, contractually, we can't mandate a common syllabus or common texts, and the courses are taught by a mixture of adjuncts [. . .] and full-time faculty members. I also direct the WAC program. So I've had to respect folks' academic freedom in their first-year comp courses— even though we have a set of common outcomes—and I've also been willing to honor the expertise of disciplinary (WAC) faculty in their expectations for writing in their fields. This has been easier for me to do than it has for some of the other comp faculty, and I attribute that largely to my NYU experience. [. . .]

Also, since I've been promoted and tenured, I find that mentoring junior faculty is extremely important to me. We all do it here, because of the culture of my department, but I do it more than most—I try to make time to talk with junior people about their courses, their concerns, and to be available to them for consultation, and to let them know that they should try to feel free within limitations (there are always limitations) to work on bringing their expertise to bear on the curriculum in a way that makes them feel invested.

We also agree that getting to shape program work as TAs has made us both more opportunistic and more responsible as full-time WPAs. At EWP, having an idea about how to improve something was only a short step from being invited to make change. For example, Denice Martone's position as Director of International Writing Courses was created because, as a TA, Denice agitated for better service to NYU's large population of international and other ESL students and then began, herself, simply to provide it. This experience has helped us not be afraid to claim authority, to seize moments at which something might get done. And while it never occurred to us that we wouldn't be allowed to do something, it also never occurred to us—as graduate students—that any work was beneath us. Unlike some colleagues who only came to administration after being faculty members, we find ourselves glad to move furniture when it will enhance conferencing, to clean up the catering after a workshop, and to see students, TAs, and faculty on a continuum rather than in starkly separate boxes. As a result, we act as if everyone deserves mentoring, and as if everyone can contribute to it.

There is also, of course, the New York City ethos of the program that was reflected in its structure—chaotic, diverse, full of strong-minded people wanting to get things done. Perhaps that is one reason we find that, having been WPAs in (between the two of us) four other programs, we still marvel at the vibrancy of the intellectual community at NYU and can see the subtle blend of guidance and freedom with which the directors nurtured it. Of the 29 people we mentioned at the beginning of this essay, many received degrees in disciplines other than composition and rhetoric; it was in teaching and talking together at EWP that they developed the skills to administer writing programs around the country.

NOTES

1. Johnson's progressive tendencies are reflected in an *ADE Bulletin* article she published in 1979, critiquing the lit/comp split, arguing for more serious attention to student texts, and anticipating how English departments might be organized on an English Studies model. Thanks to Mary Wislocki for this reference.

2. We learned some of this history informally during our time as TAs. Alfie also served as Associate Director of the program from 1991-2001, which gave him opportunities to speak at more length to teachers who had been part of the program's early years. The university's hostility to EWP's organization and curriculum is well-documented in a series of reviews by NYU faculty and administrators, each of which called for the program's abolition. It's worth noting that none of these review committees included anyone who had taught in the program. A telling and—to our ears—poignant detail of the university's attitude can be found in a pivotal exchange from 1991. The Dean's office commissioned an external review by David Bartholomae and Nancy Sommers, who began their report with a recap of the critical reports they had been given as background and the terse rejoinder that the program was quite strong—and that its major problems were caused by institutional neglect. In their report, Bartholomae and Sommers correctly refer to the program as "EWP," the locution used by students and teachers in the program. The Dean's letter accompanying the report refers to the program, colloquially, as "Expos," a term none of us at EWP ever used to refer to ourselves.

3. During our time as TAs, the Director and Associate Director of EWP held tenured positions in the English Department; the Director of Staff Development held a tenured position in the Education Department; and the Writing Center Director and Director for International Writing Courses held non-tenured positions but were both PhDs in English Education. Explaining why this collaborative structure actually worked when the English Department was so clearly hostile to the program is somewhat complicated, and after e-mail exchanges with Gordon Pradl, then Director of Staff Development, we've come to attribute it to luck. Both Jeff Spear (a Victorian lit specialist) and David Hoover (whose specialty was Old English and linguistics) served stints as Director when we were there, and both—David Hoover in particular—were respectful of composition as a discipline and trusting of their English Ed colleagues' sense that collaboration across levels was worthwhile. In our conversations, both Hoover and Pradl also acknowledged Barbara Danish, Writing Center Director, as bringing a passion to those beliefs that helped keep the program honest in moments of crisis.

4. Mentor positions were also fourth-year positions, but the nomenclature was different to distinguish mentors from the more obviously administrative jobs.

5. At the 2002 CCCC, Chuck Christensen of Bedford pointed out an NYU group to Donald McQuade—the co-editor—and explained that our curriculum was the model for the book's refashioning from *The Winchester Reader* to *The Writer's Presence*.

6. In fact, if one asked Rita today, she would be hard pressed to articulate exactly what the pedagogical philosophy of EWP was. (She leaves Alfie out of this since he had more experience in the program as an administrator.) While some of its elements certainly had a lot in common with what are generally termed expressivist philosophies—a student-centered process approach, for example, was advocated—still, the required text for the second-semester writing course was Bartholomae and Petrosky's *Ways of Reading*. While we who are now post-process might feel that it's a good idea to combine the best of several approaches and not belabor the old expressivist/social constructionist dichotomy, some instructors felt at the time that the directors might have been more explicit about the philosophical underpinnings that seemed to drive what they valued in teaching.

Works Cited

Belanoff, Pat. "Re: New York University and WPA Genealogy." WPA-L. On-line posting. 23 January 2005. 20 September 2005 <https://lists.asu.edu/cgi-bin/wa?A2=ind0501&L=WPA-L&T=0&F=&S=&P=48061>.

Guy, Alfred E. Jr. "New York University and WPA Genealogy." Online posting. 17 January 2005. WPA-L. 20 September 2005 <https://lists.asu.edu/cgi-bin/wa?A2=ind0501&L=WPA-L&T=0&F=&S=&P=37543>.

Harris, Muriel. "Talking in the Middle: Why Writers Need Writing Tutors." *College English* 57.1 (1995): 27-42.

Johnson, Paula. "Writing Programs and the English Department." *ADE Bulletin* 62 (September 1979): 46-52.

Lauer, Janice. "Graduate Students as Active Members of the Profession: Some Questions of Mentoring." *Publishing in Rhetoric and Composition*. Ed. Gary A. Olson and Todd W. Taylor. Albany, NY: SUNY P, 1997. 229-36.

L'Eplattenier, Barbara, and Lisa Mastrangelo, eds. *Historical Studies of Writing Program Administration: Individuals, Communities, and the Formation of a Discipline*. West Lafayette, IN: Parlor Press, 2005.

Malenczyk, Rita. "What I learned." E-mail to Alfred E. Guy, Jr. 21 September 2005.

"WPA Genealogy." Online postings. 15-17 January 2005. WPA-L. 20 September 2005 <https://lists.asu.edu/cgi-bin/wa?A2=ind0501&L=WPA-L&T=0&F=&S=&P=25703 1>.

21 Mentoring Toward Interdependency: "Keeping It Real"

Krista Ratcliffe and Donna Decker Schuster

While traditional mentoring assumes a "master-apprentice" model, this model is far too simplistic and fraught with cultural biases—such as, gender, race, class, and age—to engage without question (Enos 137; Rickly and Harrington 110-13; Carpenter 156-65; Ragins and Scandura 957-73; Brown et al 105-19; and Redmond 188-200). One question that emerged for the First-Year English Program (FYE) at Marquette University for us when beginning our tenures as director (Kris) and assistant director (Donna) was this: how may *mentoring* be redefined to resist the master-apprentice biases and to provide benefits for mentors and mentees? Our response to that question was to conceptualize and implement an *interdependent model* of mentoring that promoted productive administrative *habits of mind*.

Mentoring may be conceptualized as interdependent when its effects are envisioned as flowing in all directions and benefiting everyone involved, albeit in different ways and to different degrees (Wilde and Schau 174; Ragins and Scandura 958; and Brown et al 108). Despite this positive definition, mentoring toward interdependency with its multi-directional flow of effects should not be mistaken for a utopian vision, for such mentoring can be productive only when it foregrounds *real* differentials in experience and power. Indeed, at the site where these differentials intersect, commonalities and differences among people become visible and serve as sites of agency. Admittedly, the type and degree of agency is delineated by institutional structure and by power dynamics.

In such sites of agency, everyone may become not independent, but interdependent; in other words, everyone may learn how one's own agency arises in conjunction with the agencies of other people and institutional structures. Recognizing and engaging such interdependency provides mentors and mentees a means for learning how to define their own places within established institutional structures, how to negotiate these places, and how to navigate to new places. Negotiating one's agency within a program structure potentially provides new levels of professionalism for everyone involved.

Given these ideas, this essay offers stories that illustrate how mentoring toward interdependency fosters five administrative habits of mind. We ground our claims in the 2002-03 academic year when we worked together administrating the FYE program. Kris assumed directorship that summer and two institutional changes took place: she designed a new curriculum, and she negotiated for a new assistant director position, assumed by Donna. At that time, Kris was an associate professor; Donna, an advanced PhD student. Our duties, in part, included mentoring new TAs, experienced TAs, lecturers, and each other. Although our claims about interdependent mentoring emerged from our particular experiences, we believe that interdependent mentoring can be adapted by readers for their respective institutions.

To define and critique the concept of mentoring toward interdependency, we address five factors that informed our mentoring practices: (1) local institutional factors, (2) writing staff needs, (3) curriculum design, (4) staff personalities, and (5) training opportunities. Each factor is contextualized by the administrative habit of mind we cultivated. Together, these habits of mind construct a pragmatic vision of mentoring toward interdependency.

LOCAL INSTITUTIONAL FACTORS: *LISTENING* AS AN ADMINISTRATIVE HABIT OF MIND

The most important local institutional factor we faced in the fall of 2002 was the newness of our positions. Kris succeeded former directors who had defined the position and its duties clearly, although no written job description existed. To prepare for her new position, Kris merged her research interests with her administrative duties. By putting the theories of Aristotle, James Berlin, Adrienne Rich, and Paulo Freire into play and by engaging her own theoretical interests in rhetorical listening, Kris anticipated that listening could be used as an invention strategy by students for writing, by teachers for pedagogy, and by administrators for directing a program. By listening to others, she constructed a CCCC award-winning program.

First, Kris listened to experienced colleagues. The previous director, Virginia Chappell, kindly gave Kris a list of monthly duties, walked her through scheduling, and gave her copies of all program documents. The director of the writing center, Paula Gillespie, often met with Kris to brainstorm ideas for a new curriculum design. The English department chair, Tim Machan, shared his impressions of the political issues facing the first-year program, given upcoming changes in the university's core curriculum. These interactions defined the administrative tasks for Kris in terms of daily activities, program policy, and institutional politics. As these experiences demonstrate, listening as an administrative habit of mind is important for mentoring toward interdependency because, when successful, it demonstrates a respect for others, creates a space for dialogue, fosters collegiality, and encourages reflection.

Second, Kris listened to students, both graduate and undergraduate. She attended a meeting of the Association of English Graduate Students to hear TAs discuss the strengths of the existing program, define their desires/needs, and offer advice for a new curriculum. She also informally asked first-year and upper-division students for feedback about the strengths of the existing program as well as about their suggestions for a new curriculum. In all these instances, Kris listened for patterns of ideas about curriculum, training, and structural power dynamics. Once Donna was appointed, Kris listened to her ideas about curricular and training issues.

Within this context, one story that remains vivid for Kris is when Donna came to Kris's office in the second week of fall semester, confused about the program's agenda for the year and about her duties in relation to that agenda. Her peers had questioned her about these very issues, and when she couldn't provide a clear response beyond "helping with TA orientation," they assumed she was to be a glorified research assistant, which upset Donna who was committed to making genuine intellectual and practical contributions to the program. Until then, Kris had been so preoccupied by curriculum design, training, and day-to-day decisions that she had not developed an agenda for the year. Donna's desire for clarity spurred Kris to draft such an agenda and to consult with Donna about its particulars and their respective roles.

This story is important to the concept of mentoring for interdependency because it demonstrates how rhetorical listening encourages a multi-directional flow of benefits. Donna's asking for clarification became a way for Donna to mentor Kris about working collaboratively with an assistant director, a way for Kris to mentor Donna about duties of an administrator, and a way for both to mentor graduate students about learning from peers (Brown 120-6; Gunner 8-15). It also fostered a new sense of professionalism in Donna about how to shape discussions and clarify one's administrative role. Donna discovered the agency to ask, "What should I be doing?" and "How can I make a contribution and support Kris, the TAs, and the FYE program?"

Moreover, this story is important because it engendered and confirmed a dynamic of openness that had been established earlier between us. From this openness, a collaborative style for enacting new curriculum emerged. We defined an agenda of program outcomes and deadlines, we revised the job description for the assistant director position, and we ran a methodology workshop concurrently with the practicum. On a professional level, Kris began to see how her research life and her administrative life could intersect in terms of rhetorical listening as a stance of openness that one may assume in relation to self and others in order to sidestep defensiveness and facilitate genuine communication (Ratcliffe 204). On a programmatic level, listening to ourselves, each other, students, teachers, and other administrators became a habit of mind that fostered what we came to call mentoring toward interdependency.

WRITING STAFF NEEDS: *PERFORMING TRUST* AS AN ADMINISTRATIVE HABIT OF MIND

When Kris became director, she redesigned the two-course sequence in the FYE Program. As core curriculum courses, RhetComp 1 (academic literacy) and RhetComp 2 (public literacy) had specific student learning objectives that had to be integrated into the new design. Given the need to make these objectives and the new curriculum accessible to the FYE staff, Kris set up a Blackboard instructor site. There staff could download sample syllabi, lesson plans, assignment sheets, peer review sheets, grade sheets, sample student papers, and external links for each unit in both courses as well as training materials used at TA orientation and staff meetings. Instructors were encouraged to submit their own documents to the site. Kris's goal was to develop a dynamic site where instructors could access documents, revise them to reflect their own voices, and then resubmit revised versions to share with colleagues. By making the Blackboard site open to all contributors, Kris hoped to make visible her trust in the writing staff.

To generate this trust, Kris asserted that, even though each course had specific units, detailed student learning objectives, and common textbooks, each teacher was responsible for negotiating his/her own place within the program structure. For Kris, this negotiation was made visible via sample lesson plans, which allowed the writing staff to see what other people were doing in the classroom. For example, at TA orientation, the favorite session was microteaching where TAs shared lesson plans and performed them for each other. During these sessions, TAs asked so frequently if they could "steal" each other's lesson plans that a running joke emerged: "In pedagogy, it's not called plagiarism, it's called 'sharing.'" During TA orientation and later at the pre-semester staff meeting, Kris stressed that what works for one teacher may not work for another. For pedagogy is more than a lesson plan; it is dependent upon an individual teacher's beliefs, interests, talents, rhythms, and *ethos* as well as upon a teacher's embodiment of the program structure, along with an eye and an ear toward students' needs.

Within this context, one story challenged us not only to listen rhetorically but also to perform trust. Although the Blackboard site was very popular that first semester, one use of the lesson plans triggered different responses from each of us. A few TAs and lecturers were simply downloading lesson plans and using them in class, without adapting them to their own beliefs about writing and pedagogy—in sum, without thinking them through. As a result, Donna suggested removing lesson plans from Blackboard. Although Kris considered this idea, she ultimately resisted it. She wanted to give teachers time to discover for themselves what worked for them in the posted lesson plans, what did not work, and why. She wanted them to understand what she had been saying at TA orientation and the pre-semester staff meeting: pedagogy is a negotiation of the programmatic and the personal, and such negotiation takes time.

This story is important to the concept of mentoring for interdependency because it demonstrates how performing trust may foster a multi-directional flow of benefits. Donna's bringing up the lesson plan problem became a way for her to mentor Kris about how program materials were being employed, a way for Kris to mentor Donna about how staff members need time to find their own ways, and a way for both to mentor the staff about personalizing lesson plans as a means of defining their own pedagogies. Likewise, this story is important because we were able to disseminate a definition of *pedagogy* as a negotiation of the programmatic and the personal in our discussions with teachers. Concurrently, the staff began to reflect on what worked for them, and they developed faith in themselves, which provided a foundation for negotiating the programmatic and the personal. In addition, the staff recognized that their lesson plans scripted rhetorical acts whose success is dependent not only on teachers' negotiation of the programmatic and the personal but also upon their negotiation with audiences (i.e., students). On a programmatic level, performing trust became another habit of mind for mentoring toward interdependency.

But even with commitment to trusting, we still wondered how much help to provide or withhold so as to foster interdependency, not dependency, among the staff. Finding the balance was difficult because the answer to the question of how much help to provide teachers is "it depends." The amount of help new TAs need depends upon their teaching experiences and their levels of confidence; the amount of help experienced TAs need depends upon their familiarity with a curriculum; the amount of help lecturers need depends upon their previous experiences and their current career situations. Performing trust was important because we established an expected performance level in terms of intellectual engagement and appropriate behavior. If coupled with ample preparation and institutional support, performing trust engenders a reflective habit of mind for everyone involved; thus, it builds confidence in administrators and staff and promotes opportunities for confidences (pun intended) among administrators and staff.

CURRICULUM DESIGN: *PERFORMING CONFIDENCE* AS AN ADMINISTRATIVE HABIT OF MIND

As a new director, Kris walked into a curriculum focused on student's writing processes. While this curriculum was strong, it reflected the theoretical view of the former director, and Kris wanted to bring her own theoretical and research interests to bear on the program—thus, the shift to academic and public literacies. By sharing her theoretical and research interests with the writing staff, Kris emphasized the interdependency of theory and praxis (i.e., how theory can inform praxis

and how praxis can test theory) within a particular institutional structure. By reflecting on theory and praxis in the program, the staff developed as reflective practitioners and gained an intimate knowledge
of the program that, in turn, increased their confidence in their teaching. Such reflection also helped us develop personal and professional
administrative voices as well as confidence in these voices. Thus, performing confidence became for us another beneficial habit of mind.

Three factors in particular helped us perform confidence in the
FYE program and in our own roles: first, we attended a regional WPA
(writing program administrator) conference; second, Kris solicited
input from Donna on the curriculum, the custom reader, the course
guides, and the program policies guide; and third, Donna used her
location as graduate student to ask for clarifications from the perspectives of new and experienced staff and students. One story that best exemplifies performing confidence concerns a regional WPA conference
that we attended in March of 2002 prior to implementing the new
curriculum in the fall. Held at the University of Wisconsin—Madison, this conference was Donna's first exposure to WPAs, both faculty
and graduate students. These other graduate assistant directors served
as role models for Donna, establishing a professional context and providing concrete examples of their duties; her conversations with them
provided important intellectual leaps for Donna to gain professional
independence and to prepare her to make a significant contribution to
the Marquette program.

This story is important to the concept of mentoring for interdependency because it demonstrates how performing confidence may
foster a multi-directional flow of benefits. As other directors and assistant directors from different-sized schools talked excitedly about
their own programs, they mentored Donna, who gained confidence in
herself and MU's new FYE curriculum. Their information provided
her a professional overview of curriculum theory, organizational structures, and troubleshooting strategies. These overviews were invaluable
to Donna as a theoretical immersion upon which to draw when she,
in turn, interacted with Kris and the writing staff (Brown et al 113).
In the best sense, this conference helped professionalize Donna. Now
able to see multiple levels at which the program operated, she was better able to assist Kris professionally and intellectually and was also
more confident in her ability. Thus, Donna had the ability to mentor
writing staff by fielding questions, acting as a kind of initial filter for

them by reporting their questions and concerns (anonymously) to Kris. In turn, Kris became more confident not only in Donna's ability but also in the new curriculum's viability and in our collaborative efforts to "sell" it to the writing staff. She knew Donna was intimate with the curriculum and was confident that Donna could discuss course materials and curriculum without supervision; thus, Kris encouraged the writing staff to discuss problems and brainstorm with Donna, which also provided her with a certain level of administrative authority (Ragins and Scandura 958). By investing time upfront with Donna on the curriculum design and at the WPA conference, Kris saved time during the semester because the staff could work through many curriculum issues and questions with Donna.

This story is also important because it empowered Donna to incorporate current WPA research into the FYE program and curriculum and because it enabled her to perform confidently during her initial days on the job. Interacting with other program directors and assistant directors taught Donna to employ a variety of administrative strategies (such as, ways to mentor TAs and conduct workshops). It also taught her to situate herself not only within the FYE program but also within her discipline. As a literature PhD student (MU has no rhetcomp PhD program), Donna began researching within rhetoric and composition studies in order to access resources and effective training materials to support the staff. This research supplied valuable context for understanding the education cycle of student, TA, contingent faculty, WPA, English department, and institution. As a result, Donna was much better equipped to give Kris feedback on the curriculum, course guide, course policies, and introduction to the critical reader because she could intellectually situate the new curriculum in relation to the old curriculum and Marquette's curriculum in relation to other universities' curricula.

Moreover, Donna's confidence was contagious; it helped the writing staff gain confidence not only in her but in themselves because working through a problem with the assistant director often meant a shared solution rather than one dictated by a higher authority (i.e., the director). Kris's openness, her confidence in Donna, and her ability to listen helped Donna understand the interdependency of the mentoring relationship. When the staff could come to solutions without "bothering" their boss, they gained confidence. As one advanced TA and doctoral student, Tom Durkin puts it, he realized that "since the Asst.

Director in our program is typically someone closer in experience to us (i.e., no PhD by their name), there is more of a comfort level" discussing "problems" or issues with her. The "trick" as he puts it is to convince TAs to "air" their concerns to the Assistant Director. Donna used this new knowledge to act as a resource rather than to air superiority, often a problem in many doctoral programs. Only by creating an environment of trust, compassion, and performing confidence could we create this environment together. By performing confidence we established a sense of openness and shared knowledge that began in a traditional top-down model (i.e. from Kris to Donna) but then shifted in ways that supplemented, and subverted, that model.

PERSONALITY: *PERFORMING AUTHORITY* AS AN ADMINISTRATIVE HABIT OF MIND

Any administrative position garners authority from two sources: its place within the institutional structure and the person occupying the position. Institutionally, the assistant director position had been invested with authority when the department approved its creation. But the success of this new position was going to depend on the person first occupying the job. Kris was aware that her attitude toward the position would set a tone for the writing staff, so she invested Donna with as much authority as possible via inviting Donna to attend the WPA conference, asking Donna for feedback on curriculum planning, and having Donna run sessions at TA orientation. As a result, the writing staff often came to Donna for advice about their teaching. In such instances, Donna used her new knowledge as a springboard for discussions; simultaneously, she resolved to treat people with a sacred degree of respect, making a conscious effort to use her new knowledge as a means of helping other instructors find their own solutions, not as a means of pointing out what seemed like "obvious" solutions to her. In that way, she not only performed authority herself, but she engendered such performances in other teachers.

One story of authority stands out because it represents a common pattern of "gender" sensitivity that we encountered and that Kris has encountered every year since (Wilde and Schau 167)—young male students' challenging young female TAs' authority. One TA, Kristen Mekemson, describes her experience with inappropriate student behavior:

> Basically, there were 3-4 male students in my after-
> noon class (fall '02) who would sit in the corner of the
> U-shaped room set up and make negative comments
> to [. . .] one another during class, particularly during
> mini-lectures and large class discussions. Unfortunate-
> ly, this made me feel as if my authority was being dis-
> credited and [it] affected the comfort level of other stu-
> dents in responding to questions, comments, etc. This
> group of students rarely said anything loud enough for
> anyone else to hear exactly what they were saying, but
> they certainly made it obvious that they were NOT
> interested in what we were discussing and/or how we
> were broaching these subjects. (Mekemson)

Initially, Kristen ignored the behavior, but it did not stop. It became so disruptive that Kristen dreaded going to class and eventually sought advice from Donna.

When Kristen came to Donna's office, Donna discussed first how she would handle the situation either directly by asking the students to participate in class discussions or indirectly by using humor to help deflect the authority issue and shift the focus back to the material. Because of her personality, Donna would immediately address the challenges; however, Donna knew that Kristen's personality was different, i.e., less assertive and more uncomfortable about directly addressing the students and their behavior. So Donna and Kristen openly discussed these style differences; together they brainstormed solutions that Kristen would feel comfortable enacting. Because Kristen felt more comfortable addressing the students about the intellectual task rather than about the behavior, the solution was to facilitate group work that would not only split up the students but also invite each one to respond on task. Additionally, Donna and Kristen acknowledged that Kristen's age and gender played a factor in the students' behavior (according to specific comments the students made); these acknowledgements depersonalized the students' behavior and allowed Kristen to focus on becoming a professional.

This story is important because it demonstrates how performing authority may foster a multi-directional flow of benefits. First, Kristen mentored Donna about how to handle such situations; that is, Donna had to reflect upon what Kristen would be able to do, not to simply give advice. Thus, this situation gave Donna more data for reflecting on how she should use the authority of her position. Second, Donna was able to mentor Kristen, drawing upon her own experiences and upon research about microteaching and teacher assessment in ways that helped Kristen devise pedagogical tactics that would encourage desired classroom behavior. Third, Kristen was then able to mentor her students about proper behavior that is respectful not just to the teacher but to other students. Fourth, Donna was able to mentor the writing staff by making this situation the topic of a weekly methodology workshop (with Kristen's permission, of course) where they discussed different strategies for handling challenges to authority.

Performing authority is important for mentoring toward interdependency because the staff can sense when false authority or symbolic authority is placed upon someone. Kris—at her own risk—gave Donna actual responsibility, and Donna had to perform that authority, but with great respect for her peers.

Training Opportunities: *Performing One's Best Self* as an Administrative Habit of Mind

When Kris assumed the FYE director's position, multiple opportunities were already structurally embedded for training the staff. Every August, a two-week TA orientation was conducted by the director and twelve experienced TAs (all of whom were paid to work) to train new TAs (all of whom were paid to attend) to teach RhetComp 1. Before each semester, a staff meeting was held as a professional development seminar—each meeting serving as a feedback loop for assessment results and as a forum for learning about a pertinent pedagogical topic. Once the semester began, a weekly practicum afforded TAs an opportunity to discuss pedagogical strategies with the director, and a composition theory seminar was required of all new TAs. When Kris became director, she asked that the seminar be taught not by the director so that TAs could intellectually engage pedagogy and openly critique program design, and she lobbied for the assistant director's position. When Donna became assistant director, she implemented a weekly methodology workshop to help the writing staff gain ownership of the new curriculum by having them share ideas for teaching the new curriculum. The overriding goal at all these training sessions was to encourage all teachers to perform their best selves in the classroom.

The training story that best exemplifies performing one's best self is the methodology workshop. Because the curriculum was new that fall, both new and experienced writing staff had pedagogical questions and anxieties. So Donna decided to organize a weekly methodology workshop, where the writing staff (sans director) could conduct sessions for each other that responded to their own questions and needs. It provided them an outlet for performing confidence and authority—for professionalizing themselves and for engaging pedagogy as an intellectual enterprise—while Donna acted as a facilitator of topics rather than a teacher of teachers. Once a TA or lecturer presented an idea or lesson plan, other staff members discussed how it could be adapted for other materials or units and how they might have taught the material a bit differently (again reflecting differences in teaching style and persona). The minutes of each workshop were posted on Blackboard for all the staff to read. Through their participation in these workshops (either directly or online), the staff began to articulate their own pedagogies as they applied to the new curriculum; in other words, the staff began thinking about how they could perform their best selves in the classroom, and they were taking responsibility for doing so.

The story of methodology workshop is important to the concept of mentoring for interdependency because it demonstrates a multi-directional flow of benefits. First, thanks to the writing staff's presentations, our learning about pedagogy, teaching styles, and adapting materials exploded. In order to be effective at methodology workshops, Donna's performance of her best self in these sessions became her greatest learning experience because one drawback was that a competitive desire for "floor time" occasionally brought out dominant personalities, fostering competition among the writing staff. It became important for Donna to enforce her role as facilitator yet maintain respect for differences among staff to ensure that less assertive TAs received fair amounts of time to present their ideas. As such, the circumstances of these workshops required Donna to focus on her own teaching persona in which she had to prepare her best self—as a judicious, careful, deliberate and caring coordinator.

Second, the writing staff benefited from mentoring each other because, as TA Tom Durkin claims, it was useful "being able to go hear or read concerns of others" regarding the curriculum. In addition, the writing staff saved a great deal of time in the methodology sessions by using them as a forum for community lesson planning. In this way, the methodology workshop and the sample lesson plans posted on Blackboard worked off each other. If Kris had posted lesson plans for every day of the semester or if she had responded directly to staff questions, new TAs especially would have felt obligated to follow the advice of "the director." But by having a choice and by being in a "conversation" with one another and with Donna (whether online or in person), the writing staff began to see that pedagogy is a series of choices with consequence, a rhetorical performance of their best selves. This habit of mind informed Donna's work in the tasks that meant the most to her—e.g., commenting on developing curriculum, organizing and planning microteaching, conducting methodology workshops, and writing observation letters. Because these tasks had actual, realistic consequences for the writing staff, any abuse of her privilege would have created a negative backlash.

Benefits of Mentoring toward Interdependency

While master-apprentice mentoring is a well-established practice, new approaches—interdependent ones—can benefit mentors, mentees, and the staff with whom they interact, especially when the mentees are moving into a job market very different from that of their mentors. By exposing and discussing outdated modes and unspoken assumptions that feed traditional models of power and agency (i.e., master-apprentice models in a dated hegemonic structure), mentors can help mentees access agency. In turn, this agency affords everyone practical professional experience that equips them with skills for effectively navigating political environments within the academy.

By combining listening with performing trust, performing confidence, performing authority, and performing one's best self, administrators can develop and model mentoring toward interdependency. While these habits of mind may occur in any order, we organized them here to create a certain logic: *listening* creates an atmosphere of *trust*, which promotes *confidence* in self and in others and in program structures, which fosters respectful *authority* and, thus, encourages one to perform *one's best self* in administrative offices and in classrooms.

Although our stories are particular to our experiences at Marquette University, these habits of mind are not. They may be adapted to other locations. And adapting these habits of mind in order to mentor toward interdependency holds the potential to generate myriad rewards. These rewards include: developing reflective administrative and/or pedagogical stances, building morale, learning to negotiate the personal and the programmatic, establishing more equitable and productive divisions of labor, encouraging professional development, and, if you are lucky, collaborating on scholarly projects, such as this one, wherein we have focused on the positive features of mentoring toward interdependency while never losing sight of our goal of "keeping it real."

Works Cited

Brown II, Christopher M., Guy L. Davis, and Shederick A. McClendon. "Mentoring Graduate Students of Color: Myths, Models, and Modes." *Peabody Journal of Education* 74 (1999): 105-19.

Brown, Johanna Atwood. "The Peer Who Isn't a Peer." *Kitchen Cooks, Plate Twirlers, Troubadours: Writing Program Administrators Tell Their Stories.* Ed. Diana George. Portsmouth, NY: Boynton/Cook, 1999. 120-26.

Carpenter, William. "Professional Development for Writing Program Staff." *The Allyn and Bacon Sourcebook for Writing Program Administrators.* Ed. Irene Ward and William Carpenter. NY: Longman, 2002. 156-65.

Ebest, Sally Barr. "Mentoring: Past, Present, Future." Pytlik and Liggett 211-21.

Enos, Theresa. "Mentoring—and (Wo)mentoring—in Composition Studies." *Academic Advancement in Composition Studies: Scholarship, Publication, Promotion, Tenure.* Ed. Richard C. Gebhardt and Barbara Genelle Smith Gebhardt. Mahwah, NJ: Erlbaum, 1997. 129-45.

Gunner, Jeanne. "Decentering the WPA." *Writing Program Administration* 18 (1994): 8-15.

Martin, Wanda, and Charles Paine. "Mentors, Models, and Agents of Change: *Veteran TAs Preparing Teachers of Writing.*" Pytlik Liggett 222-32.

Pytlik, Betty and Sarah Liggett, eds. *Preparing College Teachers of Writing: Histories, Theories, Programs, Practices.* NY: Oxford UP, 2002.

Ragins, Belle Rosel, and Terri Scandura. "Gender Differences in Expected Outcomes of Mentoring Relationships. *Academy of Management Journa.* 37 (1994): 957-73.

Ratcliffe, Krista. "Rhetorical Listening: A Trope for Interpretive Invention and a 'Code of Cross-Cultural Conduct.'" *College Composition and Communication* 51 (1999): 195-224.

Redmond, Sonjia Parker. "Mentoring and Cultural Diversity in Academic Settings." *American Behavioral Scientist* 34 (1990): 188-200.

Rickly, Rebecca and Susanmarie Harrington. "Feminist Approaches to Mentoring Teaching Assistants: *Conflict, Power, and Collaboration.*" Pytlik Liggett 108-20.

Wilde, Judith Busch, and Candace Garrett Schau. "Mentoring in Graduate Schools of Education: Mentees' Perceptions." *Journal of Experimental Education* 59 (1991): 165-80.

22 The Reciprocal Nature of Successful Mentoring Relationships: Changing the Academic Culture

Joan Mullin and Paula Braun

INTRODUCTION

While much of the literature on mentoring attempts to give language to this human relationship, the descriptions also can reinforce a romanticized, magical notion of how mentoring works: it is a "mystery [that] lies in the inventive mind" (Yamamoto 183), comprised of "spiritual connections" between mentor and protégé (Hardcastle 27), supporting a "personal journey" traveled by the protégé (Gehrke 26). Such language masks the personal, mutual commitment required of participants, ignores the care with which mentoring agreements should be entered, and implies that the personal journey is the mentee's and that the spiritual connection doesn't happen if the *student* isn't ready to learn from the teacher. So is it no surprise that in academe, mentoring is supposed to mysteriously "happen" when students are assigned to willing volunteers, most often faculty-mentors who are seldom trained in theories vital to facilitating interactions with students, and, at best, who are given guidelines that only encourage them to "be sure to schedule regular times to meet with your assigned student" (internal memo from an unnamed academic institution)? These guidelines fail to stress the reciprocal nature of successful mentoring relationships, reinforcing, instead, the hierarchy that underpins philosophies and structures of education and that often undermines successful mentoring. Reciprocity, therefore, presents the biggest challenge to mentor and mentored because it involves a *mutual* giving and a *mutual* risking (Mullin; Cornell; Gibson, Tesone Bukalski), two qualities that challenge the traditional student-faculty relationship.

Yamamoto insists that "there must be, in both the guide and the guided, a delicate interweaving of a sense of seeing and being seen" (185). Yet the very hierarchy of academe often prevents the self-reflectivity and openness required: faculty play the role of "professor," operating like the knowing wizard behind a curtain as students embark on their journey for answers. Students, on the other hand, have often learned the risks of being open with faculty, knowing that grades may rely on their playing a role—often a passive role. Thus the decision to consciously take the risk of choosing a guide is often foreign. If students do choose a mentor, their reasons for doing so might well be linked to academic hierarchy (who is well known, who is powerful) rather than to a personal resonance with the mentor. None of these positions foster the "[t]wo elements [. . .] that distinguish mentoring, whether formal or informal, from other superior/subordinate helping relationships [. . .] reciprocity between mentor and protégé and an accomplishment of an identity transformation by each party" (Healy and Welchert 18).

This chapter will explore the need for reciprocity and risk-taking in mentoring by tracing the evolution of one faculty-student relationship—the author's. We found that successful mentoring really does depend on how receptive people are to one another; specifically, they need to demonstrate that they learn from and respect each other (Clifton). Without a mutual respect for the growth in which each is engaged, the relationship may stagnate into a typical, hierarchical association where the mentor holds authority over the mentee (Mullin 67).

While initially unequal, relationships between two participants should become more balanced as the protégé gains skill and confidence. Likewise the mentor, if responsive to a protégé's needs, will be changed by the latter's world view, and by the personal reflectivity caused by the act of mentoring (Blackburn, Chapman, and Cameron 15). Key to the association we use as an example here, as well as for others that have succeeded, is balance: Paula was a student by definition, yet Joan recognized from the beginning that the student also had a lot to teach. While by dint of age, experience and scholarship, Joan has "more knowledge" in many areas, Paula also has more in areas that Joan doesn't. This is not to say that our mentoring started out on equal terms. When we first met, Paula was trying to negotiate her way through the power structures of the academy as a Women and Gender Studies major; the power structure of academe is a territory that is familiar to Joan, a writing center director who had to learn administration in a largely male hierarchy. One point of recognition was the mutual struggle within that hierarchy.

A mutual experience and the goodwill of the people involved, however, are not sufficient for creating a positive mentoring experience. The literature demonstrates that a positive mentoring experience has the best chance of developing when there is a generative and supporting *culture* within which the participants interact. The relationship used as an example here developed in a writing center, a space which offers more opportunities for a supportive, collaborative culture than do many a center, graduate program or department. This is not to say that these environments can't create a culture that induces mentoring, but rather that they have not traditionally done so. The narrative that follows challenges faculty in any field who want to establish a mentoring program or relationship: What kind of culture can be created within a department that will foster mentoring? Besides intellectual ability, what qualities important to the scholar as professional might be used to choose mentees/students in a program? How might faculty need to rethink their own assumptions about academic hierarchies and learning if they are to create a more successful mentoring experience?

The Writing Center Context

Approaching all potential mentees with mutual respect—not constructed respect from rules or theories, but actual, honest respect—is difficult enough for many mentors; on the other hand, mentees are sensitive to hidden agendas or unacknowledged disingenuousness on the part of faculty and may create a cautious distance within the relationship. The collaborative nature of a writing center works to level the knowledge field between director and tutor. What holds true for the writers with whom they work, holds true for tutors and any mentor: not all have the same talents, nor can all be experts in every area; they need to pool their resources. This collaborative pooling plays a role in the selection process when the director interviews potential tutors, looking for those who will add to and complement center resources. The reciprocal nature of writing center work becomes even more evident through tutoring, for while it is clear that the director has years of expertise, it is equally clear that every day tutors gather knowledge about student writing, about faculty assignments and feedback practices, and about the institution as a curricular whole. This is why Joan developed tutor training policies and activities with methodology that exposed tutors to a wide range of theories and practices, but stressed the importance of tutors making their own decisions about how they would tutor in any given situation.

The importance of drawing on each others' knowledge was reinforced with a feedback loop that provided formal and informal opportunities to collaborate, stressed reflective discussion of theory and practice, and drew on individual tutorial experiences. Tutors knew they were ultimately responsible for exploring the consequences of their tutorial choices through reflective practice. Informally, they might seek feedback from Joan and other times they consulted each other; but if, at the end of the day, a tutor didn't exhibit reflective practice and seek to learn from others, that tutor didn't last very long at the writing center. The frustration of not changing their practices, of thinking they always had the same set of answers for every student writer, would be questioned if not challenged by other tutors, and would make the unreflective tutors dissatisfied with their work. This explicit contract—that all would work together, that there would be an inter-action—makes a writing center, a program, or a department an ideal mentoring environment. Tutors experience this necessity every day when they build on writers' strengths and guide them through the learning experience. Likewise, the director of a writing center, a graduate program or a department, mentors by showing students how to capitalize on their strengths as scholars, writers, and teachers, encouraging them to work together towards common goals. The game of competition, conflict and pretense as the perfect student-protégé, better than others, has no role in an environment that fosters honest reflection and mutual mentoring.

That is not to say, however, that lines don't exist between directors and tutors, even if some are crossed in various ways: directors may be tutors, friends, confidants—but they are always directors. Tutors may be smart, engaging teachers, but they are still tutors. In other words, while writing center staff may picture themselves as one happy family, they need to carefully reflect on the very real context in which they *are* situated: they are part of a professional academic office where both tutors and directors hold specific responsibilities and where accountability is a significant issue with different consequences for each. This is the reality of a relationship where there is a mentor and a mentee, but it is the definition of the role each takes on that either sustains a hierarchical relationship, results in a restrictive mentoring relationship against which the mentee feels she must eventually rebel, or grows into a mutually transformative relationship wherein the hierarchy implicit in academic structures no longer shapes the relationship (Mullin 69).

Mentoring in Action

While not true of most programs or departments, writing centers are positioned to be shaped by what Lois Zachary coined as the eight hallmarks of effective mentoring: alignment, accountability, communication, value and visibility, demand, multiple mentoring opportunities, education and training, and safety nets. These eight signs of a mentoring context provided the platform on which we successfully interacted, and the same characteristics can work for any consciously built mentoring program.

Alignment

Within a writing center, mentoring is supposed to be the culture: the director mentors tutors, tutors mentor each other, and they all mentor students. Yet a close look at this usual alignment shows the potential for a hierarchy with the director on top and students on the bottom. In our example, the director clearly was—well—the director, but tutors were very aware that they contributed to not only how tutorials might be conducted but how the office itself might be effectively run. Tutors were expected to contribute to the professionalism of the center: expected to do assigned readings and interact during meetings; expected to give input to the director and to each other. The director not only continually asked for feedback, but also made changes the tutors requested (e.g., doughnuts on late-night Tuesdays, software for students with disabilities, etc.). Joan continually asked, "Will this work for you? What do you think?" She usually, but didn't always, grant tutors' requests, but when she didn't, she provided explanations. Unlike the case in most programs and departments, the student-tutors weren't marginalized, but listened to; their opinions were sought and their scholarship and teaching accomplishments were valued and shared.

There were other equal players in that environment besides the tutors. Faculty from the university community were invited in to share their perspectives on the writing they assigned their students, and the secretary, with equal voice and respected perspective, was widely recognized as the glue that held us all together. Without sounding too unrealistically ideal, we have to admit (as will many writing center professionals) that the alignment of writing center philosophy and practice in our space gave rise to a mentoring environment that is often not even thought of in departments or programs, although the model can be applied to them in creative and generative ways.

Accountability

Zachary's claim that "Good intentions aren't enough" echoes Nancy Grimm's critique of writing centers. No matter how good the training manuals in a writing center, every director relies on tutors to help mentor the tutoring newcomers. Whatever expectations are not laid out during training tutors gain through observation and informal tutor-to-tutor interactions. In turn, tutors mentor the student writers, reflecting during the process on the theory and pedagogy the writing center promotes. Tutors need to contribute to the continued construction of the writing center because the stakes are high: students' grades can depend on their work. We also learned through alumni surveys that a student's decision to remain in college can depend on the nurturing and effective context tutors help provide. With stakes this high, tutors seek out or create together guidelines, procedures and processes for their mentoring and for students' writing. Tutors rely on and hold each other accountable, listen in on and learn from each others' tutoring sessions, and, if something questionable happens, they often confronted each other. The director might be consulted, not for punitive reasons, but for further input, instruction, or advice. This mutual engagement in achieving a personal and professional goal models effective mentoring of student/tutor-student, tutor-tutor, and tutor-director relationships.

As with all mentoring, there were also reality checks in place as tutors well knew: students would complain to Joan if they felt a need to do so, but tutors also knew she would back them up first and foremost, and protect them from abuse by either students or faculty. As director, Joan read all the tutor reports, returned some as needed, praised the ones that deserved it. Likewise, though, tutors' expectations needed to be fulfilled, and Joan was accountable to them: if she asked them to read a research article, it applied to their work since training needed to be relevant. Word would get back to Joan when things were going wrong: either tutors would bring the issue up at a meeting, a single tutor would let her know that she was not being attentive to a problem, or the secretary would inform her. It was clear that Joan's position was to reflect on the feedback to determine if the way she thought something should run was the way it should be, and if tutors' suggestions countered her beliefs, to realize that her beliefs needed to be re-examined. Accountability, as all things in a mentoring relationship, went two ways.

Communication, Value and Visibility, Demand

The writing center is built on communication that depends on respect for the contributions of all participants. All involved share a common goal and must be willing to achieve it by engaging in a dialogue that is *visible* and transparent. A writer has to risk his vulnerability, expose his insecurities, open his writing to critique; a tutor has to listen to the writer's stated needs and communicate her understanding as a reader. Together, they negotiate meaning, each working toward their mutual and individual goals until these goals intersect. It is this intersection that fosters demand and investment for all stakeholders in the tutorial, and the same pattern is replicated among tutors and directors. Value for mentoring originates from transparent and continuous communication that fosters all eight of the mentoring hallmarks.

Education and Training, Opportunities, Safety Nets

Tutors quickly learn that no student is the same as any other. While one kind of comma error in Student A is the result of poor teaching and misunderstanding of usage, another comma error in Student B might signal a lack of intellectual engagement with the subject (the student doesn't know what she's talking about). Tutors are always learning, and the director is always providing as much training as possible, but the learning and training is mutually initiated and mutually directed through communication at meetings, formal and informal. Such meetings also become the locus for generating ideas: let's create a history guideline to writing; let's start a satellite writing center in the college of engineering; let's attach tutors to writing intensive classrooms. The processes of planning, implementing, and evaluating these projects are conducted by the tutors in collaboration with the director. These projects become educational opportunities as well as *mentoring opportunities* wherein tutors initiate specific opportunities to mentor and to be mentored. Participation in these conversations about what might happen in the writing center, and observations on the part of tutors and director, determine further tutoring and mentoring opportunities for the director (toward tutors) and for tutors (toward each other). Tutors feel confident to suggest projects in which they wish to engage and be supported because within a writing center, there are always *safety nets*. For tutors this includes not just books, paper and technological resources, but very real and available human resources. While of varying levels of expertise, these human resources foster the understanding that everyone is always learning (as scholars do), and *everyone* includes the tutors, students and the director.

Our Story

Zachary's eight hallmarks for mentoring environments are useful for any department, office or group that wishes to establish a more encouraging context for faculty, staff and students. In this section, we apply her categories to our individual mentoring relationship. While the hallmarks look slightly different when applied to individuals, they nonetheless can serve as criteria on which each person in a mentored relationship might reflect, noting successful interactions, interactions that need more work, and other areas for mutual negotiation.

Paula is an example of a good student: smart, able to learn the academic system, good at reading people, quick to solve complex puzzles (writing, math or social situations), and, like many students who excel academically, without seemingly putting forth much effort, Paula exudes self-confidence. After hearing about Paula from other faculty, there was some concern, at first on Joan's part, about whether this self-confidence would interfere with Paula's tutoring sessions. Could she relate to students who didn't "get it" as quickly as she did? Yet, in high school, Paula participated in an extremely competitive academic decathlon team, where students of all GPAs were expected to help each other master college-level material in ten events: speech, interview, essay, language and literature, social science, science, math, art, music, and "super quiz" which focused on a specific current event. Through this competition, Paula learned not only the strengths and limitations of her own academic abilities and personal character; she also developed the skills needed to work very intensely with her peers, both as a teacher and as a student. At first, Joan did not know this about Paula, and yet she recognized in her a strength of character and the ability to empathize with people who struggle to learn, qualities that Joan herself admires and tries to practice.

While Joan was initially measuring Paula as a tutor to be mentored, Paula traces her decision to be a writing center tutor to a faculty development (writing across the curriculum) presentation by Joan to the math department, a day that tested this director's tenacity and belief in educating. Paula remembers thinking to herself, "I can hold my own ground against a bunch of grumpy mathematicians," and she knew at that point that she wanted to work with Joan. This recognition of each other on an affective level appears to be crucial to a successful mentor/mentee relationship. Each should have qualities they see in the other that mirror part of either themselves or some of their images of themselves. Clifton, whose research fosters mentoring relationships, gives people a personality inventory, suggesting they look for others with specific "frames" that complement theirs in order that they may reach their potential. He warns against putting people together randomly and then expecting mentoring to happen. In this case, we were both open to a mentoring relationship by what we saw in each other, and, as Clifton would note, the match made the difference: "By matching two people who have highly correlated beliefs and attitudes, the likelihood of success [in mentoring] is greatly improved" (Clifton). In these instances, the people involved align themselves with each other; they recognize not only characteristics that are the same, but a willingness to complement and collaborate—essential in a writing center director and tutor, a senior-junior faculty pair, a graduate advisor-graduate student, or an advisor and her undergraduate.

Ironically, Paula rarely interacted with Joan during her first semester as a tutor. This was partially because Joan was out of town a lot doing research, and also because Paula's shifts were during times that Joan was out of the center doing other work on campus. Yet Joan was well aware of the progress Paula had made as a tutor through reading the tutoring reports Paula, like all tutors, completed after every session. Joan's feedback on reports, and Paula's completion of them provided for each a sign of accountability: Paula would do her part and Joan would fulfill her role, providing the resources for her to do her work. Such reciprocity sets the stage between mentor and mentee for future give and take.

However, while we didn't interact that much outside of the tutor report readings and the bi-weekly tutor meetings (i.e., Zachary's education and training). The environment described by Zachary was in place, and the mentoring began to individualize the summer after Paula's first semester as a tutor when she traveled to Washington D.C. to work as an intern at a national nonprofit organization. Joan knew about the internship because during spring semester Paula worked with a fellow tutor at the writing center on her application essays and writing samples, and Joan stopped by the table to interact with the session. Joan's input didn't come across as an intrusion (i.e., hierarchical), but was perceived as a genuine interest in the exchange that took place between a tutor and writer. This was a relief to Paula who was subject to lots of advice from well-meaning faculty and others concerned about supporting her efforts to get the internship. Joan resonated to Paula's description of the pressure she felt: here was a person who could succeed in nearly any academic discipline and, like many talented students, was being pushed and pulled, both internally and externally, in multiple directions by well-intentioned people who thought they knew what she should do. Reflecting on her own response to these same pressures—resisting everything—Joan tried instead to be supportive without exerting advice or judgment. She expressed excitement for Paula and said, "What an incredible opportunity; you're going to have such a great time. Write me while you're there." And Paula did.

At first it was just to touch base to say that she had landed safely and was getting along well with her new roommates. Joan responded, and as the summer passed, the e-mails from Paula grew longer and longer. Paula was required to keep a journal as part of her final assessment portfolio for the internship experience, and so she treated her e-mails to Joan as initial free writes, which were eventually edited. Yet what Joan saw in Paula's e-mails again touched the way she herself engaged the world. Paula's e-mails were not just rambling and informative, they were entertaining and demonstrated a sharp eye and pen for social commentary; within the e-mails she would consider her role in not only her own job, but also in her relationships with others; she began to reflect on her plans for the future. The more they wrote to each other, the more we saw similarities within the other and, in seeing those, we began to each reflect on how those looked, how our attitudes operated in our own decision-making, how our own personalities played out in social situations.

Interactions of this kind can also have consequences that need to be examined when a mentoring environment is being constructed. Whether everyone is being mentored by one person, as in this case, or if different mentees have different mentors, some relationships will stand out as particularly successful. In this case, Paula was in danger of being resented by other tutors when she returned in the fall. There were many factors, however, that prevented that from happening: Joan's practices of highlighting each tutor's strengths and naming multiple tutors as experts (e.g., the engineering experts, the foreign language experts, the creative writing experts). Also, some tutors began to consult Paula either in Joan's absence or as preparation for a meeting with Joan. Rather than resentment, tutors saw this as a way of practicing their own interactions with Joan, as they came to know and trust her—and vice versa. Subject to the context of academic hierarchy, tutors and director were negotiating the risks needed to cross barriers.

As this instance demonstrates, mentoring environments (like tutoring environments) are entered into in varying degrees by the participants. For example, Margie, another tutor, was trying to decide whether to apply for graduate school; she asked Paula several questions that would have been more thoroughly answered by Joan (something Paula told Margie repeatedly). Nevertheless, Margie at first was not sure if she wanted to risk approaching Joan with the degree of uncertainty that she could exhibit to Paula. Yet, after a meeting with Joan, Margie experienced interest and support for her plans, and she thanked Paula for encouraging her to contact Joan.

As with all tutors, the more a director knows them, the more she can mentor them professionally by opening up opportunities that may challenge them and encourage intellectual and professional growth in each. Paula's ability to concisely articulate Washington DC life, to outline and then negotiate her internship, indicated to Joan that she would be an excellent tutor to mentor students and faculty in a writing intensive class, and Joan by now felt comfortable in assuming that Paula would enjoy it. Such assumptions can also cause mentoring to break down: each has the good will of the other in mind and believes to know what is good for the one (on the mentor's part) or (on the mentee's part) assumes a personal friendship and begins to take liberties with professional responsibilities. The participants unknowingly begin to erase the lines between the two, and in the process, to challenge the academic hierarchy that promotes manipulation and conflict.

Since the default position in academe pits the "knower" against the "uneducated," listening is a key in successful mentoring. The mentor needs to listen closely, respecting what the mentee is saying rather than projecting, and keeping in mind that while there are similarities with the mentee, the two are not just like each other. We clearly weren't; we came from different backgrounds and eras, had accumulated different experiences and, because of those, different self-images. The responses we gave through e-mail at first and then face to face allowed us to check those qualities and images, test them, develop or discard them, reject or accept an opinion. It was a mutual regard for our differences that kept the mentoring relationship from falling into one of the two traps that ensure failure: neither one tried to make the other just like her, and neither felt it necessary to exaggerate her differences in order to appear unique (e.g., see Zachary 52). We learned to negotiate ourselves out of the academic hierarchy while still surrounded by it and successfully interacting within it.

The negotiation was ongoing, though, and a safety net was always there: Paula would come into Joan's office like any tutor, but the conversations would be longer, more personal at times, as she navigated difficulties in her own life as well as at school. In all of this, her intelligence stood out; she turned her opportunity to be a tutor attached to a class into a research project as she did when tutoring a student with developmental problems; she had a proposal accepted to a conference with two other tutors, turned it into an article about tutor training, and had it published. Nevertheless, despite showing great promise in rhetoric and composition, Paula chose to take a different route for graduate school and pursued a master of science in mathematics with a concentration in Statistics. Joan also started a new chapter in her life and left Toledo, Ohio for Austin, Texas. Vast geographic and disciplinary differences such as these would have been enough to end most mentoring relationships, yet the friendship endured and has grown stronger. Along the way, Joan stopped seeing herself as a teacher/director and Paula stopped referring to Joan as her boss. That's not to say that Joan no longer gives Paula advice or that Paula no longer seeks Joan's input; the main difference now is that we give and receive from each other entirely as inter-generational friends. As the literature points

out, this is the last stage in a successful professional mentoring relationship (e.g., see Mullin).

CONCLUSION

While we have been explicit about some of the personal qualities of
our mentorship, several mutual characteristics have made it successful.
For example, both of us saw a high-level of self confidence in ourselves
and in each another. On a professional level, this trait made Joan both
confident and apprehensive about hiring Paula, but it also resonated personally with Joan; she knew how others' interpretations of her
confidence had been used against her in the hierarchy of academe.
Joan's mentoring reflects the guidance and encouragement she wished
she had received, and is one of the personal factors important to this
particular mentorship. This example is consistent with the research;
the individuals' experiences form the ground upon which a successful
mentoring relationship will develop.

While careful pairing after initial meetings, assessments (e.g., see
Clifton), or goal articulations should form the basis of mentoring
partnerships, personal connections nurture professional growth most
effectively when they take place in a supportive environment. These
physically and culturally supportive spaces should ensure access for
both mentor and mentee, accommodate the various levels at which
participants are able to engage, and provide opportunities to cross the
hierarchical borders that foster role-playing. To truly mentor someone
into a culture, there needs to be a mutual examination of that culture,
and that calls for reflectivity, and a willingness to learn on the part
of both participants. It is a risky undertaking that can challenge the
personal and professional identities tied to that culture, so mentoring
relationships should not be entered into as lightly as they usually have
since well conceptualized mentorships positively contribute to a profession's—and a person's—growth and evolution.

WORKS CITED

Blackburn, R.T., D. W. Chapman, and S. M. Cameron. "Cloning in Academe:
    Mentorship and Academic Career." *Research in Higher Education* 22.3
    (1981): 15-27.
Clifton, Donald O. "The Basics of Mentoring. *Gallup Management Journal
    Online.* 12 February 2003. 24 August 2005 < http://gmj.gallup.com/con-
    tent/default.asp?ci=976>.

Cornell, Charles. "How Mentor Teachers Perceive Their Roles and Relationships in a Field-Based Teacher-Training Program." *Education* 124.2 (2003): 401-29.

Gehrke, Nathalie. "Toward a Definition of Mentoring." *Theory into Practice* 27.3 (1988): 190-94.

Gibson, Jane Whitney, Dana Tesone and M. Buchalski. "The Leader as Mentor" *Journal of Leadership Studies* 7.3 (Summer 2000): 56-70.

Grimm, Nancy. *Good Intentions: Writing Center Work for Postmodern Times.* Portsmouth, NH: Crosscurrents, 1998.

Hardcastle, Beverly. "Spiritual Connections: Protégé's Reflections on Significant Mentorships." *Theory into Practice* 26 (1988): 201-08

Healy, C. C., and A. J. Welchert. "Mentoring Relations: A Definition to Advance Research and Practice. " *Educational Researcher* 19.9 (1990): 17-21.

Mullin, Joan. "Philosophical Backgrounds for Mentoring the Pharmacy Professional." *American Journal of Pharmaceutical Education* (Spring 1992): 67-70.

Yamamoto, Kaoru. "To See Life Grow: The Meaning of Mentorship." *Theory into Practice* 27.3 (1988): 183-89.

Zachary, Lois. *Creating a Mentoring Culture: The Organization's Guide.* San Francisco: Jossey-Bass, 2005.

23 Panopticism? Or Just Paying Attention?

Cinda Coggins Mosher and Mary Trachsel

In this essay we describe our shared work as mentors—or advisors—to a multidisciplinary staff of graduate instructors in the rhetoric department at our university. As we jointly reflect on our advisory roles, we find special importance in our common experience of being mentored in the same departmental advising program we now staff. In fact, both of us were mentored in our first years as Iowa rhetoric teachers (Mary in 1989, Cinda in 1991) by senior faculty member Cleo Martin. Martin, one of the university's last tenured assistant professors, espoused a "flattened hierarchy" as the ideal departmental structure and adopted a self-proclaimed "relentlessly positive" approach to teaching and mentoring that made her a legend in the department.

All new instructors in the department, whether TAs or tenure-track faculty, are required to enroll in the department's professional development program (PDP), a week-long summer workshop and semester-long colloquium on teaching rhetoric. As a new assistant professor, Mary elected to participate in Cleo Martin's advisory group. Nervous about her newcomer's status but confident of her performance in the classroom, Mary was grateful for Cleo's calm and affirming mentorship. She especially appreciated Cleo's written responses to her course materials, which inevitably contained praise for Mary as a teacher, coupled with a detailed description of the strengths Cleo found in the assignments and handouts. Now, when she recalls her time as Cleo's protégée, Mary realizes that her own advising style is largely an attempt to integrate Cleo's model of detailed, descriptive, positive feedback with a more prescriptive style of advising she believes is appropriate for novice instructors.

Cinda entered the department as a young graduate student with no prior teaching experience and was also mentored by Cleo throughout her first year. While she was thankful for Cleo's reassurance and glowing praise, Cinda felt at the time that a more critical approach might have served her better and that some of Cleo's easy-going advice was best suited to a more seasoned audience. For example, Cleo used a "collection box" to which her students submitted responses to assignments at their own individual paces throughout the semester. Cinda and other novice instructors discovered that such techniques, when not backed by Cleo's confidence and experience, could produce student complacency, leading eventually to confusion, anxiety about grades, and student demands for more prescriptive guidance.

Once Cinda experienced additional advisory models, her teaching really began to flourish. One advisor, for example, seemed diametrically opposed to Cleo. Assignments Cleo had praised as innovative drew critical concern from the new advisor; upon reviewing Cinda's first writing assignment, this advisor demanded, "What's the rhetorical purpose of this assignment? What grading criteria do you use?" Rhetorical purpose? Criteria sheet? While this new form of guidance was more hierarchical and less overtly friendly or concerned with Cinda's feelings, it dramatically improved her teaching. Her command of her classroom and curriculum grew exponentially as she integrated elements of this more structured pedagogy with some of the more relaxed techniques of Cleo's approach. Another advisor emphasized teaching as the common cause uniting advisors and advisees as institutional colleagues. His insistence on calling TAs "colleagues" told Cinda that the faculty valued her contributions and depended on her to help the department function smoothly. From this she learned the importance of respecting advisees as integral to the business of the department.

The development of our advisory styles exemplifies the "dynamic process" Margaret Compton-Hall ascribes to academic mentoring. Tracing her own development from graduate student to faculty advisor, Compton-Hall reports that she draws upon models she encountered as a student, but at the same time relies upon her "own perceptions about what [is] needed in a particular context" (157).

Personal Relationships in Institutional Settings: Ethical Conflicts

While we both felt well-served by the advisory system at Iowa, we know that mentoring can be uneasily situated in academe because many of its hallmarks—its potential blurring of boundaries between personal and professional relationships, its collaborative rather than competitive spirit, and its occasional appearance of disrupting hierarchical lines of power—violate some basic institutional norms of academic life. The sometimes awkward fit between academic mentoring programs and the institutions that sponsor them exemplifies the tension Foucault describes between the ostensibly benevolent socialization of institutional subjects and the panoptical surveillance that consolidates institutional power in the hands of an administrative elite. On the one hand, advising systems like ours seek to develop TAs' teaching skills while recognizing that becoming a teacher is a long learning process in which mistakes are bound to occur. On the other hand, the advising system serves the institutional commitment to students, parents, and citizens that the university will provide quality instruction. Advisors, as agents of the institution, employ surveillance measures to ensure that this commitment is kept.

Because our advising duties situate us as established academic subjects to promote the professional interests and well-being of less-established academic subjects through close, personal relationships, advising in our program occupies the borderlands between personal and institutional ethics. Describing these two ethical realms, feminist philosopher Claudia Card notes that both produce relationships whose structuring rules affirm the ethical values of justice and care; in both "personal" and "institutional" relationships, preserving the rights and promoting the well-being of the parties involved are equally important objectives. The two types of relationship differ, however, in defining and distributing responsibilities for relationship maintenance. Card stresses that "informal relationships are characterized by responsibilities that can facilitate relationships of attachment" (89). Such relationships are "personal" in the sense that the individual, personal identities of the parties "matter" to all participants in the relationship and are, in fact, constitutive of the relationship.

Formal relationships, by contrast, are sharply defined and constrained in ways that are publicly understood and universally applied. Individual identities of parties involved in formal relationships are far less important than the positions they occupy. Obligations to maintain and develop such relationships are predetermined by contractual agreement rather than ongoing negotiation between individuals. As Card explains, "Formality facilitates control where there would otherwise be a lack of trust or simply an inability to predict and plan" (89). An example of a formal relationship is that of lawyer-client, while friendship exemplifies informal relationships.

Many studies of mentoring programs in institutional settings suggest that protégées often find the informal aspects of mentoring relationships—their "psychosocial functions"—more significant than the formal structures of mentoring programs. Gaye Luna and Deborah Cullen, for instance, emphasize "friendship" in successful mentoring relationships, describing it as "mutual caring and intimacy that extends beyond the requirements of daily work tasks" and as "sharing experience beyond the immediate work setting" (22). Paul Schrodt et al. similarly observe the importance of "interpersonal bonding" as social and emotional support that nurtures professional identity:

> Through interpersonal bonding with mentors, an identity as a valued addition to the faculty is established [.
> . .] [I]nterpersonal relationships at work are important not only because they allow individuals to have connections that are similar to traditional friendships, but also because these types of connections allow us to get the job done. For a new faculty member who may be overwhelmed by the responsibilities of her/his new position, interpersonal bonding and social support can serve as neutralizers that balance the anxiety of organizational entry and thereby allow for increased productivity. (237)

Often, Schrodt et al. report, the most productive mentoring occurs outside of formally established mentoring programs. Formal programs, they argue, do not deliver their most important benefits directly, through assigned mentoring relationships, but indirectly, through a general atmosphere of mentoring in an institutional setting (27).

Most studies of academic mentoring programs also stress the critical importance of another quality Card finds in informal relationships—the power of individual identities to jointly construct a unique relational dynamic. Compton-Hall's study of her own evolution from graduate student to faculty advisor describes a flexible process of imitating, rejecting, and combining elements from past mentoring models to fashion new mentoring practices that meet the changing needs of individual advisees. Similarly, Jeanne Lagowski and James Vick note that while common characteristics of effective mentors can be identified, mentoring relationships must change with the individuals involved. They describe mentoring as "dynamic": "It changes and evolves as the student matures and as he or she needs change" (79).

As teaching mentors, we attempt to combine features of formal and informal relationships, but achieving this blend is not always easy or even possible. Our department's rejection of a surveillance model appears in our use of the term "colleague" to denote commonality between advisors and advisees. The same intent informs our use of the term *advisor* rather than *supervisor*, as we are labeled in official university documents. As advisors, we seek to mentor our graduate instructors—to pay attention to them and give advice, not prescriptions. We largely act as TAs' advocates as they gain experience and find their own ways in the profession. But although we value individuality and innovative approaches to teaching, we are equally committed to quality instruction in our general education curriculum. When conflicts between these commitments arise, we wonder how to be institutional selves at the same time we are personal selves, interacting with our advisees person-to-person while simultaneously relating to them as agents of the academy. What happens, for example, when TAs violate their contracts, neglect their teaching duties, or behave unethically? As advisors, how can we maintain a distinction between panopticism and just paying attention?

Disciplined Subjects: Residues of Fear and Loathing in Academe

However "personal" we may want to be, our mentoring takes place in an institutional setting that protects institutional priorities and values. Academic historians David Noble and Walter Ong describe the ethical underpinnings of academe as a monastic, agonistic, and hierarchical blend of classical and Judeo-Christian values molded by the institutional structures of the church. Espousing a transcendent, disembodied notion of Truth, an epistemology of disputation, and a vertical chain of command, the academy contributes to the institutional shaping of the modern soul traced by Foucault. In all our modern institutions, Foucault asserts, "discipline," a mode of paying attention that reinforces "internal mechanisms of power relations" (215), is an essential function. Epitomized by the super-surveillance system of the panopticon, institutional modes of paying attention to institutional subjects work to preserve and amplify institutional power, not to promote the personal well-being of individual subjects.

Studies of mentoring generally recognize its disciplinary function, variously describing it as "organizational socialization" (Schrodt et al.) "organizational assimilation" (Cawyer et al.), "incorporation" (Dixon-Reeves), "governability" (Foucault) or "management of subjectivity" (Devos). One way to measure the success of academic mentoring programs is by the protégé's level of satisfaction with academic socialization, experienced as feelings of ownership and understanding of the workplace and connectedness to colleagues (Schrodt et al.). Other assessments of academic mentoring programs ask how compatible protégés perceive their academic and personal subjectivities to be, or measure the willingness and flexibility of institutions to accommodate individual persons in their ranks. One study that describes mentoring as a process of "fashioning the academic subject," for instance, examines how discourses of mentoring steer newcomers into approved institutional roles (Devos). Through such discourse, Anita Devos writes, mentoring strives to "produce subjects who display certain modes of subjectivity or ways of being [. . .] which align personal with institutional goals, and constrain subjects from taking up modes of being considered undesirable" (71). Devos' case study of a female academic reveals a mentoring process that shapes academic subjectivity by requiring the protégé to oscillate between "active" subjectivity, in which she tries to discipline herself to become a successful academic, and "passive" subjectivity, in which she "gives herself over to her mentors to be fashioned as a suitable, successful academic subject" (77). Many assessments of academic mentoring identify a newcomer's willingness to be socialized as a critical factor. Carol Cawyer et al. observe that "individuals who need mentoring the most may reject the opportunity as a result of personality issues" and conclude that "mentoring programs may not have the desired effect if those in need of mentoring do not participate" (227).

Ideally, academic discipline is self-directed, motivated by a sense of social responsibility and devotion to a life of the mind. But in reality, academic discipline is often externally imposed and enforced through assorted penalties and threats that range from punitive grades and suspensions, to denial of promotion or tenure, and even dismissal from the institution. Such enforcement of academic discipline permeates all levels of academe. Anyone who presents Paul Goodman's "A Proposal to Abolish Grading" to undergraduates can expect students to reject Goodman's proposal, insisting that although they hate the pressure of grades, they need the externally imposed discipline—particularly the punitive discipline of grades. "If I weren't afraid of getting bad grades," they often say, "I'd never study at all."

Suspicion that academic subjects would shirk the rigorous work of the academy if they didn't fear punishment justifies the proliferation of surveillance mechanisms throughout academe—the rigorous exams and defenses, the internal and external reviews, and the tenure and post-tenure review committees that are everyday fixtures of academic life. Designed to eliminate the academically unfit and underproductive, this system of surveillance may communicate certain "bad faith" assumptions about the objects of its attention, suggesting that academic subjects merit such attention because they are probably deficient. A cynical view sees the ultimate purpose of surveillance systems to be selection of subjects whose disciplined academic service will preserve and extend institutional power. The nurturing ideals of mentoring programs like ours can be compromised by their placement in an overarching culture of institutional surveillance and cynicism. Though we try hard to maintain departmental integrity and instructional quality without implementing punitive forms of oversight, experience reveals how easily the friendly intentions of a mentoring program can become impersonal and punitive when advisors and advisees are already extensively molded as academic subjects. Informal, personally oriented relationships quickly convert to formal ones when institutional roles preclude personal identities

In institutional contexts marked by rigorous exams and evaluation procedures, any system of oversight can inspire suspicion. Our university's website listing of department-level procedures for scrutinizing tenure candidates, for instance, illustrates the disciplinary force of the academic panopticon upon individual subjects. The formal evaluation process begins with the formation of a review committee of peers, then proceeds through a complicated, legalistic series of steps requiring careful documentation and many months to complete. When equally elaborate college- and university-level procedures are added to these, the tenure trial instills fears and doubts in the most accomplished candidate—an example of what we call "bad faith contamination" by an institutional ethic of surveillance that positions colleagues to decide each other's institutional fates. The elaborate process formalizes collegial relationships; contractual obligations replace interpersonal good will when institutional criteria are at stake.

Bad faith contamination may explain why first-year faculty members in our department do not always regard their first annual "review committee" as mentors intent on fostering their professional success, but as potentially hostile monitors determined to ferret out weaknesses to store up as future justifications for denying tenure and promotion. Such conflict between the mentor's dual roles as friendly advocate and guardian of institutional standards is well recognized in the mentoring literature. R. G. Sands et al. report that it may even negate the value of well-intentioned programs: "Faculty members are peers on the departmental level. Yet those who are mentored by colleagues put themselves in an unequal and vulnerable position in relation to persons who, sometime in the future, may be making decisions about their tenure and promotion" (174).

In our department, this sense of vulnerability recently came to light in a new faculty member's annual review, leading the newcomer to request a more formally assigned mentor than the department generally provided. The request surprised senior colleagues on the committee because they regarded themselves as kindly mentors, solidly united in their intent to support their younger colleagues' professional development in the department. A fearful reaction to requests for materials therefore seemed overly distrustful. Upon reflection, however, the senior faculty came to wonder how much anxiety should be considered "too much" for those whom institutional documents label as "probationary."

The institutional culture that promotes anxiety about the judgments of others inevitably imposes its values on our department's TA advising program. Our effort to pre-empt such anxieties by describing our program as advisory rather than supervisory only partially succeeds. While we want our chosen terminology to underscore the goal of supporting professional development rather than disciplining and punishing shortcomings, some TAs suspect that behind this verbal façade their advisors are not really helpful mentors, but are instead institutional agents poised to discipline and punish.

Mentoring as *Advising*

Our graduate instructors come from many academic disciplines and represent a wide range of previous teaching experience. Regardless of their individual backgrounds, all enter our advising system by attending the teaching colloquium, PDP. Here, faculty advisors review their teaching materials and strongly encourage TAs to invite them for classroom observations. At mid-semester, advisors collect several student portfolios from each advisee and examine them to see how new instructors provide written feedback on outlines, drafts, and final versions of speeches and essays. The portfolio review is accompanied by a conference or a midterm letter from the faculty advisor. Advisors also make themselves available throughout the semester to provide additional guidance or support. After TAs have successfully completed a semester of teaching, they are considered "experienced instructors." With this reclassification comes a change in the TAs' participation in the advisory system. Experienced instructors no longer attend weekly advisory meetings, and they can petition to use independently chosen texts not included on the departmental textbook list. For as long as they teach in the department, they are assigned faculty teaching advisors to whom they submit course materials and student portfolios for midterm review. Their advisors continue offering to visit their classrooms, but unless TAs want letters of recommendation for jobs or teaching awards, they generally reject these offers.

Because our TAs arrive with varied teaching experiences and degrees of interest in teaching, they typically give PDP and the experienced advisory program mixed reviews. Faculty members, too, have mixed feelings about how the system should work. On the whole, faculty and TA responses to the advising program belie broad institutional ambivalence about the enterprise of academic mentoring. Some TAs are grateful for the close attention, while others resent and resist a surveillance system that requires them to vet their assignments with their advisors before handing them out to students. Sometimes "experienced" first-semester teachers are bored or irritated by our hands-on advisory system, considering it a waste of time and an insult to their already developed professional identities. They may regard our mentoring system as interference instead of support. Such TAs clearly feel monitored rather than mentored, and only a highly skilled, diplomatic advisor can offset this perception.

Furthermore, while some faculty enthusiastically support our current mentoring system, others equate mentoring with monitoring, and therefore see our advising system as a form of interference. While all faculty agree that some orientation to the curriculum and departmental norms is in order for new instructors, no such consensus exists about how to mentor experienced TAs. If they have already proven themselves as competent teachers, some faculty argue, we should not "burden" or "insult" them with continued surveillance. This position clearly assumes that an advisory system functions to identify and correct—possibly even to punish—the "mistakes" a teacher is found to make. Some faculty also object to experienced advising because it burdens the advisor. In a research institution, the time- and energy-consuming demands of mentoring can amount to advancing someone else's professional development at the expense of one's own. Fortunately, many of our faculty altruistically invest themselves in the informal relationships that distinguish mentoring from most other forms of academic work and are largely unrecognized by the institution. And many of our TAs respond in kind, welcoming the attention and recognition they receive from advisors. In order for these satisfying relationships to develop, however, both parties must similarly interpret the program's purposes.

But despite many advising successes and the faculty's general willingness to mentor, some graduate instructors remain skeptical of their advisors' good intentions. Given the institutional setting where our program operates, such doubts are understandable. If "probationary" faculty worry that their reviewers will find them blameworthy, might not faculty advisors similarly use teaching reviews to find their advisees culpable? And might they want to exact punishment and censure when they believe this to be the case? If a system is contaminated by bad-faith assumptions, it makes sense for advisees to avoid their advisors' scrutiny by resisting help when problems arise in the classroom or when they feel inadequate as teachers.

Such was the case in our department when an experienced instructor began to feel harassed by one of his students. Fearing that it would reflect badly on him as a teacher to "confess" his difficulties to his advisor, he tried to handle the problem himself, mainly by ignoring it and hoping it would improve on its own. Over time, however, his classroom problems grew worse instead of better; as a result, his confidence was badly shaken, and the class fell into a rapidly accelerating, downward spiral of student-teacher hostilities. Eventually, several students complained to the department chair, and impersonal bureaucratic procedures took over to manage problems the supposedly "caring" and "personal" advising system had failed to identify or address. When the problems finally came to light, the faculty tried hard to intervene in humane and constructive ways, but the intervention came too late to prevent considerable anger and discomfort among the students and the instructor.

This story of failed mentoring underscores critical obstacles to mentoring programs conceived as caring and nurturing in institutions where mentors are de facto members of a police force charged to protect institutional standards and norms. Even if such programs are not intended to discipline and punish those found in violation of standards, expectations that survival in the institution is a defensive operation may thwart even the best of intentions.

Steps Toward Fostering Effective Advisor-Advisee Relationships

While potential problems inhere in any advising situation, we try to make advising relationships comfortable and productive for all involved. Advisees need to know their advisors are not positioned to censure them. In cases of contract or ethics violations, advisors try to help advisees devise the best remedial plan and do not administer punishment. TAs also feel less singled out when they realize they actually have less surveillance than most experienced faculty members, who undergo yearly reviews that include close examination of teaching evaluations and course materials, classroom visits, and letters from the chair. Understanding that everyone is accountable to someone can make TAs and junior faculty members feel less singled-out for scrutiny because of their own inexperience or because of distrust on the part of their overseers. Knowing that you and your colleagues are all in the same boat, even if it's not a boat you enjoy, can foster a spirit of camaraderie.

Another effective approach to building collegial relationships in a vertical power structure is to focus on the benefits of the mentoring relationship. Our department boasts an excellent job placement record because our TAs have independently designed and taught writing- and speech-intensive courses. Our mentoring program has played a significant role in these job market successes as well. Advisors who maintain close contact with their TAs can write detailed letters of recommendation that highlight specific teaching accomplishments. Similarly, close advising relationships can work to a TA's advantage in competitions for teaching awards or selective teaching positions. Experience tells us that TAs' desire for strong teaching recommendations motivates outstanding work more effectively than fear of punishment for not doing what is expected. Certainly the potential for contentiousness lessens dramatically if advisees know the value of having a mentor who can help them improve and vouch for their professionalism.

Benefits come to advisors as well. Because we review our advisees' teaching materials, we are always learning from them, and we commonly introduce texts or learning activities to our own classes that our advisees have recommended. Moreover, advisors' fortunes may even benefit materially from the relationship, as when they are nominated for faculty teaching awards by their advisees. An explicit focus on such positive attributes of the advising system can foster trust between advisors and advisees and remind even the most experienced TAs of the benefits of continued "attention" to their teaching.

BALANCING PERSONAL AND INSTITUTIONAL
ELEMENTS OF MENTORING RELATIONSHIPS

While neither of us is a clone of Cleo or any other mentor, we agree with Cleo that positive reinforcement is usually a more effective advising strategy than negative surveillance. Cleo's legacy of "relentlessly positive" regard for her TA colleagues works to combat the institutional malaise we've referred to as "bad faith contamination" and defines the spirit that makes ours a mentoring system, despite the supervisory terminology the institution applies to our work. We know from experience that the personal components of mentoring relationships create possibilities for personality mismatches and even open conflicts between advisors and advisees. In facing these potential obstacles to successful mentoring, we offer advisees the opportunity to work with different advisees over time. Additionally, we aspire to approach all our colleagues with good faith, expecting that they bring the best of intentions to their professional development as teachers and strive to exhibit ethical and professional behavior. A good-faith position implies a disinclination to assume an accusatory or suspicious stance toward advisees, endorsing instead a flexibility that fosters candid, productive communication and permits a "no fault" approach to advising, whereby advisors and advisees can be reassigned without penalty when a combination is unproductive. Although our advising occurs in an institutional structure that assigns surveillance obligations to advisors, we try to show that we are not merely agents of a panoptical system;

instead, some of our most important work as advisors is just a matter of paying attention to individuals and their needs.

Works Cited

Card, Claudia. "Gender and Moral Luck." *Justice and Care:Essential Readings in Feminist Ethics*. Ed. Virginia Held. Boulder, CO: Westview Press, 1995. 79-98.

Cawyer, Carol Stringer, Cheri Simonds and Shannon Davis. "Mentoring to Facilitate Socialization: The Case of the New Faculty Member." *Qualitative Studies in Education* 15.2 (2002): 225-42.

Compton-Hall, Margaret. "Mentoring in Parallel Universes." *Reading Psychology* 23 (2002): 145-58.

Devos, Anita. "The Project of Self, the Project of Others: Mentoring, Women and the Fashioning of the Academic Subject." *Studies in Continuing Education* 26.1 (2004): 67-80.

Dixon-Reeves, Regina. "Mentoring as a Precursor to Incorporation: An Assessment of the Mentoring Experience of Recently Minted PhDs." *Journal of Black Studies* 34.1 (2003): 12-27.

Erdem, Ferda and Janset Oezen. "The Perceptions of Protégés in Academic Organizations in Regard to the Functions of Monitoring." *Higher Education in Europe* 28.4 (2004): 569-75.

Foucault, Michel. *Discipline and Punish: The Birth of the Prison*. Trans. Alan Sheridan. New York: Vintage, 1979.

Lagowski, Jeanne M. and James W. Vick. "Faculty as Mentors." *New Directions for Teaching and Learning* 62 (Summer 1995): 79-85.

Luna, Gaye, and Deborah Cullen. *Empowering the Faculty: Mentoring Redirected and Revised*. Washington D.C.: Graduate School of Education and Humanities, George Washington University, 1996.

Noble, David. *A World Without Women: The Christian Clerical Culture of Western Science*. New York: Oxford UP, 1992.

Ong, Walter. *Orality and Literacy: The Technologizing of the Word*. London: Methuen, 1982.

Sands, R. G., L. A. Parson, and J. Duane. "Faculty Mentoring Faculty in a Public University." *Journal of Higher Education* 62 (1991): 174-193.

Savage, Hallie E., Rashelle S. Karp, and Rose Logue. "Faculty Mentorship at Colleges and Universities." *College Teaching* 52:1 (2002): 21-24.

Schrodt, Paul, Carol Stringer Cawyer, and Renee Sanders. "An Examination of Academic Mentoring Behaviors and New Faculty Members' Satisfaction with Socialization and Tenure and Promotion Processes." *Communication Education* 52.1 (2003): 17-29.

24 Narrating Our Revision: A Mentoring Program's Evolution

Holly Ryan, David Reamer, and Theresa Enos

At the University of Arizona, the RCTE faculty and students actively participate in a year-long mentoring program for first-year students. This program serves to guide and support incoming students as they settle into their new surroundings.

—RCTE Handbook

Recent and growing interest in the mentoring of graduate students has come out of the increasing pressure to prepare students for the expected professionalism that will place them in a strong position when they enter the job market and beyond in their future work in the academy. Before the early to mid 1990s, there simply were no formal mentoring programs that matched individual faculty members to individual students—and certainly no structured peer mentoring programs. What did exist in a rather formal way in most programs was advising, which usually meant an appointed adviser or the program director advising each student once or twice an academic year. No doubt there was a lot of invaluable mentoring among peers but not with any formal structure or consistency. Mentoring in the 1970s and 1980s usually took the form of the master-apprentice model, with a male faculty taking as his protégé, based on similar research interests, a male graduate student. Very few female graduate students had any kind of mentoring. With the rise in the number of graduate programs in rhetoric and composition, however, and the increasing demand for hiring junior faculty in rhetoric and composition, professionalization has become a major part of many graduate programs, with formal structures of both faculty and peer mentoring emerging as part of that professionalization.

While the English Department at The University of Arizona (UA) has long had a structured mentoring program for junior faculty, graduate student mentoring takes various shapes within individual graduate programs. In the early 1990s, the Rhetoric, Composition, and the Teaching of English Program (RCTE) formalized a program for faculty/student mentoring, in part to broaden mentoring activities beyond the traditional master/apprentice model and blur rigid lines of this binary. Since 1980, RCTE has offered a required credit-bearing colloquium for first-year graduate students that deals with issues in the field and professional development (for example, managing time and preparing for the job market). Although this course is helpful in developing graduate students as professionals, it does not provide individual mentoring for new students. To that end, the Program Director also informally matched each incoming graduate to a student volunteer who was further along in the program.

Theresa Enos, as incoming Program Director in 1997, worked to more clearly delineate the goals and responsibilities of both faculty and peer mentors, so that throughout the first-year mentoring experience each graduate student would receive direction, guidance, and support in developing collegial relationships, which can lead to the types of collaborations and networking that are critical to professionalization in rhetoric and composition studies. The formal relationship with both faculty and peer mentors offers students a better opportunity to move further, perhaps even faster, toward achieving their goals. Another expected outcome is that the mentored individual is able to develop collegial relationships and to gain visibility through communicating their work and participating in professional organizations and networks.

From 2002 until the spring of 2005, Theresa worked with two RCTE graduate students, Holly Mandes and David Reamer, to improve the RCTE mentoring program and help accomplish the goals outlined above. This essay will chronicle and reflect upon our work together by incorporating moments of personal reflection and larger discussions of issues that we encountered in our work.

> *David*: When I got accepted into the RCTE program, Theresa sent me an e-mail saying I had been assigned a peer mentor. The designation didn't mean much to me, since I had always thought of a mentor as someone you

respect who has already accomplished whatever it was
you were trying to do. In our field, that meant a faculty member. But I figured Karen was someone I could
probably go to lunch with when I got to Tucson. That
was plenty for me, since I didn't know anyone in town.
And I really hate sitting in restaurants alone . . .

In the spring of 2002, second-year graduate student Holly Ryan
sent a call out to the UA RCTE listserv asking if anyone was interested in discussing mentoring of incoming students. The program had
already instituted the practice of assigning incoming students with
peer and faculty mentors to guide them through their first year, and
by most accounts this arrangement was a positive one. But although
general impressions of the mentoring program in RCTE were positive, the specifics of the program were unclear to mentors and mentees
alike. According to anecdotal evidence mentors and mentees talked
throughout the semester and occasionally had lunch, but otherwise
mentoring was an invisible presence in our program. People met with
their mentors early in the fall semester and perhaps once or twice more
during the school year, and the commitment was deemed fulfilled.
The process of assignation and expectations of mentors and mentees
went unarticulated, and until this point those involved had showed
little interest in complicating or interrogating that arrangement.

This was the context of Holly's e-mail—she was interested in looking more closely at the process and, if possible, making it more relevant
to students in the program. The response to her request was surprisingly—or perhaps not surprisingly—tepid. Only Theresa, the director of the RCTE Program, and David, a first-year graduate student,
expressed interest in assessing the program's mentoring practices. Following a series of e-mails and an initial meeting, we decided to form a
working group to evaluate and revise the RCTE mentoring program.
Theresa appointed Holly and David RCTE mentoring coordinators,
and over the course of the next two years we would work to refine and
formalize the loosely articulated mentoring program. Our work included both primary and secondary research and several presentations
of our findings and recommendations, in settings ranging from the
monthly RCTE faculty meeting to a ballroom at the 2004 Rhetoric
Society of America conference.

In the beginning, however, we focused our attention much more
locally. What, we asked, was the purpose of mentoring at the gradu-

ate level? What function did it serve in the RCTE program at UA? As we shared our mentoring experiences, we came to the conclusion that mentoring served several important functions in the program: answering basic questions, encouraging professionalization, and helping students acclimate themselves to their new surroundings. While many faculty and peer mentors were already performing these services admirably, we decided to focus our attention on how students already accustomed to the rigors of graduate student life at UA could best share their experiences.

During our conversations with graduate students and each other, we discovered that mentors and mentees in RCTE had significantly different conceptions of what the relationship was meant to entail. As there were no formal criteria for mentoring, we were not surprised to find that mentoring was occurring in many different ways, but disturbingly, mentoring was also practiced in wildly varying quantities and quality. Our first objective thus became to formalize and articulate responsibilities and expectations for mentors. We developed the following list of responsibilities for peer mentors, intended to help normalize the level and quantity of interactions between mentors and mentees:

PEER MENTOR RESPONSIBILITIES

- E-mail your mentee ASAP to make sure that moving, registering for classes, etc., is all going well.
- Arrange to meet with your mentee BEFORE the semester begins to introduce yourself and answer questions.
- Attend the social at the beginning of the fall semester with your mentee.
- Contact other mentors to arrange for small-group meetings.
- Contact your mentee on a regular basis to check progress and offer support.

We also developed a series of suggestions for encouraging professionalism and community-building among incoming students. This list (shown below) included several activities central to academic life, such as joining professional organizations and developing publications and presentations.

Suggestions for Peer Mentors

- Advise your mentee to join professional organizations such as NCTE, RSA, CCCC.
- Recommend that mentees get involved in the RCTE and graduate student communities. Encourage them to attend English Graduate Union EGU meetings, apply for professional internships, or join committees that intersect with their interests.
- Recommend that mentees attend and submit to conferences. Offer to collaborate on or workshop presentations when possible.
- Meet your mentee for lunch or dinner as often as you can.
- Help your mentee adjust to life in Tucson. Suggest good restaurants, places to visit, hot spots for nightlife, shopping locations, etc.

It was not enough to focus solely on peer mentoring, however. Faculty members were unclear about their own responsibilities to incoming students. We developed a similar set of guidelines for faculty mentoring, focusing primarily on professional development and working within the time constraints of overextended faculty members.

FACULTY MENTOR RESPONSIBILITIES

- Meet with mentees at the beginning of each semester.
- Initiate contact with your mentees at several points during the semester. Do not wait for them to always contact you. Even a simple greeting or "Do you have any questions?" can encourage students to come to you for guidance.

Suggestions for Faculty Mentors

- Meet with multiple mentees at once.
- Offer to meet with your mentees and their peer mentors.
- Encourage mentees to attend and submit to conferences. Offer feedback on proposals.
- Recommend other faculty members with similar professional interests.
- Get to know your mentees outside of the department setting by going for lunch or coffee.

- Offer to observe your mentees' teaching. This can prove to be a valuable experience for them.
- Attend social functions like the Fall Mentoring Meeting.

We realized, however, that a mentor cannot make the career for the mentee. Mentees have responsibilities within the relationship of both faculty and peer mentoring: articulating goals, taking the initiative especially after meeting with mentors the first time or two, and being committed to their professional development.

Establishing guidelines for mentoring was only the beginning of the task we outlined for ourselves. In addition to attempting to change the culture of mentoring in RCTE, we felt it was necessary to assess the strengths and weaknesses of our program as seen by our members. At the end of our first year—really our first three months—on the job, we conducted a survey of our peer mentors and mentees, asking them about their positive and negative experiences and the extent of their mentoring relationships, soliciting suggestions for mentoring activities, and seeking advice about the matching process. In particular, we were interested in what people in the mentoring program thought were appropriate contexts for mentoring and appropriate criteria for mentor-mentee matching. As we worked together over the course of the next three years, we would continue to ask these and similar questions of ourselves and our participants, both formally and informally.

David: It's the end of the spring semester. Next year's incoming class has finally been determined, and all incoming students have submitted brief autobiographical blurbs to help the mentoring coordinators match them with appropriate peer mentors. Now we're gathered around Theresa's desk, bios in hand. We unanimously match Stephen with Sally, a third-year student with similar academic histories (both entered the program with only a BA, both study public rhetorics, and both are from the east coast). We match Caren with Jessica (MA, composition studies, mountain biking). James and Jose are an obvious match (male feminist scholars). But Jeremiah is a tough one. His research doesn't correlate with anyone else in the program. He entered with a BA from a school in the Deep South, and we don't have anyone else in the program from that region. "What about Bettina?" someone ventures. "They're both African-American." "I don't know," someone else responds. "I don't think that's necessarily a valid reason to put them together. Aren't we making some assumptions about common experience?" They all ponder for a moment. "Well," the third begins slowly, "we don't have a lot of students of color here. Or faculty for that matter. Jeremiah might appreciate the perspective of someone in a similar position of difference."

While the preceding conversation is fictional, the issues raised therein are crucial to mentoring programs. What are valid criteria for matching students with peer (and, for that matter, faculty) mentors? Are academic histories and one-paragraph descriptions of personal and academic interests sufficient? What about racial and gender identities? What are the assumptions and consequences behind any match based on superficial characteristics? How can we paint a more vivid picture of the players involved so that matches can benefit everyone involved?

From the beginning we decided it was necessary for graduate students to be involved in the process. Theresa's interaction with students in the program was limited by her roles as instructor and program director, while graduate students often took multiple classes together and socialized outside of the classroom. But our combined knowledge of current graduate students was certainly incomplete—students entering with a bachelor's degree often took different courses from those entering with a master's, and levels and types of social interaction varied from person to person. And of course, our experiences were limited to current students. We knew almost nothing about those students who had recently been admitted and needed to be matched up with a mentor.

We quickly realized that personal statements and *curriculum vita* painted an incomplete picture of the people in the program's incoming class. While these documents can tell us something about the path students have taken to reach your program, they often tell very little about those students as people. After some deliberation we decided to request page-long bios from incoming students soon after they were admitted in order to give us more information to work with. These bios focused on whatever admitted students thought was important, and yielded information about everything from research interests to hobbies and family status. The bios turned out to be invaluable as we began to match incoming students with mentors—they provided a broader perspective on our incoming class, and some matches suggested themselves at once.

But even with bios in hand, matching proved complicated. Much of the information we received was superficial or nonacademic, detailing lines of scholarship or hobbies but leaving much open to our interpretation. Obvious overlaps in research or career interests make for compelling matches, but hobbies, family status, and racial and gender identities are less straightforward. While they could suggest common experiences—and thus suitable matches for mentoring purposes—we were uncomfortable ranking these criteria and placing people together based on them. Is an interest in rock climbing, for example, more likely to lead to bonding than the fact that two graduate students have children? Are either relevant for the purposes of mentoring? What about race and gender? Can we really assume that people of color will be better able to advise other people of color than whites? And what does this question say about the state of our field?

In the end we concluded that race, gender, and family status were not sufficient in and of themselves to match incoming students with mentors. Certainly they are important factors in life as a graduate student and beyond, but we are simply not prepared to make any assumptions about common experiences or shared opinions. In lieu of other compelling factors, however, these fundamental identity issues could serve as a starting point, perhaps sparking dialogue between incoming students and their peer or faculty mentors that could enrich our program and its understanding of factors affecting graduate life.

Holly: When we were invited to be a featured panel at the Rhetoric Society of America Conference in 2004, I couldn't have been more excited to discuss our research and ideas on mentoring. But when one of the participants asked "How do you handle matters of confidentiality?" I didn't know what to say exactly. We had never thought about it—at all. Certainly, our peer mentors aren't bound by any confidentiality agreements, and there is no expectation (from our perspective) that a mentoring relationship is one that requires a degree of privacy. We aren't lawyers or doctors or clergy people who were silenced by particular codes of ethics: we are mentors who are trying to smooth the transition to a new program, new school, and, often, new levels of scholarship. More significantly, none of the Web and survey research we conducted indicated that any program considered confidentiality when they designed their mentoring systems. In our program, we believe that mentoring must have boundaries.

We started conducting informal research of mentoring programs in other rhetoric and composition programs in the fall of 2004. We began by sending out simple e-mail requests to students who entered the RCTE program with master's degrees in RCTE. We asked them what kind of mentoring activities they participated in at their previous institutions, and we were surprised at the results: none of the students recalled having peer mentors, and their faculty mentors were mostly academic advisors. In one case, a student met once with a small group and her advisor to discuss teaching and to troubleshoot any teaching questions. Other than that, current students indicated that the UA was the only institution in which they ever participated in a formal mentoring program. These responses sparked our interest, and we decided to find out more about our peer institutions' programs.

In 2004, after agreeing to speak on mentoring at the Rhetoric Society of America (RSA) conference, we sent out surveys to twelve different program directors. In our survey, we asked program directors to indicate the kinds of formal activities new graduate students participate in. In general, we asked if there were formal or informal academic and/or social gatherings for students and faculty, required teacher training, colloquia for professionalization activities, orientations, and advising for students, and/or a formal first-year mentoring program with student and faculty mentors.

The response to our survey was rather abysmal with only ¼ of the schools replying back to us. Therefore, in order to supplement the information, we searched a number of university Web pages in hopes of finding information about formal mentoring programs in rhetoric and composition. We found very little online information about mentoring in any program; in fact, UA had the only page we could find where the particulars of mentoring were articulated. Occasionally, we discovered a CV in which someone would indicate she/he was a peer mentor, but that program's Web page provided no further information about mentoring.

This lack of visible articulation about mentoring as well as the limited response we received from our survey indicated to us that mentoring has been overlooked as an integral part of graduate programs. However, that is not to say that program directors, faculty, and students are not participating in mentoring all over the country. They may very well be, but the lack of information presented in a formal manner suggests that mentoring is something worth doing but not necessarily worth formalizing and interrogating in a scholarly way.

It was with this intention that we went to RSA; we wanted to have conversations about the essential, integral nature of mentoring for graduate students, and we wanted to interrogate some of our assumptions about mentoring including what we meant when we said we want to build a community and professionalize people into our field. RSA was an opportunity for those conversations and for others, such as the limits and boundaries of mentoring, that we had never thought about.

For the conference, we prepared a PowerPoint presentation that detailed how we developed our mentoring program. We explained how we organized, assessed, and restructured our program to provide a substantial experience for the incoming students and advanced students. We ended our presentation with a few key questions from our research: 1) Is community a realistic, or even a desirable, goal for a mentoring program? 2) What assumptions are implicit in this system? 3) What happens when students don't or don't want to participate? We anticipated that these questions would open up the kinds of conversations that are important to have in order to keep a program dynamic.

We expected that these questions would generate conversation, but instead, they generated more questions. In particular, the question about confidentiality sparked a considerable amount of conversation. The participant wondered how we dealt with issues of confidentiality because, at his university, faculty and students were concerned that private, personal information would be shared among the faculty and the students. This sharing could potentially harm the relationship between the mentor and the mentee because he/she might not be willing to discuss concerns or problems if the information is to be shared with others. At UA, we have decided that mentoring has boundaries, and if a student feels overwhelmed by their duties as a mentor, he/she must seek faculty assistance. We define mentoring as an academic undertaking, and not a counseling service. While we understand that a mentor may act as a confidant or as someone who soothes a nervous student's concerns, we realize we are not trained professionals and encourage students to seek other kinds of help whenever necessary. At the time of the conference, however, we hadn't confronted these issues and, in turn, had never addressed these issues with our peer mentors.

The conference made us realize that we need to continue having these conversations about mentoring, and we cannot assume that mentoring is always an easy (or even good) endeavor. By having these discussions, we can anticipate concerns and interrogate our own assumptions about what it means to be a mentor in our field.

Holly: We met with the two new mentoring coordinators to orient them to the position and the kinds of work we've done. It was strange, really, trying to summarize two years of work into two hours. Most difficult, I think, was relinquishing our vision to others knowing that they may have their own vision for our program. But it was necessary, I keep telling myself. David and I are too far into the program to have a pulse on the first-year students' needs, but I still struggle with letting go. The meeting went well, though, and we couldn't have hoped for more. The new coordinators are enthusiastic, excited, and interested in carrying through on some of our initial ideas. Still, turning over our project is an act of faith.

By their third and fourth years in the RCTE program respectively, David and Holly realized that it was time to step down as mentor coordinators. At that point in their academic careers, they were both essentially done with course work and had very little contact with first year graduate students, which they both felt was essential for keeping connected to the mentoring program. If they have regular contact with the people in the system, mentoring coordinators discover when mentoring is going well or when it needs some intervention. If the coordinators do not have this interaction, they are unable to rectify problems if they arise.

Mentoring is a dynamic process that relies on new, fresh voices and visions to keep the program alive, therefore finding suitable successors was essential. Since we never formally developed job descriptions for the mentoring coordinators, we found that we never fully articulated our positions nor had we developed a plan for replacing us. When we sent out our call for mentors, we included this call for the coordinators position: "We also need another Peer Mentor Coordinator to replace [David and Holly]. The Coordinator does the matching, organizes mentoring events, performs periodic assessments of the program, and basically just keeps the system moving." How horribly inaccurate and incomplete, we realized after we received responses from people who responded that if no one else were available, they could try to make time for the position. The coordinator does do what we called for: organizes the events, creates the matches, performs assessments, but we wanted people who would do more than keep the system moving. This "system," as we so unreflectively put it, was really a network of interpersonal relationships that contribute to the professional (and often personal) development of our graduate students. Just keeping the system moving wouldn't cut it; the coordinators needed a respect for the network (and the people within it) and a vision for its development.

We eventually found graduate students to carry on with the work that we began. The three of us feel that we've made significant changes over the course of several years. We developed job descriptions and assessment tools; we interrogated our beliefs and assumptions about what we expect from our community; we made conscious, informed decisions about our mentor matching system; and we have reflected on our own successes and failures. Our mentoring program has developed into a complex system of interpersonal relationships governed by a need for a student support system. But without people to actively and reflectively examine our program and take it in new directions, we only have a bureaucratic system that maintains its own existence without actually supporting students.

Over the last several years, scholars in rhetoric and composition have turned toward the critical to challenge their assumptions about their scholarship. We believe that mentoring deserves that same kind of close interrogation and reflection. In our experience, moments of reflection and discomfort have led us to rethink our own practices and reach out to our colleagues as we continue to define our program. We have come to realize that as rhetoric and composition scholars we can employ the tools of our discipline to contemplate the ways in which we create moments for personal and professional interaction.

25 Making It Count: Mentoring as Cultural Currency

Tanya R. Cochran and Beth Godbee

Mentoring relationships, those meaningful and often affective connections that characterize our work with students and colleagues, by their very nature, defy quantification. Even as we use the banking metaphor to describe our "investment" in others, the "return" for our time, and the "credit" we deserve, many of us who value mentoring for its qualitative and interpersonal nature resist putting our work into numeric terms. Yet in an academic culture that asks us to measure our contributions and quantify our merit, we must prove cultural capital—that we have the currency to back our reputation and contributions. Like business models that illustrate income and expenses, the curriculum vita communicates to others how we spend our professional time and energy. We must demonstrate our worth within the academic world if we are to secure tenure and promotion (like funding for a business). While we certainly believe that academic review should move away from such business and banking models, we recognize that to make such change, we must establish ourselves within this system by conveying our worth to others. To do so, we propose ways of changing the curriculum vita and review portfolio to make mentoring *count* and to establish the value of mentoring as a scholarly activity that must be valued because it is valuable to the academy.

One method of identifying instances of mentoring on the curriculum vita is already practiced to varied extents: listing the names and titles of directed readings, independent studies, theses, and dissertations. Additionally, faculty at smaller liberal arts colleges often include categories such as "Student Presentations" or "Internships Directed" that highlight projects they supervise or otherwise support. Such categories could be expanded to include student publications that develop from coursework or feedback. Since the curriculum vita has historically emphasized publication records, it makes sense to show how faculty support others' publishing. The document can bring attention to the time devoted to conferencing, advising, and otherwise supporting students and colleagues.

We can also highlight the role of mentoring in the portfolios we submit for review. Portfolio cover letters, for instance, can draw the reviewers' attention to the importance of mentoring in our professional careers and contributions. The following excerpt shows how one professor articulated her philosophy of teacher-mentoring within such a cover letter. Here she underscores the central role of mentoring in her academic life:

> Most of us do not need a book to tell us what the best teachers do.[1] The best teachers participate in their professional communities, whether by publishing, researching, attending and presenting at conferences, or keeping up with their colleagues' work. They read widely. By making every assignment matter, they challenge and even expect us to stretch our intellectual capabilities, to apply ourselves. They make learning about life and life about learning, encouraging us to confront and wrestle with unfamiliar ideas, to self-reflect, to assume control of our educations, and to collaborate with others. They insist that learning, that knowledge itself, is worthless unless we care, unless it has effect *and* affect. All of these actions suggest that, at their core, the best teachers are teachers who mentor.
>
> Teacher-mentors make us care not with lectures so much as listening, not with grades so much as careful and substantial feedback, not with homework so much as invitations to collaborate with them. What we remember is not necessarily the articles or books they have published. What we remember is their investment in us: unbelievably quick e-mail responses to last-minute questions (some at 2:31 a.m.), suggested reading lists crafted specifically to our interests, the hour it took us to reply to their query "How is your

family?" We remember having someone to emulate both professionally and personally. When tenure and promotion committees begin to value affect as equally as effect, they will finally do what teacher-mentors ask: to care. As you consider some of the unconventional materials in my portfolio, I request that you be such a committee, one that recognizes, appreciates, and rewards the commitment required to care.

While the content, tone, and style of such a cover letter will reflect the individual professor as well as take into consideration departmental politics, the letter above offers another example of what we can do to begin altering the current system of tenure and promotion and revising what counts as professional activity.

Other components of the tenure and promotion portfolios are recommendation letters solicited from co-workers, publishers, and scholars in the field. In addition to these letters, we might ask for ones from students and colleagues who have benefited from mentoring relationships. Often students ask their mentors for recommendation letters or referrals; to reciprocate, they could write letters for faculty to include in their portfolios. The following excerpt from one such letter illustrates how mentoring can be overtly recognized and documented:

> I am writing in support of tenure and promotion for Dr. Lisa Burrell[2], the Director of the Writing Studio and Assistant Professor of English. I have worked with Lisa Burrell for two years, and she has been the most positive and influential part of my master's experience. In fact, she has inspired me to continue my studies through a doctoral program in composition and rhetoric. Lisa's interests in the field have certainly shaped my own, as she has exhibited for me what it means to be an academic in the broadest sense of the word.
>
> In the two years we have worked together, Lisa has devoted large amounts of time to my academic and professional development. In the fall 2002, I enrolled in Lisa's special topics course on writing centers, and there I began several projects on tutoring, composition, and feminist pedagogy that led to directed studies as well as my first publications.

The letter goes on to provide detailed information about collaborative projects, the publications Lisa supported, and how the mentoring relationship influenced broader personal and professional development. Such letters might appear alongside ones from esteemed colleagues who praise the faculty member's research, publishing, or other professional contributions. In this way, mentoring becomes an equally important part of their academic pursuits.

In addition to letters from students and colleagues, review portfolios should contain a variety of artifacts that support the value of mentoring and illustrate the time involved with mentoring activities. Just as faculty collect copies of their publications, workshop handouts, and other materials, they should assemble documents that highlight the role of mentoring in their daily work. Such artifacts might include the following:

- Office hour sign-up sheets showing frequency and length of conferences
- Copies of written feedback given on student papers
- Transcripts of video or audiotapes of conferencing
- Directed and independent study course designs or reading lists
- Copies of recommendation letters and referrals
- Journal entries or reflection pieces describing mentoring collaborations
- Samples of student work that resulted from conferencing and other feedback
- Evaluations or reflective writing from students and colleagues

Such documentation makes clear the time and intellectual engagement devoted to mentoring activities. It further acknowledges the centrality of mentoring to ongoing academic work.

We hope that these strategies may help us not only gain recognition for our mentoring but also generate new thinking about how to represent and make known the work we do with advising, conferencing, and otherwise befriending students and colleagues. We argue that mentoring *is* professional activity and that outcomes of the relationships with colleagues and students should be weighed more heavily in career decisions. Mentoring should be included not only as a line of the curriculum vita but especially as a substantial component of annual reports and reviews. In tenure and promotion decisions, letters from students and colleagues should be taken seriously and required as part of the review process. As we assemble teaching and professional portfolios, we might provide evidence of mentoring relationships and discuss how mentoring plays out in our personal and professional lives. By taking some of these steps, we can move towards a system of tenure and promotion that is more balanced and more reflective of how the best teaching and learning actually occurs.

NOTES

1. If you would like such a book, though, see especially Ken Bain, *What the Best College Teachers Do* (Cambridge, MA, Harvard UP, 2004).

2. Pseudonym used.

26 Reflections on Mentoring

Michelle F. Eble

While the idea for *Stories of Mentoring: Theory and Praxis* materialized in response to our positive experiences with mentoring and the abundance of scholarship on the topic, we recognized early on that this collection of essays would need to go beyond simple descriptions of positive, meaningful mentoring relationships. Instead, our purpose was to provide snapshots in time, a portrait of mentoring as it exists in the field of rhetoric and writing studies. We hope this composite picture will illuminate effective models of mentoring and provide heuristics for building mentoring programs that view mentoring as a scholarly activity. The collection achieves this end by incorporating personal mentoring experiences understood through various theoretical and historical lenses, reflective practice, and prior research. This final chapter offers a reflection on some of the common threads running throughout the collection and discusses the implications this work might hold for the future of research on mentoring in rhetoric/writing studies and academia at large.

Given the abundance of scholarship on the topic and the large number of proposals we received for this collection, mentoring is vital to the education of academic administrators and teachers/researchers, along with the future of academic programs. Clear sets of strategies and practices are in place—often referred to as professional development—to initiate newcomers into the profession. The theory and praxis of mentoring discussed in this collection moves beyond the common strategies and practices for professional development. This work defines mentoring in a wide variety of contexts, compiles approaches to mentoring, documents successful mentoring relationships and programs, and provides new ways of thinking and reflecting on mentoring metaphors and historical uses of the term. Several chapters illustrate best practices while also cautioning against mentoring based on one-to-one relationships, mentoring based on the power of the mentor and subordination of the mentee, and those mentoring relationships based on exclusivity or exclusion.

The notion and practice of mentoring can be complicated especially for those who have not, for whatever reason, had experiences like the ones discussed in this collection. More importantly, what's omitted from this collection is as instructive as what we include and provides insight into future areas of research on mentoring. By no means do we proffer this work as a definitive volume on mentoring in academia, nor is it necessarily a "how-to mentor" treatise. In fact, ultimately, this collection provides a point of departure from which scholars might continue thinking about mentoring and building on the rich research and practices discussed here.

Throughout the twenty-five chapters in this collection, contributors characterize mentoring relationships as professional and personal, flexible, and nurturing. These relationships are described as colleague-building, collaborative, multifarious, beneficial, complex, and life-changing. According to most of the volume's contributors, these relationships occur through interaction, communication, and collaboration—actions that are mutually beneficial and reciprocal. Mentoring programs attempt to create such environments and focus on community-building and peer mentoring. Drawing conclusions from the research and practices discussed in this work is difficult, but a majority of the mentoring relationships described became collegial provided that two elements existed: mutual benefit and respect. Several chapters point out that an emphasis on community-building and generative relationships help lead to successful collegial partnerships. Aren't all students, especially ones interested in employment in higher education, striving towards supportive and respectful collegial relationships? An emphasis on this perspective of mentoring (building colleagues) is key to both the current and future discussions of mentoring.

As evidenced in these chapters, mentoring takes many forms—from formal mentoring programs to peer groups; from co-teaching to dissertation directing; from advising to fostering mutually beneficial relationships (based on respect and reciprocity); and from collaborating within meetings and producing scholarship to modeling effective administrative and professional activities. This volume collectively asserts that mentoring, as a scholarly activity, should be valued and rewarded much like teaching, research, service, and administrative work. Several chapters provide heuristics for thinking about how to both value and evaluate mentoring. Almost all the pieces in the collection were written collaboratively as if writing about mentoring is in and of itself a collaborative process. The chapters also account for the locations of mentoring occurring in varied contexts—in departments, programs, universities, conferences, writing groups, meetings, special interest groups (SIGs), caucuses, and coalitions, etc. Mentoring relationships occur across ranks as well. For example, tenured faculty may learn just as much from their graduate students and/or junior faculty when it comes to technology (as has often been my experience) as the junior faculty member learns from their colleagues about the department culture and history and/or research opportunities in the field.

Contributors to this volume agree that mentoring (whether individual, group, or in a program) should be viewed as a scholarly practice. Once the act is documented as such, people can begin to research mentoring more formally and collect best practices. We see this book as one step in that direction and the pieces collected in it as illustrations of practices worth valuing. For so long, the predominant theory of mentoring—master-apprentice model—was problematic and based on exclusion and tokenism. Only the lucky were mentored, and the predominant mentoring model was difficult to institute and promote. Over time, we think as the pieces in this work illustrate, the theory of mentoring has changed, and as a field we are beginning to understand the importance of this practice within the academy, not just for the token few or the ones who make it through the academic bureaucratic hoops but for all those who want to take advantage of engaging in relationships that are mutually beneficial and generative.

What has contributed to the rise and interest in programmatic mentoring in higher education? Many of the chapters point to the relationship between mentoring and the teaching of writing because in many ways, writing program administrators become mentors by the nature of their positions as they help professionalize teaching assistants (TAs). Several chapters point out how mentoring can have positive effect on programs and the teaching, learning, and research that occurs within them. Partly, mentoring exists because of program and student needs, but we also argue that mentoring has intangible benefits to hiring departments as well. Those students who have been mentored and encouraged to engage in professional development activities in graduate school often become cooperative colleagues because they learned as students to collaborate and work in mutually beneficial relationships. This experience translates into a more effective, less traumatic transition to tenure-track or other professional positions. Departments who mentor junior faculty not only provide a smoother transition to the job and academic culture, but also help acclimate junior faculty in ways which ultimately lead to hiring retention and more collegial departments.

Of course, one of the problems inherent with attempting to provide a snapshot is that inevitably elements get left out. This edited collection is no different. The majority of the contributors to this collection are women, but we do not interpret this to mean that a majority of mentoring is done by women. We know of many men who have been mentors in our field; several of them contributed to this volume, yet a collection like this, in some ways, continues to foster the notion that most mentoring is done by women. Is this because women are seen as more nurturing? For the most part, the contributors to this collection do not see mentoring as synonymous with nurturing, and we hope others will explore these myths and assumptions about mentoring. Contributors to this work also point out that scholars of color and women are often expected to shoulder a greater burden of mentoring to help diversify the field. Clearly, future work on mentoring should focus on fostering mentoring relationships that occur across boundaries of race, ethnicity, class, gender, sexuality, and disability. Also at issue are mentoring programs based on conscription—programs that focus on compliance rather than productivity or collaboration. A couple of chapters raise these issues and touch on possible models that may help further conversations about the implications of mentoring. What about those students and new faculty who don't have mentors—because they don't know to find one or because none are available? Can mentoring happen through other means? This collection provides only a couple of options for those who don't have access to mentoring, and we know the voices collected here are not exhaustive. We recognize that resistance to mentoring exists and power/authority struggles are real. We don't want to minimize these tensions in mentoring relationships; however, we hope this collection will serve as a starting point for other conversations.

Obviously, mentoring can take on a wide variety of forms: from individual relationships between faculty and students, WPAs and graduate students, major professors/dissertation directors and their mentees to formal mentoring programs. Mentoring can also happen in various contexts and may include peer mentors (experienced TAs mentoring new TAs), professional development seminars, writing groups, collaborative endeavors, internships, and assistantships—whether administrative, teaching, or research. Lynée's rewarding experience in graduate school working with Win Horner prepared her to serve as my mentor from our very first meeting when as a graduate student, I took teaching composition from Lynée. Win's collaborations with her graduate students led Lynée to envision collaboration as beneficial to students, program development, and ultimately the mentor herself. As a result of our earlier relationship, Lynée (then the WPA at our institution) recruited me to serve as assistant WPA—a new position that she created. Together, with the help of others, we implemented a mentoring program whereby experienced visiting instructors and TAs mentored new TAs. We initiated a series of mentoring seminars that TAs were required to attend. It was an incredibly rewarding experience for all of us involved in the process. I was able to take these experiences with me to my own institution where I continue to mentor technical and professional writing students as they complete their Master's degrees and advise undergraduate English majors as well as PhD students. Lynée and I have also collaborated on a number of research projects, published an article, and worked on this edited collection. Because of Win's philosophy of mentoring, Lynée and I are also conducting these same professional activities with other colleagues and our individual advisees.

Informal and formal mentoring takes place in innovative and sustaining ways at many universities and colleges. This became obvious to me when, as a new assistant professor, one of my new colleagues and I realized right away that we taught professional writing in similar ways. One of my previous mentors and my new colleague completed their PhDs at the same school and had been part of a highly respected professional writing mentoring program. While I realize that not all new hires have such serendipitous experiences, talking with a new colleague about their teaching or research is one small way to begin to build a mutually beneficial relationship.

The examples of mentoring appearing in this work occur across time and place, beginning in graduate school, through motherhood/fatherhood and tenure, throughout whole lifetimes, and across race, gender, and age. We are inspired by the life-changing, mutually-bene-ficial, generative relationships depicted in this work. Mentoring helps build a community of scholars and ensures that knowledge-building continues in each new generation.

I found myself in such a position only recently as I began to advise a graduate student on her dissertation topic. I was introduced to the field through my mentor, Lynée; after all these years (ten to be exact), we are colleagues who continue to generate new projects and bounce ideas off each other, to present collaboratively at conferences, to hold each other to deadlines, and to introduce each other to new colleagues and new projects. As we put the finishing touches on this manuscript, I find myself going up for tenure. It seems in many ways that Lynée and I have come full circle, as one of my first acts as Lynée's assistant was to help her put her own tenure file together. What an invaluable experience that process holds for me today. I realize that the real value in mentoring is the legacy that continues through each generation and act of mentoring.

We are aware of the providential nature and the role personality plays in most of the collaborations described in this work. We received very few angry or highly critical submissions on mentoring, but we know these stories and these unfortunate relationships do exist. We also recognize those who don't have any mentoring stories to tell. Our intent in this work has not been to exclude these stories or these expe-riences. We want to encourage readers, researchers, teachers, students, program administrators, and advisors to build relationships with stu-dents, professors, and colleagues based on common interests and goals. The one motif that stands out in all the chapters of this collection and our own experiences includes this mutual, two-way relationship where each person receives some benefit. We want to promote mentoring that matches or reflects the experiences described in this collection, and we call for continued research and scholarship on mentoring in order to make these positive experiences available to as many students as possible.

Contributors

Diana Ashe is an Assistant Professor in the English Department at the University of North Carolina at Wilmington and the mentee designée for her coauthor, Elizabeth Ervin. Her research focuses on writers and controversies in environmental rhetoric and technical communication, and she serves as the director of UNCW's Professional Writing Program.

Ken Baake is an Associate Professor of English at Texas Tech University in the technical communication and rhetoric program. He is the author of *Metaphor and Knowledge: The Challenges of Writing Science* (2003) and also researches the different ways that people understand their environments—in particular, the water-starved American West.

Stephen A. Bernhardt is the Chair of the Department and Professor of English at the University of Delaware. He holds the Andrew B. Kirkpatrick, Jr. Chair in Writing, from which position he promotes strong writing and communication skills across the university. He teaches scientific, technical and business communication at all levels. Professor Bernhardt is widely published in leading journals, with research interests centering on visual rhetoric, computers and writing, workplace training and development, and the teaching of scientific and technical communication.

Paula Braun is an analyst at the Government Accountability Office. From 2002 to 2004, she worked as a writing tutor at the University of Toledo. In 2003, she chaired and participated in a panel presentation at the IWCA-NCPTW joint conference that explored the directive versus non-directive paradigm, found in most tutoring manuals, in light of post process writing theories. In 2005, the *Writing Lab Newsletter* published a synopsis of the presentation.

Meredith Kate Brown is a PhD candidate at the University of Louisville where she is currently working as a Graduate Teaching Assistant and as an Assistant Director of the Writing Centers Research Project. In 2007, Kate was the recipient of an International Writing Centers Association research grant to help support research for her dissertation, *Breaking into the Tutor's Toolbox: An Investigation into Strategies Used in Writing Center Tutorials.* Her most recent scholarship has appeared in the *Writing Center Journal.*

Eva R. Brumberger is an Assistant Professor in the Professional Writing program at Virginia Tech. She teaches undergraduate and graduate courses in visual rhetoric, document design, technical editing, professional writing, and business writing. Her research and publication areas include visual rhetoric and document design, international communication, and the pedagogy of professional communication. She has taught as an instructor at the University of Wyoming and as an adjunct at the University of Alaska, Johnson and Wales, and the New England Institute of Technology. She also worked as a technical writer in the computer industry and continues to do freelance writing, editing, and design work.

Rebecca E. Burnett is Director of Writing and Communication at Georgia Institute of Technology and Professor of Rhetoric in the Department of Literature, Communication, and Culture. Her research interests include risk communication, workplace literacies, communication-in–the-disciplines, collaboration and teamwork, and international technical communication.

Lisa Cahill is a program manager for the writing support program at the Arizona State University Learning Resource Center. Her research interests include writing center theory and writing in the disciplines. Her work has appeared in edited collections.

Jennifer Clary-Lemon is Assistant Professor of Rhetoric at the University of Winnipeg. She is co-editor, with Peter Vandenberg and Sue Hum, of *Relations, Locations, Positions: Composition Theory for Writing Teachers.* Her research and teaching interests include examining the rhetorics of representation, as well as composition history and disciplinarity. She has published in *Composition Studies* and (with Maureen Daly Goggin and Duane Roen) the *Handbook of Research on Writing.*

Tanya R. Cochran is Assistant Professor of English at Union College in Lincoln, Nebraska. Her research focuses on cultural studies, composition and rhetoric, and faith and learning. She has published in a variety of journals and has book chapters included in *Televising Queer Women: A Reader* (Palgrave, 2007) and *Modern Mythology in the New Millennium* (Lang, 2008). In addition to chairing the Science Fiction and Fantasy Area of the Popular Culture Association and serving as an editorial board member for *Watcher Junior: The Undergraduate Journal of Buffy Studies*, Tanya is the coeditor, with Rhonda V. Wilcox, of *Investigating* Firefly *and* Serenity: *Science Fiction on the Frontier* (Tauris, 2008).

Barbara Cole received her PhD in Poetics from SUNY Buffalo. Her current research focuses on modernist "difficulty" and the problem of critical reception, most notably in the work of Gertrude Stein.

Michele Comstock is an Assistant Professor in the Department of English at the University of Colorado Denver. She has published articles on gender, youth, and digital media literacy. Currently, she is collaborating on a book-length project on public space and the privatization of writing and teaching.

Kelli L. Custer, a graduate student at Indiana University of Pennsylvania, is finishing her dissertation, "Driven Identities: How the Personal and Professional Identities of 13 Past CCCC Chairs Relate to the Identity of the Field." The piece is scholarly creative non-fiction with travelogue overtones, as the interview-based research-collecting road trip was approximately 12,000 miles. Her research interests include issues surrounding identity, particularly the development of professional identity by beginning teachers, teacher training, and writing program administration.

Doug Downs is an Assistant Professor in Rhetoric and Composition at Montana State University. His research interests center on cultural conceptions of writing shared by the public and the academy, and how those conceptions impact writing instruction and instructor preparation. Much of his current mentoring focuses on undergraduate research, as he is an editor for the national undergraduate Writing Studies research journal *Young Scholars in Writing* and active in mentoring the research and presentations of students in his own department.

Katherine Durack worked as a writer, editor, and consultant in the computer industry before joining the faculty at Miami University. Her research has received several awards, including outstanding article awards for publications in *Technical Communication, Technical Communication Quarterly,* and the *Journal of the Association of Proposal Management Professionals* and the Outstanding Dissertation Award in Technical Communication, sponsored by the Conference on College Composition and Communication Committee on Technical Communication for 1998. She is currently exploring her interests in the patent genre.

Angela Eaton is an Assistant Professor of Technical Communication and Rhetoric at Texas Tech University. She studies professional and technical communication practice and pedagogy, especially within online environments, and teaches courses in editing, grant writing, and research methods. She is also a contract technical communicator, editor, and grantwriter.

Michelle F. Eble is an Associate Professor at East Carolina University where she also serves as Director of Undergraduate Studies in the Department of English. Her work has appeared in *Computers and Composition, Technical Communication,* and *Technical Communication Quarterly.*

Carol Ellis is a member of the writing faculty at the newest University of California campus in Merced, California. Her PhD in English is from the University of Iowa in Iowa City. Carol writes in a variety of genres and has presented many papers, including presentations at MLA and CCCC. Her most recent published poem in *The Comstock Review* will be followed by her essay on disability as an idea. Carol is working on a book of her poems for publication.

Jessica Enoch earned her PhD from Penn State in 2003. She is now an Assistant Professor at the University of Pittsburgh. Her work has appeared in *College English* and *College Composition and Communication.*

Theresa Enos is currently Professor of English and was Director (1997-2004) of the Rhetoric, Composition, and the Teaching of English Graduate program at The University of Arizona. Founder and editor of *Rhetoric Review,* she teaches both graduate and undergraduate courses in writing and rhetoric. Her research interests include the history and theory of rhetoric and the intellectual work and politics of rhetoric and composition studies. She has edited or coedited ten books and has numerous chapters and essays published on rhetorical theory and issues in writing. She is the author of *Gender Roles and Faculty Lives in Rhetoric and Composition* and co-editor of *The Promise and Perils of Writing Program Administration* (Parlor Press, 2008).

Elizabeth Ervin is an Associate Professor in the English Department at the University of North Carolina at Wilmington and the mentor designée for her coauthor, Diana Ashe. Her essays on public discourse, composition pedagogy, and rhetorical theory have been published in numerous journals and collections, and an ethnographic study on feminist mentoring appeared in *Women's Studies: An Interdisciplinary Journal*. Professor Ervin is the author of the textbook *Public Literacy*, now in its second edition, and is currently working on a book about the concept of *copia* as it relates to rhetorical ethics.

Bruce W. Farmer spent a career at TRW, the aerospace firm in Redondo Beach, California. He was driven to pursue a PhD by his increasing recognition that good communication practices are at the heart of high-functioning technical and business work environments. At New Mexico State University, his coursework bridged departments of business, communication, and English, with an emphasis on finding the common threads in the research on organizational communication, management, and productivity. Following a dissertation on the socialization of workers into organizations, Bruce returned to TRW, where he finished his career.

Jenn Fishman, Assistant Professor of English at the University of Tennessee, teaches and researches at the intersection of rhetoric and composition, performance studies, and eighteenth-century studies. She is currently at work on a book entitled *Active Literacy*.

Julie Dyke Ford received her PhD from New Mexico State in 2001. She is currently Associate Professor of Technical Communication and Director of the Technical Communication program at New Mexico Tech, located in Socorro. She has published and presented in the areas of engineering communication, technical communication pedagogy, organizational communication, and medical writing. Julie serves as a member of the ATTW executive board and is the faculty sponsor for New Mexico Tech's student STC chapter.

Dorinda Fox earned a PhD in the History of Rhetoric from the Florida State University, as well as an MA in Technical and Expository Writing from the University of Arkansas at Little Rock. Her dissertation examined sophistic rhetorical practices inherent in the work of Chris Rock and George Carlin and how their work could be used to teach composition. She specializes in teaching online writing courses.

Catherine Gabor is an Assistant Professor (and mentor) of Rhetoric and Composition in the English Department at California State University, Sacramento. Her teaching and scholarship focus on service-learning and electronic writing spaces/tools.

Lynée Lewis Gaillet is Associate Professor of Rhetoric and Composition at Georgia State University. She is the editor of *Scottish Rhetoric and Its Influences* and author of numerous articles and book chapters addressing writing program administration and the history of rhetoric/writing practices. Currently, she is co-editing with Winifred Bryan Horner the 2nd edition of *The Present State of Research in the History of Rhetoric*.

Cheryl Glenn is Liberal Arts Research Professor of English and Women's Studies and co-director of the Center for Democratic Deliberation at Penn State University. In the summers, she teaches courses in rhetoric and writing at the Bread Loaf School of English (Middlebury, Vermont, and Santa Fe, New Mexico). Her many scholarly publications include *Rhetoric Retold: Regendering the Tradition from Antiquity Through the Renaissance, Unspoken: A Rhetoric of Silence, Rhetorical Education in America, The St. Martin's Guide to Teaching Writing, The Writer's Harbrace Handbook, Making Sense: A Real-World Rhetorical Reader*, and *The Harbrace Guide for College Writers*. With Shirley Wilson Logan, she co-edits the Southern Illinois University Press series, "Studies in Rhetorics and Feminisms."

Beth Godbee is a doctoral student in composition and rhetoric at the University of Wisconsin-Madison, where she works in the writing center and teaches composition. She has published in *Southern Discourse, Praxis*, and *Writing Lab Newsletter* and serves as the graduate student representative of both the International Writing Centers Association (IWCA) and Midwest Writing Centers Association (MWCA).

Dayna Goldstein is a PhD Fellow in the Literacy, Rhetoric, and Social Practice program at Kent State University. Her research interests include posthumanism, information literacy, disciplinarity, and assessment. She is presently serving as the graduate assistant to the KSU writing program and a senior writing center tutor.

Baotong Gu is Associate Professor of English at Georgia State University, where he teaches technical communication with an emphasis on electronic media and technology. His publications include two co-edited collections: *Contemporary Western Rhetoric: Critical Methods and Paradigms* and *Contemporary Western Rhetoric: Speech and Discourse Criticism.*

Alfred E. Guy Jr. is the R.W.B. Lewis Director of the Yale College Writing Center, which coordinates Yale's WAC requirement. He has previously served as Director or Associate Director of the writing programs at Johns Hopkins, Princeton, and New York University, and has been an Associate of the Bard College Institute for Writing and Thinking since 1993 (where he is also a member of the Advisory Board). His composition scholarship focuses on how students learn academic discourse and how graduate student teachers become professionals.

Thomas L Hager is currently working at IBM in the Financial Services Sector as global client director for Deutsche Bank. In his job, he is responsible for total IBM sales to Deutsche Bank. Thomas joined IBM during the course of his PhD program in Rhetoric and professional communication at New Mexico State University. While working in various IBM technical writing, development, corporate communications, and marketing functions, he completed his research and finished his dissertation.

Amy C. Kimme Hea is an Associate Professor in the Rhetoric, Composition, and Teaching of English program at University of Arizona. Her research interests include Web and wireless teaching and learning, teacher training, and professional writing theory and practice. She has published on articulation theory and methodology, visual rhetoric, WWW design, hypertext theory, and service learning projects. Her collection *Going Wireless* is part of Hampton's Computers and

Composition series, and her other work appears in journals including *Computers and Composition, Kairos, Educare/Educare, and Reflections: A Journal of Writing, Service-Learning, and Community Literacy.*

Amy Hodges Hamilton is Assistant Professor of English at Belmont University. Her research and teaching interests center on personal writing, writing and healing, feminist theory, and healing and the arts. With Wendy Bishop, she co-authored "Letter Writing and Loss" (*Trauma and the Teaching of Writing*, SUNY 2005), which explores writing as a way to heal both private and public traumas. She has served on panels as an expert in writing and healing, and also leads writing and healing workshops in her community.

Bill Hart-Davidson is an Assistant Professor in the Department of Writing, Rhetoric, and American Cultures at Michigan State University and a co-director of the Writing in Digital Environments Research Center. His research interests lie at the intersection of Technical Communication and Human-Computer Interaction in such areas as visualizing knowledge work processes and user experience design.

Winifred Bryan Horner is University of Missouri Professor of English and Texas Christian University Radford Chair of Rhetoric Emerita. She has published twelve books on rhetoric and composition and has lectured widely both nationally and internationally. Her many students are well-known active scholars in the field of Rhetoric and Composition.

Robert Kramer has worked extensively in the field of visual communication, including Web development, photography and digital video. Prior to joining the Los Alamos National Laboratory in New Mexico, he worked as a writer for IBM, and he also was part of a multi-state, federal grant project at New Mexico State that produced multimedia materials for teachers. His most recent publication in *Technical Communication* concerned single sourcing. Currently, Robert is designing Web spaces and interactive media, developing streaming servers, and shooting new portfolios of technical and scientific digital images.

Janice Lauer is Distinguished Professor of English, Emerita at Purdue University, where she directed the graduate program in Rhetoric and Composition. She received the CCCC Exemplar Award and has published on invention, disciplinarity, empirical research in composition, and classical rhetoric. Her most recent book is *Invention in Rhetoric and Composition*.

Anna Leahy is the author of *Constituents of Matter,* which won the Wick Poetry Prize and was published by Kent State University Press. Her poems appear regularly in literary journals such as the *Connecticut Review, Crab Orchard Review,* and *The Journal,* and she is a guest poetry editor for *Fifth Wednesday.* She also edited *Power and Identity in the Creative Writing Classroom,* which includes an essay by Wendy Bishop and, in part, led to Leahy's collaborative essay in this collection about mentoring. Leahy collaborates, too, with an art historian and with a computer scientist in other scholarly endeavors for publications such as *English Language Notes* and *Curator.*

Carrie Leverenz is Associate Professor of English at Texas Christian University, where she teaches courses in writing, composition theory and pedagogy, rhetorical criticism, and cyberliteracy. Her current research focuses on ethics and writing program administration and on the challenges new media writing poses to the field of composition. She currently directs the New Media Writing Studio at TCU, after serving as Director of Composition for 7 years. Prior to coming to TCU, she Directed the Reading/Writing Center and Computer-Supported Writing Classrooms at Florida State University.

C. Renée Love teaches Composition, Professional Communication, and Literature courses at Lander University. She is particularly interested in interdisciplinary approaches that create bridges or that synthesize polarities, the space between personal and academic, literature and composition, community and classroom, private and civic.

Andrea Lunsford is the Louise Hewlett Nixon Professor of English and Humanities and Director of the Program in Writing and Rhetoric at Stanford University. She has designed and taught undergraduate and graduate courses in writing history and theory, rhetoric, literacy studies, and intellectual property and is the author or co-author of many books and articles, including *The Everyday Writer; Essays on Classical Rhetoric and Modern Discourse; Singular Texts/Plural Authors: Perspectives on Collaborative Writing; Reclaiming Rhetorica: Women in the History of Rhetoric, Everything's an Argument,* and *Exploring Borderlands: Composition and Postcolonial Studies.*

Arabella Lyon, Associate Professor of English at SUNY Buffalo, winner of the W. Ross Winterowd Award for *Intentions: Negotiated, Contested, and Ignored,* is currently working on two book-length projects, one on transnationalism and comparative rhetoric, the other on deliberative democracy, human rights, and speech-act theory.

Rita Malenczyk is Professor of English at Eastern Connecticut State University, where she has directed the writing program since 1994. Her work, which focuses primarily on the rhetoric and politics of writing program administration, has appeared in the journal *WPA* and in several edited collections, including *Administrative Problem-Solving for Program Administrator as Theorist* (eds. Rose and Weiser, Boynton-Cook/Heinemann) and *The Outcomes Book* (Utah State UP) which she co-edited with Susanmarie Harrington, Keith Rhodes, and Ruth Overman Fischer.

Katherine S. Miles is an Assistant Professor of English Writing and Rhetoric at St. Edward's University in Austin, Texas. Her dissertation, written under the direction of Dr. Rebecca Burnett, investigates the rhetorical situation of a virtual reality chamber and the effects of multimodal contexts on technical communication pedagogy. Currently, she is investigating technological multitasking and its implications for student learning and workplace practices.

Susan K. Miller-Cochran is Associate Professor of English at North Carolina State University and Director of the First-Year Writing Program. Her research focuses on the uses of technology in teaching writing, especially with second language writers. She is especially interested in the ways that different technologies can facilitate writing, research, and collaboration, both in a classroom and at a distance. Her work has appeared in *Composition Studies, Computers and Composition*, and *Teaching English in the Two-Year College*, and she is also an editor of *Rhetorically Rethinking Usability* (Hampton Press, forthcoming) and *Strategies for Teaching First-Year Composition* (National Council of Teachers of English, 2002).

Jerry Moore graduated in 2005 from Texas Tech University with a Bachelor's degree in English specializing in Technical Communication. In addition to English, his academic interests include military history and Homeric Greek. Prior to attending college, Jerry served in the United States Air Force for ten years.

Tom Moriarty is an Associate Professor of English and Director of the Writing Across the Curriculum program at Salisbury University. He is the author of *Finding the Words: A Rhetorical History of South Africa's Transition from Apartheid to Democracy* (Praeger/Greenwood 2003) and is currently co-editing a collection for Utah State University Press on the development of undergraduate degree programs in Rhetoric and Writing.

Cinda Coggins Mosher is a Lecturer in Rhetoric at the University of Iowa where she assumes many duties including the directorship of the Speaking Center. Her research interests include Writing Center pedagogy and contemporary media.

Joan Mullin has taught writing and initiated and/or directed writing centers and WAC programs at the Universities of Toledo and at Texas in Austin. Mullin has published in writing center, WAC and disciplinary journals; recent publications have included studies of the intersection of visual/written texts, disciplinary definitions of plagiarism, and student-faculty mentoring in classrooms. Currently chair of English Studies at Illinois State, Mullin consults and studies international sites of writing instruction and serves as a consultant-evaluator for the Council of Writing Program Administrators.

Nancy Myers is Associate Professor of English at the University of North Carolina at Greensboro where she teaches composition, linguistics, and the history of rhetoric. She received the UNCG Alumni Teaching Excellence Award in 2002. Along with Gary Tate and Edward P. J. Corbett, she is an editor of the third and fourth editions of *The Writing Teacher's Sourcebook* (Oxford). In addition to her other articles, she most recently published essays in *Relations, Locations, Positions: Composition Theory for Writing Teachers* (NCTE 2006) and *The Locations of Composition* (SUNY 2007).

Stacia Dunn Neeley is Associate Professor of English in the Department of Languages and Literature at Texas Wesleyan University in Fort Worth, Texas. She teaches composition/rhetoric and women's studies, and her scholarly interests include critical pedagogy, cultural studies, and feminist rhetoric.

Lorelei Ortiz is Associate Professor of Business Communication at St. Edward's University's School of Management and Business in Austin, Texas. Ortiz developed and teaches International Business Communication courses, serves as mentor and advisor to International Business majors, and is founder and faculty advisor for the Hispanic Business Students Association at St. Edward's University. She received the "Outstanding Faculty Advisor" award in 2006 and continues to mentor students as a QPR Suicide Prevention instructor and as co-organizer of the SEUganda Mission Support Program, benefiting the Women's Center in Uganda. Ortiz has published in the Journal of Business Communication and the Journal of Writing and Technical Communication.

Veronica Pantoja is an English faculty member at Chandler-Gilbert Community College, in Chandler, Arizona. Her current research interests include writing centers and computer-mediated composition and pedagogy. Her work has appeared in *Teaching English in the Two-Year College*, and various edited collections.

Tim Peeples is Associate Dean of Elon College, the College of Arts and Sciences, and Associate Professor of English at Elon University in Elon, North Carolina, where he continues to teach courses in the Professional Writing and Rhetoric English major concentration as well as first-year composition. He has edited a professional writing reader, co-authored a first-year composition textbook, and published a number of articles on issues related to writing program administration.

George L. Pullman is Associate Professor of English at Georgia State University where he teaches electronic writing and history of rhetoric. His articles have appeared in such journals as *Computers and Composition*, *Rhetoric Review*, *JAC*, and *Rhetoric Society Quarterly*.

Krista Ratcliffe is Professor and Chair of English at Marquette University in Milwaukee, WI, where she teaches undergraduate and graduate courses in rhetoric and composition theory, writing, and women's literature. She has served as MLA representative to the Division on Teaching Writing, as CCCC Representative and Chair of NCTE's College Forum and as President of the Coalition of Women Scholars in the History of Rhetoric and Composition. Her research focuses on the intersections of rhetoric, feminist theory, and pedagogy. Her publications include *Anglo-American Feminist Challenges to the Rhetorical Tradition*, *Who's Having This Baby?* (with Helen Sterk, Carla Hay, Alice Kehoe, and Leona VandeVusse), and *Rhetorical Listening: Identifi-*

cation, Gender, Whiteness (2006 JAC Gary Olsen Award; 2007 CCCC Outstanding Book Award); her work has appeared in edited collections, as well as in *CCC, JAC, Rhetoric Review, and College English.*

David Reamer is a PhD student in the Rhetoric, Composition, and the Teaching of English program at the University of Arizona. His dissertation, "Ethics, Professionalism, and the Service Course: Rhetorics of (Re)Framing in Technical Communication," examines the technical communication service course as a site for outreach, not only through pedagogies that address the needs of local communities, but also as a site of ethical, professional, and civic instruction for students in disciplines outside of the humanities. His work on technical communication pedagogy and civic participation has appeared in *Composition Studies.*

Larissa Reuer currently resides in Chapel Hill, North Carolina.

Rochelle L. Rodrigo is an English faculty member and instructional technologist at Mesa Community College in Arizona. She has taught writing, film, and literature classes and has presented at institutional, local and national, disciplinary and interdisciplinary workshops about technology and writing. Her work, which explores interactions between humanities and technology, has appeared in *Computers and Composition, Teaching English in the Two-Year College, Journal of Advancing Technology, Flow,* as well as various edited collections.

Duane Roen is Professor of English at Arizona State University, where he serves as Head of Humanities and Arts in the School of Applied Arts and Sciences. Since his days as an undergraduate, he has been interested in how teachers can help students learn more effectively. Duane enjoys making connections among disciplines, which means that he draws on many fields in his scholarship—rhetorical theory, composition theory, literary theory, linguistics, psychology, sociology, feminism, anthropology. Because his interest in collaboration writing is more than an abstraction, he has collaborated on most of his books, chapters, journal articles, and conference papers. He finds collaborating with graduate students to be especially exciting.

Linda Rothman graduated in August 2007 with a BA in English with an emphasis in Technical Communication from Texas Tech University. She works as a medical transcriptionist and enjoys editing and proofreading for friends and colleagues.

Holly Ryan is a doctoral candidate in the Rhetoric, Composition, and Teaching of English program at the University of Arizona. A teacher of undergraduate courses in composition, her current interests include rhetorics of the body, specifically disability rhetoric, writing program administration, and peer tutoring in online spaces. She is coordinator (along with David Reamer) of the RCTE mentoring program, and recently published "The Idea of a Writing Center Meets the Reality of Classroom-Based Tutoring" in *On Location: Theory and Practice in Classroom-Based Writing Tutoring*.

Donna Decker Schuster earned her PhD in English at Marquette University, where she currently teaches. Her dissertation, "Exclusionary Politics: Mourning and Modernism in the Work of Elizabeth Barrett Browning, Amy Levy, and Charlotte Mew," explores connections among gender, literary modernism, and nationalism. She has published articles on Toni Morrison's *Beloved*, Elizabeth Barrett Browning and nationalist poetry, and The Heritage of Irish Elegy in Neill Jordan's "The Crying Game." She recently co-edited an essay collection entitled *Women's Literary Creativity and the Female Body* (Palgrave MacMillan, 2007).

Wendy Sharer is Associate Professor of English and Director of Composition at East Carolina University. She is the author of *Vote and Voice: Women's Organizations and Political Literacy, 1915-1930* (SIUP 2004), co-author of *1977: A Cultural Moment in Composition* (Parlor Press, 2008)), and co-editor of *Rhetorical Education in America* (U of Alabama 2004). Her work has also appeared in *Rhetoric Review* and *Rhetoric Society Quarterly*. Her most recent project is an edited collection about archival research methods in composition and rhetoric.

Jessica Smith works as the Institutional Research Coordinator for the University of Mary Hardin-Baylor in Belton, Texas and as a freelance technical writer and editor. Her scholarly works focuses on technical editing, information architecture, and developing user-friendly interface design.

Susan N. Smith is currently finishing her dissertation in Rhetoric, Composition, and the Teaching of English at The University of Arizona. Sue studies heuristic tools that students use in analysis of professional writing, and she currently teaches the writing component of a Management Law and Ethics course at Eller College at UA.

Randi Spinks received her BA in English with a specialization in Technical Communication from Texas Tech University in August of 2004.

Betsy Strosser will soon receive her Master's degree in Technical Communication at Texas Tech University. In May, 2004, she earned a BA degree in English with an emphasis in Technical Communication and a BA degree in Dance with an emphasis in Ballet.

Susan E. Thomas is Teaching Development Coordinator for the Faculties of Arts, Music, and Education, and Director of Academic Writing for the Faculty of Arts at the University of Sydney, Australia. Her teaching and research interests include rhetoric, academic and professional writing, and philosophies of teaching and learning. She is the editor of *What Is the New Rhetoric?* (Cambridge Scholars Publishing, 2007) and the author of several articles and book chapters. Susan is the treasurer of the Australian Association of Writing Programs and was the 2007 recipient of the University of Sydney's Vice Chancellor's Award for excellence in teaching. She is currently completing a monograph, *Teaching Writing Beyond US Borders*, a history of the writing program she designed and implemented at Sydney University.

Mary Trachsel joined the Rhetoric faculty at the University of Iowa in 1989. As a faculty member in a department that employs over 100 graduate instructors each year to teach entry-level Rhetoric courses, she serves as a teaching advisor to new or experienced graduate instructors every semester. Her research addresses rhetorics of the emergent field of Animal Studies, with particular attention to the subfield of Ape Language Studies.

Stephanie Vanderslice teaches at the University of Central Arkansas. She served, with Leahy, on the Pedagogy Team for the Association of Writers and Writing Programs. She, with Kelly Ritter, is editor of the collection *Can It Really Be Taught? Resisting Lore in Creative Writing* (Heinemann 2007), to which Bishop contributed.

Carolyn Vickrey is the Associate College Librarian/ Instruction and Reference Services Librarian at Austin College in Sherman, Texas. Before going to NMSU for her PhD, she worked in two different companies as a Technical Editor. Her dissertation focused on collaborative writing, especially with regard to collaborative planning using electronic communication. Currently, she creates Web pages and brochures for library patrons and imaginative print handouts for classes in library instruction.

Catherine Warren is a senior at Texas Tech University. She is a dual major, majoring in both International Business and French. Upon graduation, she will pursue her dreams of traveling around the world as a professional writer and photographer.

Jennifer Wells is the Reading and Writing Specialist at Mercy High School in Burlingame, California, where she directs the writing center and is a literacy coach. She is also doctoral candidate in English Composition at Indiana University of Pennsylvania, and is interested in both high school and college composition, writing center theory and pedagogy, adolescent literacy, and creative nonfiction.

Robin Woody received her BA in English from Texas Tech University in 2004. She currently works as a Business Relationship Manager in the Enabling Technologies department at United Supermarkets, LLC.

Michael J. Zerbe teaches rhetoric, composition, and professional writing and editing courses at York College of Pennsylvania, where he is an Assistant Professor of English and Humanities. He is the author of *Composition and the Rhetoric of Science: Engaging the Dominant Discourse* (Southern Illinois University Press, 2007).

Index

LaVergne, TN USA
17 January 2010
170278LV00003B/5/P

9 781602 350724